P9-CCO-752

Gracious Living

in a

New World

ALSO BY *Alexandra Stoddard*

Mothers: A Celebration

The Art of the Possible

Alexandra Stoddard's Tea Celebrations

Alexandra Stoddard's Book of Days

Making Choices

Grace Notes

Creating a Beautiful Home

Daring to Be Yourself

Gift of a Letter

Alexandra Stoddard's Book of Color

Alexandra Stoddard's Living Beautifully Together

Living a Beautiful Life

The Postcard as Art

Reflections on Beauty

A Child's Place

Style for Living

Finding Joy

in

Changing Times

WILLIAM MORROW AND COMPANY, INC.

New York

Gracious Living

in a

New World

❋

Alexandra Stoddard

Copyright © 1996 by Alexandra Stoddard

All rights reserved. No part of this book may be reproduced or
utilized in any form or by any means, electronic or mechanical,
including photocopying, recording, or by any information storage
or retrieval system, without permission in writing from the
Publisher. Inquiries should be addressed to Permissions
Department, William Morrow and Company, Inc., 1350 Avenue
of the Americas, New York, N.Y. 10019.

It is the policy of William Morrow and Company, Inc., and its
imprints and affiliates, recognizing the importance of preserving
what has been written, to print the books we publish on acid-free
paper, and we exert our best efforts to that end.

Library of Congress Cataloging-in-Publication Data
Stoddard, Alexandra.
Gracious living in a new world : Finding joy in changing times /
Alexandra Stoddard.
p.   cm.
ISBN 0-688-14337-7
1. Conduct of life.   2. Stoddard, Alexandra.   I. Title.
BJ1581.2.S754   1996
170'.44—dc20   96-20078
                                                           CIP

Printed in the United States of America

First Edition

1 2 3 4 5 6 7 8 9 10

BOOK DESIGN BY MARYSARAH QUINN

TO *Alexandra, Brooke,* AND *Peter*

Contents

A LETTER TO MY READERS   XI

ONE ✳ *Redefining How We Want to Live*   3

TWO ✳ *Reawakening Our Five Senses*   47

THREE ✳ *Expressing with Heart and Hand*   77

FOUR ✳ *Working with Grace*   113

FIVE ❋ *Gracious Solitude* 163

SIX ❋ *Family Graces* 183

SEVEN ❋ *Celebrating with Grace* 223

EIGHT ❋ *New Horizons* 266

NINE ❋ *Let Us Live as Poets* 300

TEN PRINCIPLES OF A GRACIOUS LIFE 317

ACKNOWLEDGMENTS 322

A Letter to My Readers

Dear Readers,

We are living in a new world, one that challenges our peace of mind and our inner grace. With its frenetic pace and constant state of flux, modern life often feels chaotic and unstable, and leaves us unsure of the ground we walk on. Technology, while providing us many advantages, encourages us to race through our days so that we no longer know what we'd do if we were to slow down. Labor-saving devices seem not only to have failed to enhance the quality of our lives and free up more time, but get be-

tween us and the immediate, sensory pleasures of life and
increase the pressures on us to do more. Many of us feel
cut off from life's blessings, from our neighbors, from
the wonders of nature, and from a sense of our own significance in the scheme of things. Modern life leaves us
feeling spiritually starved.

In our rush for newer, quicker, better, we seem to be
missing out on what we fundamentally crave, a calmer,
gentler, sweeter, and more gracious life. Is it easy to
achieve such a life? Definitely not. Is it possible? Absolutely, positively, certainly, yes. (Don't look for impossible from me; I've never found a solution in cynicism.)

When my husband and I began spending more time in
our little cottage in a small Connecticut village, we discovered a new path, a slower path that can be followed
any time, anywhere, by anybody. This road is a very old
road. Gandhi spoke of it when he urged, "We need to
learn to be still in the midst of activity and to be vibrantly
alive in repose." Awareness, attentiveness, and appreciation are the energies that light our path toward gracious
living.

We're on a pilgrimage together in this ever-changing
world. But the pilgrimage always takes us back to the same
place, back to ourselves and the basic, essential pleasures
that constitute a rich and fully lived life in any age. We
can put first things first and determine for ourselves what
we need and what we can live without. By changing the
direction of our gaze toward our inner needs we can begin
to see what really holds us together.

Whom do you know who is grace-filled? What are their passions? Have they simply been blessed with good fortune, or did they have to learn to strive for what's important? When you take a closer look at a person who lives graciously, whether he is nine or ninety-nine, you see an energetic, spirited, loving person who has a zest for living and enjoys the miraculous gift of life. The world is extremely interesting to a joyful soul. We are surrounded by opportunities for living with grace—our own hands and our own hearts are all the tools we'll ever need.

We have so much to learn. We have rushed past the fundamental joys of living, but we can find our way back. Life is so wondrously rich with possibility. The more we welcome and value each day, the more we can do to restore grace and meaning in our lives. Look for the spirit of grace as it unfolds everywhere before you. To find grace-filled opportunities, all you need is to be open and enthusiastic. We have so much to share. Our grace adds rays of brightness in times of adversity as well as in times of relative peace. Grace begins within each of us and flows out to our families, to our neighbors, and to the whole universe. Together, let's celebrate the gift of grace.

Grace to you,

Alexandra Stoddard

Alexandra Stoddard

Gracious Living

in a

New World

$\mathcal{O}ne$

❖

$\mathcal{R}edefining\ \mathcal{H}ow\ \mathcal{W}e$ $\mathcal{W}ant\ to\ \mathcal{L}ive$

Lessons from a Village

In the village of Stonington, Connecticut, where my husband, Peter, and I have the good fortune to spend precious time in our small but lovely eighteenth-century cottage, everyone buys the daily newspaper at Frankie Keane's "news office." No one in Stonington has the newspaper delivered. At seven o'clock Frankie's store bubbles with activity; everyone there has either jogged, bicycled, or walked their dogs over to enjoy the simple pleasure of picking a fresh newspaper off the pile and sharing a few moments with neighbors. When Peter picks up his *New York Times* every morning, Frankie has already penciled in "Pete" on the top left-hand corner of the paper. No one calls my husband Pete but Frankie Keane. As Frankie completes his transactions, he closes his cashbox, punctuating the gesture with a contented "Eeah," leans against the counter, crossing his arms, and tells a story about his almost ninety years in Stonington, where his mother owned the store before him.

For beauty, truth, and goodness are not obsolete; they spring eternal in the breast of man.

—EMERSON

There are lots of things we can do here by phone, fax, car, or any time- and energy-saving device, but somehow it's always sweeter to take the time and physical energy to do things ourselves. If we're not in the mood to cook, we don't simply pick up the phone and wait for our meal to be delivered to our door. We go to the fish store at the dock, select a lobster, and ask that it be boiled and shelled. The exchange with the lobsterman is usually accompanied by a friendly argument over whether we will come back for our lobster or wait. Every time we flip a coin to decide. Either way, we like to take our time. Who knows what will happen in the stolen minutes while waiting? A chance to reflect, rest, maybe happen upon some friends, or watch a boat go by. . . .

Here the people seem to possess the secret of tranquility and to live lives of more than surface contentment.

—LOUISE
DICKINSON RICH

In Stonington everyone has an easy smile. No one rushes. There's never any need to. Life has a steady, reliable pace. There's always time to smell the roses; we welcome the day and look for opportunities to let life unfold. Emerson wrote, "To find the journey's end in every step of the road, to live the greatest number of golden hours is wisdom." After we pick up the paper, often we stop off at The Yellow House, a local tea and coffee shop owned by a friend who lives across the street. Water Street swings up to High Street, where the shop is located; hanging out at a table on the café sidewalk is a great way to see the village and all the people coming and going. On the way back to the cottage, we wave to the shopkeepers, sometimes stopping for a brief visit to exchange views with the owners as well as the other customers, who are often our neighbors. In restaurants, we mingle, friends come over to our table, and sometimes we pull up chairs to sit together. The post office is a meeting place where we invariably see friends; here everybody exchanges a few cheerful greetings. The lumberyard is another favorite place to poke around at leisure, where you may discover just the right nail or piece of wood for a home improvement project while running into fellow villagers.

Time softens its edges in the village, becoming a con-

The aim of life is to live, and to live means to be aware.
—HENRY MILLER

The greatest revolution of our generation is the discovery that human beings, by changing the inner attitudes of their minds can change the outer aspects of their lives.
—WILLIAM JAMES

tinuous stream of engaging moments where we're more in tune with our senses and the rhythms of nature.

My life is like a stroll upon the beach, As near the ocean's edge as I can go. . . .
—HENRY DAVID THOREAU

There's always time to go to the nursery to buy more grass seed, brew iced tea, pick herbs from the garden, and have an afternoon siesta. The fresh bread, strudels, and cookies are transported warm from the oven of a restaurant a few blocks down the street. I never stock up on anything because I enjoy having certain errands to run each day.

We all take time to drop things off. Our house is on the way to the beach and the Point, so we often receive a handwritten note tossed through our letter slot in our front door. If there's information a neighbor knows you'd be interested in, it will show up in your box or basket. A friend next door takes pictures of us with friends at our front door

To do as you would be done by, in the plain, sure, and undisputed rule of morality and justice.
—LORD CHESTERFIELD

or at the gate and drops them off later in the week with a one-line note. Once when we were away, Margie photographed our window boxes brimming with geraniums because she thought they looked so pretty. The interactions are never obtrusive; always there is gentle communication.

Every house in this cozy little village reflects the cheerful, unpretentious spirit of the people who live here. Some houses are big, others quite small, like ours. But inside every home one senses a juiciness and love of life. Everyone's window box brims with pansies or geraniums. Houses and picket fences are repainted each spring. Since our town is on a peninsula, many of the homes are set near the water. Our cottage is not on the water, but we enjoy a view of Long Island Sound over a neighbor's garage—a view that we love climbing up to admire any chance we get. We have regular sunset gatherings at each other's homes all around town. We all take a special pleasure in sharing the wonder of nature in the arms of our community.

People look out for each other here. My neighbors and I think of each other as extended family. We all know each other by name and genuinely care about each other's welfare. When Peter was sick several winters ago, friends brought us homemade soup and preserves, logs for the fire, fresh strawberries, yellow roses, and warm letters. If the season is right, bunches of ripe tomatoes and petunias will appear on our doorstep.

One's first appreciation is a sense that the creation is still going on, that the creative forces are as great and as active today as they have ever been, and that tomorrow's morning will be as heroic as any of the world. Creation is here and now.

—HENRY BESTON

We all tend to regard every little errand as an opportunity for a visit. Friends often stop over on their way to do chores. Whether we go to the lumberyard to get some nails, to the bookstore to pick up a new biography, to the library to do research, or to the market to get some of Donna's freshly baked Portuguese sweet bread, everyone does their daily rounds with

an eagerness for life and the gratification of connecting
to a few friends along the way. We greet, often with a hug,
and always with lively conversation.

*Enough is abundance
to the wise.*

—EURIPIDES

Peter loves doing errands, moving about
the village, meeting and greeting. Wherever
you go here, people love to tell their favorite
stories, from Doug the barber to the wait-
ress Julie, who doubles as a corrections officer during the
week. One of the most successful real estate brokers in
the area works at a local restaurant as a bartender on Friday nights just so he can stay in touch with everyone in
town. The waitress at Noah's, another local
restaurant, is a graphic designer; she always
fills us in about her current projects. The
waiter owns the nearby bookstore and makes
certain to tell us about new books we should
read. Ministers and masons have breakfast
at Noah's, where they debate local matters
and world affairs.

*But what happiness
except the simple
harmony between a
man and the life he
leads?*

—ALBERT CAMUS

We all make a special effort to create an
air of good will. In Stonington, people want to get to
know each other in an easy, relaxed way. We share this
blessed, spirited peninsula, but our connection to each
other goes well beyond its borders.

What the Village Can Teach Us

Ever since we purchased our cottage in 1989, Peter has been studying village life. He believes there is an exquisite importance in the friendship and privacy that exist here. As our houses are all close together and near the road, we have mastered the art of genuine friendliness and caring without being obtrusive.

Villages are made up of numerous exchanges at shops and restaurants. There's a great emphasis on the significance of fair dealings, which strongly affect the fabric of all of our lives. Sometimes in a large, impersonal environment people are careless, cut corners, and are indifferent in business transactions. In a city you often have to be on your guard so you won't be shortchanged or overcharged. In our village, everyone bends over backward to ensure fairness. If there's a miscalculation in a transaction, it is dealt with right away. If someone takes the wrong package from a store by mistake, it is immediately understood as having been inadvertent. No one would ever be accused of a deliberate wrongdoing.

Everyone is concerned with others' well-being. For example, if someone is experi-

What is the value of preserving and strengthening this sense of awe and wonder, this recognition of something beyond the boundaries of human existence? . . . Those who contemplate the beauty of the earth find reserves of strength that will endure as long as life lasts.

—Rachel Carson

encing some sort of difficulty, one of the local ministers will be informed and will pay a friendly visit to the family's home in the spirit of helpfulness. Everyone is helpful. One August afternoon, we had a large shipment of books delivered in a gigantic van. No one could miss the sight, and several villagers dropped by to witness the scene. As Peter and I began to work up a sweat from carrying boxes, a neighbor came from across the street with a pitcher of fresh lemonade. Then the traffic along our narrow street started to back up, and we noticed a friend had parked her car. Elizabeth and her husband were on their way home and saw that we could use some strong bodies to help out. Miraculously, the enormous job got done in a fraction of the expected time.

With only plain rice to eat, with only water to drink, and with only an arm for a pillow, I am still content.

—Confucius

Peter believes there is a generosity of spirit in a village often missing when the human scale is lost. One day I admired the incredibly beautiful roses at a local restaurant and inquired who grew them. Late that afternoon a fragrant bouquet was delivered to our cottage by a friend with a note that read, "My aunt was so touched you admired her roses, she wanted you to have this as a gift. Her husband just died, and it meant a lot to know her roses are bringing others pleasure."

Villagers also donate much of their free time to community projects. They understand that the more effort they put into improvements, the better their collective lives will be. They prefer volunteer participation, where individuals take pride and interest in doing things themselves, rather than waiting for government funding which defeats the spirit of enterprise. There are always projects to beautify certain areas, and people join forces to see to it that the work gets done. For example, if you walk down Elm Street, you will see a square with a fountain. Cannon Square, a memorial with two cannons, is where our village defended itself against the British in 1814. It is also where we have our Fourth of July celebration. A permanent committee was set up to raise funds to repair and maintain Cannon Square because it is an invaluable piece of history and heritage for villagers. A small village often lacks funds, so a school may double as a community center, a theater, or a recreational facility. There is imaginative multi-use for space, with no sense of excess. In old New England villages, local governments sat in meeting houses that were also churches.

> *Let your speech be always with grace, seasoned with salt.*
>
> —COLOSSIANS 4:6

> *I will speak ill of no man and speak all the good I know of everybody.*
>
> —BEN FRANKLIN

Among the thinkers whose work has had a profound effect on my and Peter's thinking about the advantages of village life in the modern world is Dr. René Dubos, the author of the seminal work, *A God Within.* Dr. Dubos was a microbiologist and philosopher. In his book, he muses on his own childhood in France: "The very small French village in which I grew up was then and has remained to this day outside the mainstream of the modern world. Even though it is located only thirty miles north of Paris, its name, Hénonville, is not on any map. Yet, limited as village life was, it provided a rich variety of experiences which are still alive in my memory and which are indeed incarnated in my whole organic being. . . . This enchantment, using the word in its strong etymological sense, has conditioned my whole life. It continues to color all my feelings. . . ."

Dr. Dubos found in his village an ideal microcosm, a small representative system having elements of what is large. In his small world he found fertile soil for play, learning, comradeship, and wonder. In a pond he found elements of nature that inspired him to become an internationally recognized microbiologist. He was a great believer in the value of living within range of the sound of church bells. Dr. Dubos teaches us the necessity of an appropriate scale for our needs as human beings. He believes we can only *know* a few hundred people and we can have approximately a dozen intimate friends. By breaking bigness down, we're able to know ourselves and others better, and we're able to participate more because we can understand the dynamics of our interchanges.

The mind and will of man must work their way strenuously to a higher unity in which the primitive "direct experience" is manifested on a higher level.

—Thomas Merton

In the village, our collective talents and skills are put to use for our own enjoyment and for the improvement of the whole community. One day Mark Pescatello came by in his shiny white truck and saw me on tiptoe trying to put up our flag. Within a few days, Mark and his assistant arrived with a huge slab of granite as a plinth for Peter and me to stand on when we raise and take down the flag. We call it Mark Rock.

Once after a storm I noticed a cracked windowpane in our bedroom. A contractor friend took a look at it and told us how easily it could be fixed. "The lumberyard will replace it within a few hours. Here, let me take it down for you." There's no indifference about anything, no matter how small. Everyone cares about everyone and everything. While the pace is easy in a village, there's no indolence. There isn't a portion of the community where people don't do anything. Everyone makes contributions. There's a spirit of graciousness, not passivity. People here move their feet.

Teach us delight in simple things.
—Rudyard Kipling

Stonington Village is a borough with its own internal government. The borough warden, our mayor, is the wife of a chef at a restaurant they own on Water Street, where they live upstairs. Everybody agrees that the less control the better, though we also concur that in some areas control is beneficial and fair for everyone. For example, if anyone wants to make substantial changes to their houses, they have to have the changes approved by the borough, which decides whether the changes would unfairly impinge on another building. The village people voted down our area becoming a historic district, which would have

The great and glorious masterpiece of men is to live to the point.
—Michel de Montaigne

subjected it to more outside control. Yankees don't like being told what to do. But there seems to be the right balance, sufficient control and government to meet the tone of civility. If this were not so, the village would vote to change it.

Every village has to be economically self-sustaining. To do this, many people wear several hats. Our town treasurer is also the village mason, who contributes to beautifying the village as well as coaching football at the local high school. Mark's daughter works part time at The Yellow House.

In a small village, any tensions that may arise from religious differences are defused. Inhabitants are apt to be more ecumenical, joining forces for leadership to help the community. When there is this common commitment to help, religious diversity only adds to the richness of community.

Grace was in all her steps,
heaven in her eye,
In every gesture dignity
and love.

—JOHN MILTON

For me, the village is a kind of Platonic archetype, a model of what we can aim for in order to live graciously in the modern world, wherever we may live. Once we see what makes the village work so well, we can find these blessings anywhere.

The village is somewhat sheltered from the rapid changes of the modern world. Today, we sometimes live anxiously because our busy lives are so subject to change from every side that we are deprived of the continuous sense of meaning derived from stability. Today, no sooner do we get used to one mode of life when it's transformed into another. The office where my daughter Brooke works just upgraded its computer system. She says she was just getting used to the old one!

My career requires that I travel frequently, both inside and outside New York City. Getting around in cities has become only more difficult and time-consuming as the years go by. If I have a meeting in midtown two miles away, it could take me up to an hour to get there by taxi because of traffic congestion. We used to keep a car in the city, but it became too expensive to keep it in a garage in a safe neighborhood, and to leave your car parked on the street, if you can find a spot, is an invitation to have it broken into and vandalized.

Friendship, compounded of esteem and love, derives from one its tenderness and its permanence from the other.

—SAMUEL JOHNSON

There are also longer delays at the airports today due to air traffic control and heightened security. I've learned to be Zen about such shifts over which I have no control. I always leave early, and ride out the delays by reading, working on a book chapter, and writing notes to friends. I prepare for the worst when I travel, knowing that I could be stranded for several hours waiting for a single flight.

There's been a steady, pervasive disintegration of trust and confidence in the city due to people cheating and threatening one another. Ever since I began decorating in New York in 1961, if you had established credit, you could conduct business transactions over the telephone in good faith. Now, everyone requires a signature and deposit before any work begins, which causes delays. The workroom that builds furniture for my clients has been burned so often by slow payments that they now require that the final bill be paid before the furniture leaves the showroom, rather than waiting for the client's final approval after they receive their pieces.

Last year, after we taped a television show in Norwalk, Connecticut, our taxi to the train station was half an hour late, causing us to miss the train back to New York City. Because I had a meeting in the city that afternoon, I asked the driver if he could take us all the way into New York, a forty-five-minute trip. The fare was one hundred dollars, but I had no choice. As we zoomed along Interstate 95, the driver asked us for the money. I knew I didn't have enough cash, and neither did my colleague Elisabeth, so we said that we would have to write a check as soon as we arrived. "No, cash only. Pay now, or I'll let you out." After reaching into every pocket and compartment possible, counting even nickels and pennies, we still didn't have enough. He then pulled over onto the shoulder of a crowded highway and I feared the worst. We were like sitting ducks. Thankfully, we did another search and miraculously came up with the difference.

In a village, everyone performs services and then sends you the bill. There's a sense of empathy, where everyone helps out to fill another's needs. In a city, you are usually forced to go through impersonal channels, such as re-

Wisely and slowly; they stumble that run fast.

—WILLIAM SHAKESPEARE
ROMEO AND JULIET

sponding to an advertisement in the newspaper. In the village, a window or bulletin board at the liquor store may provide a free communication service by posting help-wanted ads or notices about baby-sitting services or a lost puppy.

In less sophisticated times, when the pace of life was slower, there was a fundamental grounding in everyday life. We need to find some modern equivalent to feel rooted in our lives today not only to enjoy each day, but to soften the fall when we are thrown by life's inevitable difficulties and tragedies. Change is slow to take hold in the village. The small scale of life makes apparent the values that people cling to, the underlying support for a simple, rich, fulfilling, and gracious life: home, family, friendship, community, loyalty, accountability, respect for the individual, a shared sense of tradition and history, continuity in customs and rituals, the pleasure in the simple life, and a general sense of joy and connectedness to beauty and to all things in the natural world. Village life provides a powerful example of the worth and dignity of human life. In the village each person is valued. Here no one is a stranger. If our garbage container is left on the sidewalk after recycling, and we're not in residence, someone will put it inside our gate or walk it to the back, out of sight. If you have to go to the hospital in an emergency, the ambulance team are dedicated volunteers from the neigh-

If you get simple beauty,
and nought else,
you get about the best thing
God invents.

—ROBERT BROWNING

borhood and always arrive within a few minutes. No forms to fill out, you go. If you need landscape work done, there are people who will come to help out and do it with care. No one is too proud to earn a little extra money to help out with family finances. If your roof has water damage from the 1996 blizzard, the contractor who lives in the neighborhood comes over to check it out and give advice. If the cab doesn't pick you up in time to get to the Mystic railroad station, anyone with a car is glad to take you. If a package comes while you are away, your neighbors will hold it for you until they see your lights on, and then they'll run it over to you. If it's snowing, a friend will pick up and deliver your newspaper to save you from leaving your cozy spot by the fire and going out into the cold.

To lead a simple life in reasonable comfort, with a minimum of possessions, ranks high among the arts of living. It leaves us the time, resources, and freedom of mind we need for the things that give life value: loving, helping, serving, and giving.

— Eknath
Easwaran

One of the waitresses in a local restaurant has an abundance of lilies of the valley in her yard. Often she'll take the time to gather up little bunches of the fragrant, delicate flowers and put the miniature bouquets on each table as a sweet and gracious gesture. If a good deed is done, or if there's good news, it gets around, via word of mouth, fast.

Village life is rich in meaning because everything that happens within it is of consequence. A loss to one is a loss to all. In a city where life is busier, we can create this same continuity and community through loyalty in our daily interactions. In every city, there are elements of village life, a sense of cohesiveness available to all who seek it in their neighborhood. I greatly appreciate the people who are part of my daily life in New York. When I rented my first apartment in 1961, one block away

The great artist is the simplifier.

—Henri-Frédéric
Amiel

from where we live now, I found friendliness available if you're willing to show genuine interest in people's lives wherever you go.

All these years later I remember Stella, who did my dry cleaning. She advised me never to serve guests "a spread finer than you have when you're alone." Such good advice, a wise tidbit you wouldn't receive if you were in a rush. On the corner where I live is the YMHA, where we vote and where they have day and evening programs seven days a week. There are forums, sports activities, a swimming pool, and other facilities. Authors give talks and readings, and journalists, doctors, spiritual leaders, actors, and actresses speak and perform. Often music ensembles will give concerts. When you participate in the YMHA and its activities, you have a stake in a village community right in the heart of a crowded city.

All the churches, temples, and synagogues have activities for everyone in the community to become involved in. All we have to do is call up and put ourselves on a mailing list for their newsletters. I took an exercise class at the Brick Church across the street, for example, where they also hold Alcoholic Anonymous meetings. There are shelters, soup kitchens, tutoring, art exhibits, and adult education classes as well as forums, all inviting us to get involved in the community. In front of the Heavenly Rest Church at Ninetieth Street and Fifth Avenue, you not only can take part in the activities at the church, including afternoon and evening concerts, you can also enjoy Central Park and the reservoir, where you can observe horseback riders and runners, who are perhaps in training for one of the city's many races.

Existence is infinite, not to be defined; and though it seems but a bit of wood in your hand, to carve as you please, it is not to be lightly played with and laid down.

—LAO-TZU

I joined the Yorkville Emergency Alliance when there were federal budget cuts in the 1980s. We met regularly to see what we could do in our neighborhood. We established dozens of soup kitchens and shelters, and helped out with local educational programs. Peter has always been involved in political clubs in our immediate neighborhood, known as Carnegie Hill.

Carnegie Hill Association serves the community, assuming the same function as a borough. The association is primarily concerned with safety, especially for the several schools in the area, and beautification. It deals with all kinds of environmental issues, including building specifications. If you come to New York in the springtime, you will be greeted by thousands of Dutch tulips in the island dividing Park Avenue, all paid for directly by the association and by the residents. Later the tulips are replaced with begonias. During the winter holidays, fir trees are decorated with tiny white lights every block.

The more you know people in your neighborhood, the more you care, which helps you to make meaningful connections with others. Patty, who now does our dry cleaning, is hardworking and bright, and a conscientious mother. I gave her one of my books, which she reads to her nine-year-old child, who wants to be a writer.

One night when I wasn't feeling well, Peter wanted to pamper me with some delicious food, not the usual take-out variety we all eat and get tired of over time. Peter and I go to a restaurant near our apartment that reminds us of being in a small village in Normandy. Because Peter has such a friendly relationship with the owners, they were delighted to fix their first "to go" gourmet meal, and ran it up in a taxi. These kinds of interchanges and give-and-take of good deeds create the texture of village life wherever you live. Village life is all about people and community. Acts as simple as dropping off a note or some flowers to a neighbor, or inviting friends over for an impromptu, casual dinner, can turn a city even as large as New York into a friendly village.

In the village we slow down and enjoy doing everyday things. We're not starved for new experiences. The sunsets at the Point, the colorful gardens in our front- and back-

Cheerfulness keeps up a kind of daylight in the mind, filling it with a steady and perpetual serenity.

—Joseph Addison

yards, the walks, the visits with neighbors, the sense that there is time for everything—these never pale in comparison to what might be "out there." We always have the day before us and the sky above us. Village life shows us that the joys of living are simple joys. Here we still have time to get back to our senses and live a more deliberate, quality life. You can see this in the faces of the people on our streets. Mark Twain once observed, "Wrinkles should merely indicate where smiles have been." There are no frowns or downcast glances, no moping around. The face lines all turn up. There's an upbeat quality to the atmosphere, perfuming the moment with heavenly mist.

If a man is capable of leading a responsible life himself, then he is also conscious of his duties to the community.

— CARL JUNG

If we rush for newer, quicker, better, we miss what we really crave: a calmer, gentler, and more gracious lifestyle. "This is the way it should be," says a friend from our village. This is the way it should be everywhere: Then we can exhale and relax, and feel a sense of peace that the important things still hold.

We make the important things hold value by valuing them deep within ourselves. Our next-door neighbors who share our floor in our apartment building in New York have a big, white Wheaton terrier, William, who is not only loved by his owners, but also by all of us who see him come and go daily. We always invite him into our apartment for a quick run around and visit when we hear him shaking his collar outside our front door.

When we spent weekends in New York before we bought our cottage, Peter would invite a small group of friends to come over for a visit after church every Sunday. When the new minister arrived, we had a dozen parishioners over to welcome him. Our living room has been the setting for countless fund-raisers and special dinners for community causes, whether to benefit my daughters' day school or to fund special projects overseen by church groups.

THE GRACE OF COMMUNITY

Village life has an intimate scale. Here people feel connected, knowing that they matter to each other. When we are in the village we know that we belong; we never feel lost here. When we're here, we're home. Today, perhaps living far away from family and loved ones, many of us feel we've lost this sense of home, this connectedness, this intimacy. But we can create home wherever we are. When we walk down the village street we see the people among whom we live and work. We share the streets. We know that we

Man is not possessed by free will for good works unless it be assisted by grace.

—JOHN CALVIN

need each other to make this little society work. We need each other to survive. When faced with a hurricane or a blizzard, we unite as a community because we know that together we have enough strength to handle any natural disaster. We take care of each other when there is an illness or death, and we take pride in one another's achievements as well, such as a sports victory at school, a college acceptance, or a new job. We are not only physically interdependent, but spiritually, too. When people do good for each other, the whole town feels blessed. It feels good to be alive among such people. Each year, a group of villagers organizes Stonington Village Kitchens: A Walking Tour, a charity event involving group tours of several kitchens in the area, including my own. The money raised by the one-day event is contributed to the Child and Family Agency of Southeastern Connecticut. The public library also hosts a variety of events, including an open house complete with lectures and music, to support its own existence. Peter and I jump at the opportunity to teach art and writing classes at elementary schools in the area, encouraging students to be creative and study hard.

To see a World in a Grain of Sand And a heaven in a wild flower, Hold infinity in the palm of your hand And eternity in an hour.

—WILLIAM BLAKE

City life, because of its hustle and bustle, sometimes requires that we try that much harder to do good for each other. I find that much of the community work I do involves my career as an author and a designer. I love to volunteer my services to teach adult education seminars and to give lectures to raise money for educational programs. Often I donate a library of my books to local auctions that are raising funds for hospital programs or other projects. When I am invited to participate in an "author-to-author luncheon" for charity, I'm there.

How unfortunate when we become more preoccupied with getting ahead of each other than in supporting each other. When we anxiously compete, erecting barriers to protect our claim on what is ours, then we've lost one of our fundamen- tal joys in life: our connection to other people. Racing to get ahead, we may turn around and discover that we are alone. Re- gardless of where we live, we must make sure that there is enough to go around.

Happiness is the light on the water.

— W ILLIAM
M AXWELL

"We are by all odds the most persistently and obses- sively social of all species," writes Dr. Lewis Thomas in his fascinating book *The Medusa and the Snail,* "more de- pendent on each other than the famous social insects, and really, when you look at us, infinitely more imaginative and deft at social living." Once we see how a sense of community is central in living a gracious life, we can work to create a community among our neighbors anywhere.

I try to be on a first-name basis with all the people I encounter regularly in my daily life. This custom adds a great measure of familiarity that provides a touch of village warmth wherever you live. I never shy away from asking people's advice and showing my interest in their various areas of expertise. I like to take the time to really talk to the people I come into contact with. If you're rushed, you may give others the impression that you feel you're too good for them, that your time is too valuable for you to take a few minutes to visit. You will find that everybody has a fascinating story that they're eager to tell. In the city we can join community boards, we can set up reading groups with friends and neighbors, we can organize block parties, rebuild our local parks and gardens. We can get to know our neighbors better. Have an open house. Start a book club. Get to know your local grocers, bakers, and butchers, and develop a rapport. You'll find people are always eager to make a connection; and you're likely to learn something new from these experienced hands. Any time you reach out, extending yourself in a personal way to others, regardless of the size of the city, town, or village in which you live, you can make daily life a blessing. The seeds to grow a more gracious life can be planted anywhere we live. Not long ago I received a special delivery from my butcher of over thirty years, Leon Lobel. He had been in Florida on vacation and had noticed a picture of me in the living section of the local paper. He passed the article on to me, with a note attached: "Congrats. You look great." The sweet gesture brought an immeasurable amount of cheer to my day.

We ascribe beauty to that which is simple; which has no superfluous parts; which exactly answers its end.

— EMERSON

In the village we learn to relax, let down our guard, and see that it is other people who make life good. In each other's company we feel pleasure and warmth, an enrichment of feelings. Because of its larger scale and greater diversity, city streets sometimes make us turn away from others, focusing our eyes straight ahead. But this is a mistake. The city is filled with wonderful possibilities for friendly, neighborly encounters. I love it when a tourist in New York City asks me for directions, or when I can help someone who is nervously clutching a piece of paper, looking around to find an address. Helping others find their way is always an opportunity for making connections. I love extending myself to others, as if to say, "This is a great town. We New Yorkers care about people." A friend was telling me recently about her first trip to New York when she was a college student visiting her roommate over the summer. Pam had been warned of the "unfriendliness" of the natives and told to keep to herself. When she arrived at Grand Central Station, she immediately followed signs to the appropriate subway train and hopped on, careful not to stare at a soul. Not long after the train started to move, she began to panic. She could not understand one word of what the conductor said, and feared she would miss her stop and end up in a dangerous part of the city. Her eyes welled with tears when a young woman sitting across from her offered to help. When she mentioned her stop, another person standing near her announced that he would be getting off at the same stop and would walk her out to point her in the right direction. "Everybody was so thoughtful and eager to help, I couldn't believe New

You will know your own innocence again when you can see the love that breathes within every iota of creation.

—DEEPAK CHOPRA

Yorkers had such a mean reputation," Pam exclaimed. "Ever since that first trip to 'the big city,' I have loved coming back."

Respect for life is a blessing. Caring about each other and knowing that it is people who determine the quality of our lives is an inspiration. Why would we choose to deny ourselves so fundamental a joy?

A SENSE OF LOYALTY

Modern life can be impersonal. So many times we read that people today feel alone, alienated, cut off from each other and from nature. Though technological advances have brought us many blessings—cures for illnesses and new ways of expressing ourselves and communicating with others—machines have also given us the illusion that we need them more than we need people. Today, we have less and less of a sense that people count; we have greater respect for technology than for the people who create it.

O day of radiant gladness, O day of joy and light.

—HYMN

The anonymity of the corporation, which dominates so much of life for many of us, also gives us a feeling of disconnection from each other. Loyalty, too, is a disappearing value. It's difficult to feel a sense of loyalty when we no longer work for an organization for life. Statistics now show that, on the average, people will change jobs more than eighteen times during the course of their lives. All of this isn't necessarily bad, some of these shifts provide opportunity: Change keeps us on our toes and often gives us a new chance to grow. But we are nevertheless suffering for the loss of old certainties and old connections, which creates entirely new problems.

Still, there is no problem that doesn't have within it the seeds for its solution. When faced with an impersonal business atmosphere, we can make a special effort to bring our own touch of humanity to our jobs. For example, I often prefer to write my business letters by hand using social stationery and colorful ink rather than to type them up on a computer and simply sign them at the bottom. When I complete my first draft of a book, I always hand-deliver the manuscript to my literary agent and my editor rather than hiring a messenger service or "overnighting" it by mail. The act of placing the box containing my book into the hands of the two people who will be the first to read my creation is an essential part of the writing process that I will never abandon for a more efficient method.

And leisure (which is not to be confused with empty time, but which is time through which free, life-enhancing currents flow)— leisure in these days is something to be sought and cherished as a rare and priceless boon; leisure to think, and talk, and write, and read.

—PROFESSOR JOHN
LIVINGSTON
LOWES

We can find ways to reconnect to each other, even in a corporate setting. We can find a source for feelings of loyalty. Once we become aware of what is at the heart of gracious living in any age, we can take steps to reinvent and transform those values for our time. The village is a good place to look for reminders of what matters.

This Day

I recently read in a survey published in *Psychology Today* that in 1983, 25 percent of adults reported always feeling "rushed." Eleven years later, the figure jumped to 40 percent. If this keeps up, according to a book by economics professor Juliet Schorr, *The Overworked American,* "by the end of the century Americans will be spending as much time at their jobs as they did back in the 1920s." Does this sound like a better life? How did we get here? When did we decide that doing more in less time was to be our ultimate goal? Over the past few decades, our definitions of "urgent" and "emergency" have changed significantly in response to modern technology. Computers, fax machines, call waiting, voice mail, Federal Express, E-mail . . . how did we manage without these time-savers? We've paid a price for these advantages: We expect everything to happen immediately. We have to have everything and do everything right now, for fear of losing out somehow, or falling behind. "I need this *yesterday*" is our general modus operandi.

> *In this world, you must be a bit too kind in order to be kind enough.*
> — Pierre Carlet de Chamblain de Marivaux

Magazine editors call it "time crunching" or "time

compressing.'' Whatever name we give it, as a society we have put ourselves in a chronic state of speeding, of having to catch up. We never do catch up; we just keep adding more to our schedule. Often we feel we will never get out from under our load. Thanks to technology and labor-saving devices, the easier things are to do, the more compelled we are to cram in more. Then we'll really feel productive, goes the thinking. Returning to the work schedule of the 1920s sounds like a step backward, not forward.

The art of art, the glory of expression, and the sunshine of the light of letters is simplicity.

—Walt Whitman

We've paid for our speeded-up lives with a loss in the quality of our time. Our chronic lack of time has robbed us of the ability to understand that the truth of living is found in the experience of being, and that life cannot be put on hold while we're trying to produce more. Writer Simone de Beauvoir expressed this so well when she wrote, ''The time that one gains cannot be accumulated in a storehouse; it is contradictory to want to save up existence, which, the fact is, exists only by being spent.''

When we slow down, we have a chance to enjoy the experience of living rather than trying to race the clock. We need to take off our watches periodically and spend a day, or even part of a day, with absolutely nothing on our agenda. Only then can we truly follow our spirit and be spontaneous. Have you ever taken off from work early, with no destination? I love to spontaneously give my two employees, Elisabeth and Julie, the afternoon off. Once

I phoned from Stonington to announce that the following
day would be an office "snow day" and advised them to
sleep late and spend the day "playing in the
snow." Why cling to the modern, complicated craziness of being busy all the time,
filling our days with obligations, appointments, and engagements? We have a horror
of having nothing to do, so we eagerly take
up doing more only to discover that we're too rushed to
enjoy doing anything. In this frenzy we may often have a
sense that life is passing us by and we will never get what
we are looking for. In our hearts I think we know that by
rushing and overproducing we are running away from any
real hope of happiness. The truth is that nowhere in our
lives is there a richer potential for gracious living than in
the present moment.

*Elegance does not
consist in putting on
a new dress.*

— C OCO C HANEL

"Slow down," says the village street. Here we ride bi-
cycles or walk to everything. We do have cars, but people
use them so infrequently that traffic jams are unheard of
on our narrow streets. We'd rather have a garden patch
than garage space. We're not exactly roughing it. We do
have electricity, plumbing, and telephones. Yes, we even
have fax and Xerox machines. But modern craziness, the
race for more, rarely encroaches on us. When it does, it's
noticeable. One tiny restaurant in town tried to enter the
modern world by purchasing an electric pepper grinder.
Whenever they used the machine it made such a startling
buzzing noise that to our collective ears it could have been
mistaken for a chain saw cutting down a redwood. Need-

less to say, the electric pepper grinder didn't survive even its first night. We never needed it to begin with. I'd prefer using an old-fashioned pepper grinder over some new gadget, any day. There is something lovely about the ritual of grinding the pepper, transforming it with one's own hands from hard little beads to flavorful powder. It's not churning your own butter, but it's a satisfying process. The gesture of grinding has a ceremonial aspect that brings a certain stillness to the table.

You must give some time to your fellow men. Even if it's a little thing, do something for others—something for which you get no pay but the privilege of doing it.

—Albert Schweitzer

When we begin to slow down we see that there are many opportunities for ceremoniousness everywhere in our lives. Not only can we do without certain machines and possessions, but our lives are improved by doing things with our own hands; the experience is calming and rich beyond measure. Activities as simple as walking to work, growing plants in a window box or on a windowsill, baking bread from scratch, or squeezing oranges for fresh juice in the morning can become illuminating experiences.

Village life helps me self-regulate, to mosey around at my own pace, listening more closely to my inner rhythms. I've learned to walk at this pace in my busy city life where I often take the long way home after lunch with Peter. I love to gaze in the windows of antique shops and other stores to see if anything catches my eye and lures me inside. My experience in Stonington has taught me that I can take back my life by an exuberant determination to slow down all the racing and the striving. I can clear the muddy waters kicked up by too much rushing by becoming aware of my deep need for grace in every possible moment. I've learned that, no matter where I am, as the writer Goethe so beautifully expressed it, "Nothing is worth more than this day."

SIMPLIFY, SIMPLIFY

The need to own and to consume more and more "things" seems finally to be leaving many of us cold and empty. Many of us have begun looking within ourselves for a vision that will sustain our deeper longings. Today, in more and more books and magazine articles, on more and more radio and television talk shows, we, as a nation, are asking ourselves: How much or how little do we *need* to be happy? "Knowing what one wants," wrote Rollo May in his classic book, *Man's Search for Himself,* "is simply the elemental form of what in the maturing person is the ability to choose one's own values. He works not merely from automatic routine, but because he consciously believes in the value of what he is doing." The simple verities of village life have helped show me the way back to gracious living. How

The universal soul is the alone creator of the useful and the beautiful. . . . Here the omnipotent agent is Nature . . . the representative of the universal mind.

—EMERSON

much do we need in order to live a fulfilling gracious life? Not as much as we have been led to think.

Today we're told that we must have a food processor in order to cook a meal efficiently. Yesterday it was a microwave in order to cook more quickly. What will we need tomorrow? And though we can populate our kitchens with more gadgets than ever before, fewer and fewer people today are sitting down to a home-cooked meal. Many don't even cook for their friends and family anymore.

We've bought so many things beyond kitchenware. We have video cameras and VCRs. We have stair machines and cross-country skiing machines. We have computers, CD-ROMs, and giant-screen televisions. Are we living any more graciously for having them? No.

The peace of mind that you're looking for is present all the time.

—JOAN BORYSENKO

How often do you find that today's luxury becomes tomorrow's necessity? And often that unused luxury becomes a plant holder or a clothes rack. To make matters worse, now we have to find the time to use all these new gadgets, only adding to the list of things that press on our time. We exchange one labor-saving device for another, but somehow we still never have enough time to do what we want. But we don't stop; we just accept our condition of rushing. I recently met a man who had spent thousands of dollars on a special "shiatsu chair," which massages your upper body while you sit in it. He also bought a high-tech exercise machine that covers all muscle areas for "efficient relaxation and exercise." I couldn't believe my ears as he explained that he's used them no more than five times in the past year because he doesn't have the time.

We have paid for "new and improved." We have increased our standard of living and now must work hard to maintain it, leaving us little time to enjoy what we have. In addition to "time poverty," we feel doomed never to have enough money to support our lives. But when we stop and explore what makes life rich and fulfilling, we find the answer not in all our accumulated possessions, but in our simple ability to take pleasure in the moment, in what is all around us, free for the taking. We have been overworking for things we don't really need, chasing technology in hot haste. We have become more mechanical and less spiritual. "On its own, no amount of technological development can lead to lasting happiness," instructs the Dalai Lama. "What is almost always missing is a corresponding inner development."

Life in Stonington confirms, over and over again, that I gain more spiritually when I crave less materially. Happiness itself, explained Emerson, "depends not on property but on expression." When we experience life in all its dimensions—sensual, spiritual, and practical—when we begin to see that much of what we want and think we need in order to live a good life is unnecessary, we are relieved to find that we can be happy with what we have.

To create a sense of balance, we've kept life simple here

Friends, books, a cheerful heart, and conscience clear Are the most choice companions we have here.

—WILLIAM MATHER

in Stonington. I've tried to bring that appreciation for simplicity into my city life as well. In Stonington, people seem to have discovered life's true pleasures. You'll find more appreciation for a flower than for a fancy piece of jewelry. A beautiful sunset is valued far more than an extravagant evening of dinner and dancing. A brisk walk around the village and down to the water is preferable to an aerobics class or twenty minutes on the stair machine. Reading a book outside in the fresh air is far more rejuvenating than a facial and a trip to the beauty salon. The gift villagers give themselves is the present moment, which they hold as their treasure. There's a greater emphasis on the pleasures of a simple good life than in ambitious undertakings that would take us far away from our sunsets and fresh air and the sound of church bells, laughter, wind chimes, children, dogs, and seagulls. There's always a fishing boat coming or going for the watchful eye. At Ice Cream Alley, the regulars under five get free cones. The attendance is way up in the church on Church Street, and not just because of the wonderful minister and his family: Half the year the stained glass windows are open to reveal a breathtaking view of Narragansett Bay. Not bad scenery for a prayerful awakening.

It is the treating of the commonplace with the feeling of the sublime that gives to art its true power.

—Jean-François Millet

I try to take the inner rhythms and harmony of our village with me wherever I go. I prefer to walk to my destinations when possible and have conversations with all the people I encounter during the course of my day. The village is implanted in the center of my being as a reminder of a simple, more gracious life that will guide me wherever I am. We can slow down and scale down anywhere. We don't need to get everything done *today*. We can go twenty-four hours without turning on our computers, or checking the fax machine for messages. We can take the time to sit down for breakfast and start our day with our spouse or to read the *whole* paper, even if it means getting up half an hour earlier.

True elegance transcends eloquence.

—PASCAL

WITH "ONE'S OWN EYES"

The nineteenth-century poet William Wordsworth saw even in his time the price we pay for buying our way to happiness: "The world is too much with us; late and soon, /Getting and spending, we lay waste our powers; /Little we see in Nature that is ours; /We have given our hearts away, a sordid boon!"

A rainy day is the perfect time for a walk in the woods.

—RACHEL CARSON

We can take back our hearts, and live more graciously in the modern world, by reawakening our senses to everything around us. Through our senses we draw our experience of what it means to be alive. In observing nature we observe the essence of living. We *are* our senses. Whenever we open our eyes, our hearts, and our minds, we can

expand our sense of discovery, of wonder, and of pleasure—our aliveness to life.

In the village and everywhere in my life I'm drawn by
so many beautiful natural rhythms. I love to sit at my small
pine desk set in front of an open window where I can
overlook the harbor. I delight in seeing the light hitting
a cobweb at the window, or in sitting quietly enjoying the
sun setting over the water. I crowd this tiny
space with many pleasures: a bud vase with
some pansies freshly picked from the garden, pictures of the girls, paperweights, a
small brass bucket full of fountain pens. I
love to look out of windows, anywhere I am.
Here I love to watch the boats coming and
going; for me it's a never-ending fascination. I watch a friend walk his dog. I hear
laughter across the street where two young

There's absolutely no reason for being rushed along with the rush. Everybody should be free to go very slow.

—Robert Frost

girls happily announce, "Ice-cold lemonade! Twenty-five
cents! Ice-cold lemonade! Twenty-five cents!" I look out
at a cornflower-blue house that turns lavender when the
sun sets. The white bark of the birch trees looks so pretty
swaying against the blue paint. I remember carving hearts
in the white bark of other birches as a child, putting a
boyfriend's initials in the wood.

I think of how much I love blue. The sky is an intense,
penetrating blue with huge puffy blue-white cotton ball
clouds that remind me of the clouds in a John Constable
painting. I peek out of my window, looking down to the
picket fence and window boxes. How could geraniums be

so red? The color is identical to a boiled lobster shell. Is it the salty sea air that makes them thrive? Is this the same air that exhilarates my spirit so? I hear halyards chiming in concert with the sound of cheerful shouts from the little entrepreneurs across the street.

It is always possible to stop what you're doing to take in the day, even if just for a few moments. Even on my busiest days in New York, when my schedule is filled with meetings, interviews, and writing deadlines, I work by the living room fire or at my marble-top table facing a window that looks out upon the Brick Church. All I need to do is look up at the fire or out the window to have a moment of pure serenity while I work. Sometimes I light a scented candle or incense so I can continuously enjoy the aroma as I focus on what needs to be done.

We all have moments when the universal seems to wrap us round with friendliness.

—WILLIAM JAMES

Often Peter is at his desk just a few feet away. He flashes me a smile every now and then, which replenishes my energy. We learn where grace can be found by paying attention, reawakening our senses to the indescribable delights around us, and by our capacity to appreciate and love all living things.

Nineteenth-century writer George Sand captured the simple truth about how we retain joy and connection to living when she explained, "The whole secret in the study of nature lies in learning how to use one's eyes." We open a world to ourselves when we use all our senses, and

May you live all the days of your life.

—JONATHAN SWIFT

keep our eyes, ears, nose, taste, and touch alert to life. The sound of the bugle is for me a sensory symbol of awakening going back to my childhood days at summer camp. Bleary-eyed kids, we would be revived from sleep each morning by the muffled sound of reveille off in the distance. *Da da, da da da. Da da, da da da. Da da, da da da daaaaa da.* The bugle sounds grace in the evening sky as well, singing, "day is done, gone the sun."

I love the thought of poet Emily Dickinson's father ringing church bells in their village of Amherst, Massachusetts, about which she wrote in her poetry. He would ring the bells when he wanted everyone to stop, pause, and absorb the breathtaking beauty of the sunset.

Our desires here in Stonington are limited. There's no more land for development in the village; there hasn't been for a hundred years so that few buildings were built after the late 1880s. Here and there are condos tucked discreetly along the water's edge, but the village maintains a human scale that suits our sensibilities. Everyone is enriched by the natural beauty here and we all deeply appreciate what we have.

Thinking a smile all the time will keep your face youthful.
—FRANK GELETT
BURGESS

I know I'm living with grace when I feel so content just being alive. Here in this friendly village, in our little cottage, the sight of the wind vigorously tossing the bleached white café curtains stirs my soul. Each morning that Peter and I wake up here we think, Where would we rather be? I feel blessed by this special place, because being here has taught me so much about being alive to life wherever I am. In nature and at home, whether we're in a small village or in a big city, the more meaning we find in everything around us, the greater our opportunity for pleasure and gracious living. We can look up at the evening sky, watch the moon outside our window, welcome the morning with a vase of flowers, and say goodnight with a kiss no matter where we live.

OUR DAILY WALKS AND OTHER GRACEFUL RITUALS

Village life reminds us of the pleasure we take in the rituals of everyday living. Rituals give our lives a sense of continuity. In the city we can meet for drinks after work, join for coffee after dinner, or perhaps take a quick trip to a museum during lunch. People in Stonington delight in their daily walks. At least once a day, everyone seems to enjoy a walk out to the Point, the tip of the village, which is a peninsula pointed at Watch Hill overlooking Little Narragansett Bay. Some go at five A.M. Others go at dusk. But everyone seems to find the way there every day. Some of us find this ritual so refreshing we travel by foot to the Point several times a day. Watching the boats sail across the entrance to Block Island Sound and onto the Atlantic, or the waves lapping at the shore, is equaled only by the beauty

The world is enlarged for us, not by new objects, but by finding more affinities and potencies in those we have.

—EMERSON

of the sunrises and sunsets. Our four-year-old grand-daughter, Hillary, is in love with all the sailboats and their colorful sails. She calls them "tall ships" and dreams of the day she can live on one. Under the twinkling stars we feel a sense of the utter mystery of our being, grateful that beauty can move us to the depths of ourselves. Such walks!

Villagers partake in several customs and rituals characteristic of their culture, including festive Fourth of July parades and Labor Day auctions. One of the most significant traditions maintained by the villagers is the annual Blessing of the Fleet. On this midsummer day, twenty-seven boats called daggers, owned and operated for generations by Portuguese fishermen, enter the harbor. Festooned with ribbons and flags, the boats parade through the harbor with a large crowd cheering them on at the Town Dock. Here priests and bishops bless the fleet because ocean fishing is arduous and dangerous in all seasons. The event is a spirited celebration with food, drink, and prayers, a colorful panorama with a poignant village theme going back to the beginning of memories.

Quality—in the classic Greek sense— how to live with grace and intelligence, with bravery and mercy.

—THEODORE H.
WHITE

In the midst of the hustle and bustle of city life we can create meaningful rituals and customs, too. We can have weekly Sunday dinners with friends, making a meal together or meeting at a neighborhood restaurant. We can plan for one Broadway show or concert as a monthly treat, or go to a different museum or art gallery each weekend.

Peter and I love to go to afternoon movies, and sometimes we see as many as three in one week! By setting these patterns of tradition, we can develop an appreciation for a sense of history anywhere we live.

THE OPPORTUNITIES FOR SERENITY

When we're not in a constant state of haste, all our senses become more alert, and our potential to enjoy life is expanded immeasurably. We live more graciously in the modern world by reawakening, and it is in this state that we truly find ourselves. When we slow down we can live more fully in the moment and more deeply within ourselves.

I'm grateful that although I have always worked hard I have been lucky to discover free time amid all the activity of a busy modern life; this is the path to serenity. For us to put modern life on hold, we must turn off the machinery and tune in to ourselves. When we slow down long enough to find ourselves, we discover new depths in our experience of life. People who live contentedly have the chance to discover themselves. One of our friends, an immensely successful businessman who specialized in aviation, now studies painting at the Old Lyme Academy, a distinguished art school nearby. On his days off, he looks out the window of his sunporch and inspiration is right there in front of his easel.

There is a certain majesty in simplicity.

—ALEXANDER POPE

Juan's father was an artist, and he didn't find time to paint until he moved to Stonington. When we bought our eighteenth-century cottage, Peter discov- *I never had to go* ered a passionate interest in architecture, *anywhere to find my* which he has been cultivating ever since. *paradise.*

Wherever we are, we can slow down —Emily enough to reveal passions we never knew we Dickinson had. A client of mine who later became a close friend decided to start walking the forty blocks to his office at a midtown investment firm. He chose a route that took him by Central Park each morning. Before long, Hank became so enamored of the natural beauty he began to set his alarm for five o'clock in the morning to give himself two serene hours in the park before going to the office. He has since become a nature buff and bird-watcher, involved in a variety of en-vironmental organizations and wildlife expeditions.

Inner Grace in Any Age

The easy grace of Stonington has taught me about the blessings of life available to us in any age: Faith in the good sense and coherence of everyday life sustains us. Here I have learned the value of taking the time to find comfort in the simple things, not letting myself become inured to what is around me every day. When I'm in the village I can smell hot brownies a house away. I delight in basic human transactions, like picking up the morning paper at Frankie's. I expand with a sense of continuity doing errands and enjoying daily rituals with my neighbors. I enjoy the solitary pleasure of watching the boats in the harbor. I try to build community and connectedness by talking and working with local proprietors, friends, and neighbors, helping out any chance I get. Life is a joy when we stop racing around in a feverish search for a new, vague "something" out there. When we live in a state of endless expectation of what could be, we never experience exaltation in what is: being alive to what is here for us every day. All gracious living—whether in a small village or a big city—requires this development of inner grace.

The individual human is still the creature who can wonder, who can be enchanted by a sonata, who can place symbols together to make poetry to gladden our heart, who can view a sunrise with a sense of majesty and awe.

—ROLLO MAY

Gracious living today is not confined to village life, but is an attitude toward life that comes naturally in the ideal village setting. Kindness, courtesy, and elegance—these are gracious values in any age. Elegance means "ingenious simple and effective," according to the *New Oxford English Dictionary*. This way of living isn't beyond our reach today. By rearranging our priorities we can enjoy all the virtues of the village in a new world.

Two

❋

Reawakening Our Five Senses

GRATUITOUS GRACE

Some mornings when I wake up, I look around my room and I think, How good is this day. How good to be alive. As my eyes scan the walls, I feel contentment in the lemon yellow, azure blue, spring green, pink, and lilac colors in our paintings as well as in our quilts, the "Joy" pattern of our bed hangings, our paperweight collection, and the flowers. I am moved by the light streaming in from the window or, if it's raining, I feel cozy with the sound of the rain pounding against the glass. I take in the art, the paintings that say so much to me, the family photographs, the pictures of friends, and I smile to myself. I smell the rich, roasted coffee brewing in the kitchen; I hear the sound of Peter padding across the room; I feel the cool white sheets against my arms and legs; I notice the beauty of the yellow tulips that I bought in the store yesterday or the pink peonies that I picked from the garden, beautiful not only for their shape and color but because they are life itself.

How meaningful life can be when we celebrate the sensory gifts that are available to us each day. Each one of our five senses is a gateway to inner life and experience. Beautiful music, a lovely poem, a breathtaking landscape, or a powerful painting; the taste of a seven-hour roast leg of lamb and the perfect red wine to go with it; the smell of roses; the feel of a baby's skin or the lips of our beloved; these make a heaven of our life on earth. Emerson wrote of this "direct, personal, unmediated experience [where] life is an ecstasy." We don't have to turn to anything beyond the world of our senses—the loveliness of a warm breeze or the feel of grass under bare feet—to know how we can feel most fully alive. When we are open, our senses

How simple and frugal a thing is happiness: a glass of wine, a roast chestnut . . . the sound of the sea. . . . All that is required to feel that here and now is happiness is a simple, frugal heart.

—NIKOS KAZANTZAKIS

alert, life resonates within us. We calm down, slow down, unplug our machines, and take in the moment; this restores meaning to life.

The twentieth-century English visionary Aldous Huxley wrote about spontaneous moments of appreciation for life. He called these "moments of gratuitous grace." There are moments, unbidden, when we experience the wonder of life in the simplest things. By recognizing the awesome potential for gratuitous grace in each day, we increase our appetite for life.

In every sight and sound around my house, an infinite and unaccountable friendliness, all at once, like an atmosphere, sustaining me.

—HENRY DAVID THOREAU

Whether we are happy or sad, whether we feel lucky or lost, whether we feel lightness of being or the heaviness of pain, what's important, ultimately, what makes us feel most alive, is our alertness to the richness of experience. When we savor this desire for awakening as a hope and a possibility, we can always feed our souls and make contact with our inner life. This is what makes life precious.

I live for the possibilities of the moment. I don't neglect the broad picture of life, the needs of others, or a sense of my larger responsibilities. But I am always alert to snap up those illuminating moments when I feel open to all the rhythms of life. "As human beings we have our roots in nature," wrote Rollo May, "not simply because of the fact that the chemistry of our bodies is of essentially the same elements as the air or dirt or grass. In a multitude of other ways we participate in nature—the rhythm of the change of seasons or of night and day, for example, is reflected in the rhythm of our bodies, of hunger and fulfillment, of sleep and wakefulness, of sexual desire and gratification, and in countless other ways."

The competitive busyness of modern life often makes us feel cut off from our own sensual rhythms and appetites. But why vie with our neighbors when we can enjoy the grace of breaking bread with them? Often, we're so busy we only have time to sample the appetizer at life's banquet, when we could be sitting down to enjoy the whole meal.

The flowers appear on the earth; the time of the singing of birds is come, and the voice of the turtle is heard in our land.

—SONG OF SOLOMON

When I was a little girl I kissed everyone who came to the door. I still love to hold hands and kiss the family and friends I love. I have some friends I give such a strong bear hug to I feel our ribs press together, and when I see certain children I run toward them and let them jump up on me. The aroma of baby shampoo in their hair, the chocolate smudges on their faces, and the stickiness left behind by lollipops all make me nostalgic. I adore playing airplane with babies, and blubbering their tummies until they can't stop giggling. I give them butterfly kisses with my eyelashes, and never lose an opportunity to give a love pat or a squeeze on the shoulder. Brooke loves me to massage her arms and hands, and

Alexandra adores it when I rub scented cream into her feet and toes.

I have a hunger, a thirst, a yearning, and a deep longing to taste it all.

The Alchemy of Sensory Experience

Sensory pleasures have a way of folding into one another. One sensation creates a mood, which opens us to other sensations, memories, and pleasures we've enjoyed. We feel lifted up out of this one moment, which seems to open out onto eternity. Interestingly, we travel the path to these spiritual heights on solid ground. We take a bite of a buttermilk biscuit and it links us to earlier emotional memories and experiences; we hear the clicking of heels on the street below and remember listening for

Reason is founded on the evidence of our senses.

—Percy Bysshe Shelley

our mother returning from an evening out. What our senses take in on one level reverberates on another. When a violin string is plucked, the untouched strings vibrate in synchrony. There is a subtle alchemy at work here. I pursue these waves of experience, this connectedness, with the same passion I give to my children, to Peter, to friends and family I love, and to my work.

In his remarkable novel, *Remembrance of Things Past,* the French writer Marcel Proust captured for all time the phenomenon of how one sensual experience brings forth a flood of powerful memories which tap into our inner life. He called this experience "involuntary memory." In

If you work at it, you can smell the smell of autumn leaves burning or taste a chocolate malt.

— F R E D E R I C K
B U E C H N E R

his novel the main character, upon tasting a madeleine pastry, is overcome by memories. This special moment in the present unlocks the door to a continuous present in which the past is still taking place, erasing any differences between past, present, and future. In this bite was a taste of eternity.

Peter and I recently celebrated our anniversary in Paris, on a trip which, on the last day, blessed me with this sense of past and present merging into a time out of time. Paris has charms that never fail to call up my sensual memories. Maybe it's the beauty of the city, so old, its architecture so lovely. Maybe it's the delight Parisians take in sensual pleasures. Everywhere in Paris, at any time of the day, you see people walking down the street with either a delectable pastry in hand or a crispy baguette tucked under an arm. On this particular trip we stayed in a tiny hotel, on perhaps the narrowest of streets in all of Paris, on the bohemian Left Bank. Our enchanting room was a duplex with a skylight and a window facing north into a tiny walled garden with an exquisite fountain. The hotel was a fifteenth-century cloister and our room had originally served as the attic. This intimate place inspired decorating ideas for our cottage. I imagined that we could conceal lighting in the rafters, tuck in some skylights, and be on top of the world.

On the Sunday morning that was our last day in Paris, I lay on my back looking up at the clouds moving across the skylight; a few birds fluttered across the sky. The cool starched linen sheets soothed me as I anticipated this last day. We had the entire day free to do whatever we pleased. Peter asked the waiter to leave our breakfast tray on the coffee table. When I became aware of the fragrance of hot, freshly baked croissants, I rose up out of my reverie. Then I smelled the chocolate. That was it! The night before we had deliberately ordered coffee and fresh squeezed orange juice and no pastries for breakfast, knowing we would be feasting the rest of the day from lunch to tea to dinner. But once those deep aromas wrapped their tentacles around me, I was enthralled. I leapt out of bed, scampered to the balcony, and there I saw

Tell them . . . that if eyes were made for seeing,
Then Beauty is its own excuse for being.

—EMERSON

a pretty tray with a bud vase holding Sonja pink roses and white freesia and a basket brimming with hard rolls, sweet bread, chocolate-filled pastry, brioches, and croissants. I could hardly speak. As I wrapped myself in the huge, cozy, white terrycloth bathrobe provided by the hotel, tying the sash tightly around my waist, I instantly knew I was lost. The feast would begin at breakfast!

How can orange juice taste so sweet? How could it be so delightfully pulpy and refreshing? Caught up in an orgy of delight, the next thing I knew I was fondling the miniature jars of cherry, strawberry, and Concord grape confiture! Maybe this should be a honey day, or should I have the orange marmalade? My only agony was that I couldn't decide which topping to choose for my perfect, buttery croissant; ah, Paris . . . we should always have only such problems. I debated until I could no longer resist twisting the lid off the marmalade. As I did so I remembered dozens upon dozens of experiences of such sensuous euphoria when I was equally content and happy with so little. Taste and smell are only one point of entry.

As I leaned forward to break open the moist and flaky croissant, I placed on my lap a starched white cotton napkin, which I noticed had a lovely basket-weave design. A few inches of my periwinkle blue-and-white—striped nightshirt peeked out from under the terrycloth robe, reminding me of a beach towel. I grew keenly aware of how comfortable I felt in this old soft cotton nightshirt; how soft, like the texture of silk velvet, the shirt had become over the years.

When you have only two pennies left in the world, buy a loaf of bread with one, and a lily with the other.

— C H I N E S E
P R O V E R B

I noticed the room, decorated entirely in blue-and-white toile de Jouy, a traditional textile of eighteenth-century France. The colors reminded me of a ranch in Texas that I had decorated, where I had used a similar blue-and-white design in the guest room. I loved to stay in that room whenever I visited there.

The sense associations kept unfolding before me that morning in Paris. I could envision being at the ranch, eating succulent fried chicken, taking sunrise walks on roads through vast open spaces. As I

looked around me I felt a sense of overwhelming serenity. Peter sat next to me on a blue chair and we both
paused a few moments before reading our
Herald Tribune. We looked into each other's
eyes and toasted life with our stemmed orange juice glasses. We sipped coffee, tasted
the pastries, and looked up at the very
same moment toward the open window.
Dozens of churches clanged their bells in
concert for more than ten minutes. The
sweet, delicate, crunchy marmalade-
drenched nose of the croissant was still on my tongue.
I felt aware of my whole being and I was moved to tears.
I had the sensation that similar past experiences were
merging into this ever-present moment.

> *A light, a glory, a fair luminous cloud Enveloping the earth.*
>
> —SAMUEL TAYLOR COLERIDGE

The origin of my feelings that morning in Paris may
have been as simple as the sound of a gentle rain, or the
cheerful birds chirping away in the courtyard below our
window, the church bells, or the marmalade. However
near or far away the source, my body responded with a
potent pounding in my chest. However unscientific, however simple, physical experience and unconscious memories blended to transport me to a higher state. I think
about this experience over and over again. How do such
blessed moments of convergence come about? How we can
use them to understand our lives and live more fully? This
knowledge, this experience is timeless, available to us in
any age. When we experience this alchemy, the modern
world seems eons away.

THE VAN GOGH CONNECTION

On another trip to France, this time to a small village, Auvers-sur-Oise, where the artist Vincent van Gogh spent his last summer, painting seventy paintings in seventy days, I once again experienced this wonderous convergence of past and present. One day Peter and I shared lunch with the founder of the van Gogh Institute at the Auberge Ravoux, a restaurant van Gogh frequented. I was thrilled to sit at one of the tables where the master had eaten his lunch and dinner. I was aware that he had been everywhere in this room, walking on this same black-and-white building-block pattern on the inlaid tile floor. The tables and chairs were the ones he sat at, and the Swiss-embroidered white cotton floral design of the curtains is an exact replica of the panels that hung in the windows long ago. From where I sat I had a wonderful view of the whole space. I imagined I could hear the clip-clop of horses and carriages on the street, once again bringing people to this same spot that they came to over one hundred years ago. In the restaurant there are painted replicas of van Gogh's paintings of every place he set up his easel, from the wheat, corn, and sunflower fields to the gardens.

I felt van Gogh's presence everywhere. I glanced up at

Every day look at a beautiful picture, read a beautiful poem, listen to some beautiful music, and if possible, say some reasonable thing.

—JOHANN WOLFGANG VON GOETHE

the bar, on which a relief work in copper depicted a basket
of wheat. Above the bar hung dried salamis, the same type,
I'm told, that van Gogh had enjoyed. When
our bread arrived at the table I knew it was
the same kind of bread baked for the
painter. It was sliced on a cutting board,
perhaps the very same one used to slice his
bread. The smell of garlic, butter, and
soupe de poisson emanating from the
kitchen flooded my senses. I had to have
everything I knew he'd enjoyed; so I went
all the way and ordered la spécialité de l'Auberge Ravoux:
gigot d'agneau de sept heures, the seven-hour lamb, which I
learned was van Gogh's favorite. It was inexpressibly delicious. The meat was so moist, tender, and sweet, it simply melted in my mouth. I can still taste this remarkable
meal.

No spring, nor summer beauty hath such grace,
As I have seen in one autumnal face.
—JOHN DONNE

And what is a perfect dinner without a sublime dessert?
Dominique Janssens, the founder and owner, who was a
repository of historical information, told me that van
Gogh loved the *mousse au chocolat,* and urged me to taste it.
A twelve-inch crock of chocolate mousse was placed at the
center of our rectangular table, smelling like brownies
baking in the oven. Shavings of chocolate
decorated the top. What can I say? The
mingling of the lamb and the chocolate
mousse stirred up memories.

As I licked my spoon that day in Auvers,
I thought of my mentor and friend Eleanor

The brain is the citadel of sense perception.
—PLINY THE ELDER

Brown, who ended every meal with chocolate ice cream, chocolate mousse, or a piece of Godiva chocolate. I savored the sweet ecstasy of the moment, the vibrant color, the spirit, the intimacy, the passion of van Gogh's paintings, Eleanor Brown's beautiful designs, my husband's gentleness and love. All of these converged into an exalted moment. The sense of history, the timelessness of human pleasure, our connectedness to each other nourished and sustained by our senses, filled me with awe that day, and held me in a timeless embrace.

There is pleasure in the pathless woods, There is a rapture on the lonely shore, There is society, where none intrudes, By the deep sea, and music in its roar: I love not man the less, but nature more.

—LORD BYRON

Modern technology and advances in the forms and varieties of entertainment cannot match the richness of our own sensory experience. The gifts of daily life are the simple things that surround us. When we pay close attention to these we discover the magical inner life of all things we encounter every day.

THE INNER GRACE OF OBJECTS

In Auvers I experienced everything as part of another continuum as well: the continuum of my own daily life. The ladderback side chair where I sat was an ideal height for enjoying a leisurely conversation—its back was just about an inch higher than the table—allowing one's arms adequate freedom of movement. I was aware that these chairs had the same rush seats as the chairs we bought at an antique shop near Giverny, impressionist painter Claude Monet's hometown. We have a collection of these chairs in the kitchen of our cottage. These sturdy, simple side chairs allow us freedom of movement and a solid comfortable seat. Their design and charm give us a feeling of physical and emotional comfort that enhances well-being. I was also aware that the table at the auberge was the same size, shape, design, and fruitwood as the writing table in my Zen writing room in Stonington.

The older I grow the more do I love spring and spring flowers.

—EMILY DICKINSON

The furniture we sit on, the atmosphere of where we live, and the objects that surround us, have their own grace. We can see this so clearly in the beauty of Shaker furniture, in the simplicity and unembellished practicality of its design. These are an expression of the Shakers' highest spiritual values, plain, practical, and simple. Shaker furniture has such timeless and spiritual appeal. In no other design is the minimalist aesthetic clearer than in this inherent beauty, eloquence, and grace in form that follows function. As an interior designer, I find this fascinating: Purity of design with clean lines, without any superfluous decoration, the Shaker hallmark. We become attached to the objects in our immediate midst because they are far more

That which above all others yields the sweetest smell in the air is the violet.

—FRANCIS BACON

than mere matter, they are symbols, providing deeper meaning to our daily rituals. The French farm table where I write is from Provence, so I'm mysteriously transported to another country as I sit quietly in Connecticut and write. The butcher-block table in our kitchen was used by two strong men in the nineteenth century, and all those undulations in its surface add charm and texture.

I have been here before,
But when or how I cannot tell:
I know the grass beyond the door,
The sweet keen smell,
The sighing sound, the lights around the shore.

—DANTE GABRIEL ROSSETTI

Objects tell a story, as people do, and whenever we know their provenance—their source or origin—or understand the guiding principle behind the form, our pleasure increases. Years ago I fell in love with an eighteenth-century pine hutch we now have centered against a prominent wall in the dining room. The bottom section was designed for live chickens, a detail I enjoy knowing.

Looking around our cottage awakens me to the importance of handicrafts as an integral part of the energy of our rooms. When an object is made by skilled hands, it has a soul that is felt. I have a collection of old baskets placed under a large fruitwood dessert table. The workmanship is so fine. One of these baskets is Shaker, strongly delicate and handsomely beautiful. We use everything, regardless of its age and value, because all the objects we surround ourselves with are functional as well as pretty. When we incorporate our favorite things into the fabric of our daily lives, we are elevated into a higher aesthetic. The art of living with grace is available to each of us, right here, where we live.

OUR SACRED SPACE

Recently, I was moved and exhilarated by an exhibition of paintings by the seventeenth-century Dutch master Jan Vermeer at the National Gallery in Washington, D.C. Almost all of his paintings are set in rooms that he has transformed into sacred, intimate spaces, where you observe ordinary people in a simple household setting performing personal activities. These paintings are heartbreakingly beautiful. Looking at them we're transported, grasping a sense of the actual life taking place in each room: In one a woman reads a letter, in another a woman pours liquid from a pitcher, and in still another, a woman sews a piece of lace. In one a young woman stands at a virginal, a period musical instrument. She is exquisitely dressed in pearl-colored silk taffeta with a sky-blue shawl, entertaining an unseen visitor. Could it be the viewer? Vermeer's voyeuristic style invites us to enter into this sacred space. In all of these paintings the action gives us the sense of something taking place in the moment, yet the stillness, the quietness around these

While with an eye made quiet by the power
Of harmony, and the deep power
of joy
We see into the life of things.

—WILLIAM
WORDSWORTH

scenes gives them an aura of eternity. There is a sense of peace contained in each of these rooms, which are finally more than rooms. They are sacred spaces of peace.

Sunlight is painting.

—NATHANIEL HAWTHORNE

Vermeer uses light to convey spirituality, combined with jewel-like colors, love letters, and pictures of cupids to allude to discreet undercurrents of sexuality, allowing us a glimpse into a Dutch lady's most intimate moments. Perhaps her husband is a sea captain, off to sea for months at a time. She was able to amuse herself, often alone but never lonely. The love doesn't disappear when the lover is away. Through Vermeer's paintings, we learn a great deal of the history of the house as a private place for a family, a sacred space where a woman can do her housework and show her skills as an interior decorator. Her reward is the creation of an atmosphere where she wants to participate in a stream of present moments. The rooms become animated because of her presence. When a child or man appears, the woman is calm and receptive.

If the doors of perception were cleaned, Everything would appear . . . as it is, infinite.

—WILLIAM BLAKE

Ever since I came to New York in 1959 to study interior design, Vermeer has been a favorite artist. No other painter captures privacy and reverence so movingly. The sensuality he conveys in the immediate experience as well as the sense of eternity he expresses through light and color and composition is truly unique. He used light streaming into oversized windows, allowing us to look inside and observe an austere, simple, clean space, filled by a woman's sensuous as well as mystical presence. If you missed this great show last year in Washington, right here in New York, at the Frick Museum, are three of his paintings, and the Metropolitan Museum of Art has five.

The rooms we live in physically, and the metaphorical room where our spirit lives, our heart and our mind, are connected. Such rooms present untold opportunities for grace. I know I'm living with grace when I feel content just being in the blessed spaces in my home. I have always tried to transform every place where I spend my time into a sacred space, where Peter

It's not a bad life to be serenaded by birds and church bells.

and I and family and friends can create memorable moments morning, noon, and night. At home we can explore all the possibilities for gracious living in the modern world. We try to expand these possibilities by adding sensual texture and by awakening to serendipitous moments of grace in our midst.

At the cottage we delight in rearranging our paintings and objects. We set the dining-room table for breakfast with care and beauty, as though it were a royal banquet. We enjoy using our parents' dessert dishes and a variety of one-of-a-kind cups and saucers, handed down in our families through generations. We like to paint a watercolor from memory out in the sunlight of the Zen garden. We never tire of polishing the surface of a sweet old table or rubbing brass until it gleams. All our treasured things add variety and enjoyment to our everyday rituals. When we use a favorite bar of lime soap Brooke brought us from Paris, the chartreuse color and the hint of lemon and cocoa butter scent open us up to finding everything we do a gift. We dry our hands on pretty kitchen towels, different colors and designs each day. Why use only stripes or plaids when we can also enjoy checks? We enjoy arranging flowers, paying attention to the vase we select to assure it complements the color and mood we want the arrangement to convey. I put candies in hand-spun colored-glass dishes, smiling every time I add to the supply, happy to be part of sweetening a loved one's moment.

You will inhale happiness with the air you breathe, without dwelling on it or thinking about it.

—JOHN STUART MILL

All spaces in our cottage are worthy of respect, and we consecrate them because they are manifestations of our collective souls. The buttery is a walk-in closet, so filled with treasured objects we've gathered over time from our travels that this space is a living family autobiography, too rich to close the door upon. The shelves hold pottery, china, and glass—flower containers, pitchers, teapots as well as mustard pots—and we can remember the good times wrapped around each object. Where we were on that particular trip, what we ate for lunch that day, all bring more meaning to the simple, often humble objects we collect along our journey.

I look out the window and find a riot of colored spinnakers, the large, colorful triangular boat sails set so they swing opposite the mainsail, gliding by. These vibrant sails balloon out in front of the boats in bold patterns of reds, yellows, blues . . . flags puffing in the breeze. The faces in the bouquets of pansies on my desk make me smile. On the wall to the left of the window hangs a watercolor of pansies painted by a friend in England. What is it about a pansy that makes it so dear to me?

Because I love every room in this cottage, everywhere I turn I find inspiration. My favorite appliqué quilt is a vibrant green with white panels, like windowpanes filled with flowers; the quilt is as old as I am. Looking at this beautiful quilt I am stirred into memories of my mother's flower garden and my childhood. I look at our books, our objects of affection, remembering each place where they were purchased or found. Many of my favorite objects were found here in Stonington, picked up right on Water Street at one of the many antique shops. Since we've come to the village, we haven't had a car, so I'm often seen dragging an old shutter or windowpane mirror down the street. My hands have become strong from this. I like to touch and carry the objects I love. I love sitting in my favorite rustic ladderback side chair, which we found down the street. It's been painted several times in various shades of off-white, but most of the paint has sloughed off, exposing the ash, a homey rye-toast color. No one could fabricate the charm of this "found" object. I also love to move things around the house all the time so I can touch

A morning-glory at my window satisfies me more than the metaphysics of books.
—WALT WHITMAN

them, put them in new places where they thrill me all over again. I display my four different-colored quilts—yellow, white, pink, purple, and green—the colors of pansies, on a large mahogany rack. I love it when everything around me feels present, vivid, and alive. No cloistered rooms gathering dust for me!

Outside the open window the morning air is all awash with angels. Love calls us to things of this world.

—RICHARD WILBUR

Grace becomes ours when we pull together the increasingly fragmented pieces of our lives and integrate them into a sustained pattern of meaning. Our lives are enriched and grounded in the time spent enjoying our home. I never feel our cottage is a work trap, though Peter and I spend many hours working inside its walls. On the contrary, it is a sweet place where we can idealize daily life. I know I am living with grace when I'm just sitting in one of our flower chintz–upholstered swivel chairs, which is as wonderful as being in a garden (and the down cushion makes it more comfortable); or repairing the loose leg on an antique end table we found in Italy in 1976. We work as a team, so one glues while the other holds the wood together. This loving of objects makes them alive to us. We rearrange some tulips, selecting a smaller vase, and after changing the water and cutting down the stems, we give new life to the cut flowers and our spirit. We light a chubby candle held in an antique match striker. Now that safety matches don't work on these ribbed outer surfaces, we've turned our collection into candle holders. To take an object we love and find new, inventive uses for it brings these favorite things new glory. Just because we don't make rich gravies every day doesn't mean we should relegate the gravy boat to a high shelf in a dark cupboard. By using it for a chopped tomato, onion, and balsamic vinegar dressing, its presence in our lives is continual.

Writing a letter with a favorite fountain pen with lavender ink on our Nile-blue cottage stationery, using a floral stamp, lends enchantment to the writing process, allowing us to find the present moment rich with spiritual overtones. While we may not have a collection of enamel objects like those created at the house of Karl Fabergé in Moscow at the end of the nineteenth century, the objects we use can be a delight to the hand, the mind and the eye. When we have refined objects that add elegance, wit, and charm to life, continuing the ideal marriage of materials and design, we tap into the mystery whereby man's love of nature inspires great beauty in his creation of objects. We should have nothing profane in our home. Nothing has to lack imagination and spirit, or be dull. When I put my ink in a cut-crystal inkwell with a brass lid, the light catches the glass and shimmers. Even something as prosaic as a covered copper pot for soup can be charming, especially when you polish it at the kitchen sink while talking lovingly to a child.

I haven't understood a bar of music in my life, but I have felt it.

—IGOR STRAVINSKY

Where we place our objects in our home and how they function for us has great power over our well-being, our feelings of contentment and our spiritual illumination. Here life is rich with opportunities for increasing our appreciation of the gift and mystery of life. I feel deep contentment just being home in this sacred space.

Whatever that principle is which feels, conceives, lives, and exists, it is heavenly and divine, and therefore must be eternal.

—C I C E R O

Our homes are places where we can express and enjoy many pleasures. Here we can be free and creative. Our home is a canvas on which we paint many things: still lifes, landscapes, portraits, and anything that moves us in a deeply personal way. We design our homes for spiritual as well as physical comfort. In the right atmosphere, lying on a hardwood floor, gazing up at a dreamy blue ceiling, looking around at flowers, paintings, and objects of personal meaning can transport us into other worlds, out of body and time. Lie on the floor in a favorite room, bend your knees to protect your back, and muse. The kind of furniture you select and where you place it helps you to feel spiritually elevated. It's important to free yourself from the frustration of having objects in your space that don't mean something to *you.*

Last winter I took on the huge project of repainting our bedroom in our New York apartment. I was writing a book about the home and inspired myself to tackle one of my favorite spaces in the world. How can four white walls, four doors, two windows, a sand-colored bleached floor and a heavenly sky-blue ceiling become a boundless garden where the air is perfumed by flowers and the paintings become windows onto beautiful scenes? Six floors up from the cement sidewalk below, we live in a dream, a garden in bloom, evoking my awakening as a little girl to the beauty and wonder of flowers from Mother's garden. As I painted, Peter polished the brass on a dressing table I inherited from my mother. I could almost feel her brushing my hair before braiding it, remembering how she sat in front of a dormer window where this sweet piece of French provincial furniture was placed. The sentimental antique walnut dressing table doesn't really go with our Canadian maple four-poster bed and all the white wicker, but the room wouldn't be as sacred if Mother's table, along with all the loving memories it evokes, weren't here. Our homes are stitched together out of pieces of personal history, aesthetic taste, and the fabric of comfort, continuity, and support. Home is our little corner of eternity.

I've often told my decorating clients that they should love everything in their house. My French peasantware lamp, a lady in an apron holding a huge pale blue umbrella, is silly but lovely. Whenever I look at it I think of Brittany, where it comes from. Just the other day I used a white linen cocktail napkin with the monogram J for my maiden name, Johns. It made me remember my parents' Chippendale tea table and see my mother using these very napkins. I have only one and it's precious to me. The more meaning we surround ourselves

He was a rationalist, but he had to confess that he liked the ringing of church bells.

—ANTON CHEKHOV

with, the greater our opportunities to find meaning in life.

When I was on *Oprah Winfrey* for the first time, her producer asked which of the rooms in our apartment was my favorite. I immediately said that our bedroom was. Oprah sent her film crew to the apartment to capture the spirit of this soft, airy space. After the shoot, I walked into our bedroom through our narrow angular hall, turning the corner, as always surprised by the sheer beauty of this room. On the window wall is a twenty-four-inch-deep ledge, with bookcases underneath. Flower bouquets adorn the ledges in front of each window and are reflected in the panes of glass. That day, I had placed a black umbrella near an antique white wicker chair with a pastel floral chintz cushion; the pairing made a beautiful still life, as though the umbrella were a parasol. In that instant I saw the room through the cameraman's eyes. The "umbrella visit" lasted only three or four minutes but was such a memorable, delightful surprise; an unexpected opportunity for new inspiration and a new way of experiencing this sacred space. Everywhere we look we can create an animated still life, a scene that suggests, points, and triggers our consciousness, and makes us more aware of our humanity.

Why is it I so enjoy sharing my sacred

Musical or not, sound wends its way into the very core of our being. The proof is that traces of it remain hooked, like ragged tatters, in the soul's inward recesses.

—F. Gonzales-Crussi

The sky is the daily bread of the eyes.

—Emerson

spaces with others? I guess it's because I imagine that others will derive the same pleasure as I do from the shine on the old brass andirons or the reflection of the polished green Vermont marble of the hearth. We want our space to be worthy of our friends and people we care about. Our sacred space taps into a universal experience of place, both physical and spiritual, that we all long for.

Sense and Sensibility

Our ability to experience, to be fully open to life through our heart and our senses is within our control. All the new and improved machinery of modern life can never replace the richness of direct, unmediated experience of the world around us. Emerson wrote of the "direct, personal, unmediated experience [wherein] life is an ecstasy." The most common situations are rich in possibilities because everyday life is the rich soil from which we grow. Only when we remember to keep alert to the deeper power within these daily experiences do we have the opportunity to tune into a more vivid life. It's really a matter of our sensibility, of our ability to be aware of and responsive to emotion and taste.

In youth and health, in summer, in the woods or on the mountains, there comes days when the weather seems all whispering with peace, hours when the goodness and beauty of existence enfold us like a dry warm climate, or chime through us as if our inner ears were subtly ringing with the world's security.

—William James

The day after we returned from our anniversary trip to Paris I was still overflowing with the experience. I rejoiced again to find daily life at home equally rich in sensuous possibilities. Wherever we live there are sights and sounds that can reach deep into our souls, whether it's the sound of children playing on the street or a view of the sky outside our front door; the opportunities for gracious living are ever present.

I love it, I love it;
and who shall dare
To chide me for
loving
that old arm-chair?

— ELIZA COOK

After our return, the Paris church bells continued to cast a profound spell over me. One night I was startled awake by a thumping inside me; I sat up in bed in our apartment in New York City and listened as the church bells chimed. It was four o'clock in the morning but I was still on Paris time, where it was already ten o'clock in the morning. This glorious "wake-up call," however, was too strong to allow me to just roll over and go back to sleep. So I made use of the time. After preparing some coffee, I went to the laundry room to put in a load of clothes from the trip. I'd converted two old-fashioned maids' rooms into useful work spaces next to the laundry room. They're peaceful retreats, unusually quiet for a New York City apartment. Through an open window, facing the courtyard, I heard only the patter of gentle rain.

I passed the next two hours in a dreamlike state, relishing and deliberately prolonging my sensations of the experience of the trip. I sipped coffee as I ironed. I pulled out the blue-and-white–striped nightshirt I had worn in

Paris and spray-starched the white mandarin collar and cuffs. As I folded it neatly, I squirted on it a spritz of orange-scented *eau de toilette*. (Jean Lapart's Paris cologne has lemon and grapefruit scents and also gives a clean twist to the smell of freshly laundered clothes.) When I sprayed on the scent, the "croissant/marmalade moment" surfaced inside me. I was able to bring that rhapsodic Sunday morning in Paris right into my tiny laundry room. I love to spray natural room fragrances around the house; they have a way of engaging all my senses, invoking sensual memories of orange groves in Florida or a visit to a friend's garden perfumed by lemon trees in Provence. There is a company called Citrus Magic that offers these pure, lovely, natural room fragrances—should you wish to partake of these aromatic pleasures for yourself. You can find them anywhere from a spa where you go to have a massage to a hardware store where you stock up on light bulbs.

Later in the day, I couldn't wait to call our daughter Brooke, who spent the year in Paris after she graduated from college and is the real Francophile in our family, to tell her about our trip. I told her about every meal, each pastry, every view of the Seine, every café, every boutique, every museum, every postcard, every park, every scene; I didn't

Tasting, seeing, experiencing living— all these demonstrate that there is something common to enlightenment— experience and our sense experience; the one takes place in our innermost being, the other on the periphery of our consciousness.

—D. T. SUZUKI

want to lose a minute of that wonderful experience. When I told her about the church bells in Paris that Sunday, she gasped with recognition. And then she told Peter and me about the moment when she was twenty-one and decided to move to Paris. She was living in Santa Barbara the summer after graduating from college, and one evening, while she was talking on the telephone with a college friend who was living in Paris, she could hear the sound of church bells clanging at the other end of the line. "A bell went off in me," she told us. "I asked myself, What am I doing in California when I could be in Paris where those beautiful bells are ringing? I'm moving to Paris." That's all it took . . . well, maybe a few more variables came into play. But Brooke lived with her friend in Paris for a year, on the Left Bank, close to where our hotel was located. She, too, was profoundly moved by the symphony of church and cathedral bells and by the sensory feast of Paris.

Then the song of a whitethroat, pure and ethereal, with the dreamy quality of remembered joy.

—Rachel Carson

A Passion for Bells

The ringing of church bells always elicits mystical, magical sensations in me because of the many memories it evokes. I remember the power of the bells from Grace Church in Wilmington, Delaware, where my grandfather Benjamin

Morley Johns was the minister when I was a little girl.
When Peter and I were married at St. James Church on
Madison Avenue at Seventy-first Street, we arranged for
the church bells to ring out for more than twenty minutes
so our friends could walk to my apartment
on Sixty-third Street with the joyous clanging of the bells following them along the
way. The sound echoed in our souls, like a
favorite hymn or a song you keep with you
long after you've heard it.

*We become in part
what our senses
take in.*

—Eknath
Easwaran

    Across Park Avenue we hear the bells of
the Brick Church. Our bed is deliberately
placed near the windows so we can have a close view of
the colonial architecture with its Georgian details, Corin-
thian columns, and towering steeple with a copper ball
finial and weather vane. Every time we hear the bells we
pause, our emotions stirred. The church bells at the Second Congregational Church in Stonington wake us up as
well, with their deep-throated bonging resonance. Those
bells have been ringing out in exultation since 1824!

    I have discovered that I am not alone in my passion
not only for bells, but for all of life's sensual delights. "Beauty is so important to
me, Alexandra," one woman told me last
year on a visit to Winston-Salem, North
Carolina. "I'm at a banquet every time I set
a pretty table for a family meal or when my
husband and I have friends over. I'm nour-

*Colors are the smiles
of nature . . . they
are her laughs, as in
flowers.*

—Leigh Hunt

ished by the colors, the textures, the flowers—even before I taste the food I feel satisfied.''

Every little pine needle expanded and swelled with sympathy and befriended me. I was so distinctly made aware of the presence of something kindred to me, that I thought no place could ever be strange to me again.

—HENRY DAVID
THOREAU

This richness of sensation, this openness to life itself is powerful and precious. So powerful, that sometimes I am overwhelmed by it. Recently I was having a moving conversation with a close friend over lunch in a French bistro. We talked about our deepest yearnings. "Why is it," I found myself asking her, "we can sometimes feel so alone when we have these stirrings and sensations?" My friend answered, with a smile, "It's because most people don't feel or express these things to one another. If they heard us they would probably think we're crazy." We laughed and kissed and hugged good-bye, nourished by our lunchtime rendezvous far more than by our salads and iced teas. Walking back to my apartment I felt as light as air. Maybe we are crazy. But how wonderful to feel so alive.

Three

✣

Expressing with Heart and Hand

THE JOY OF DOING

The one sure way I know to restore grace to my hectic life is to work with my hands. I love to touch the soil, to feel the wet earth between my fingers. I've tried wearing gardening gloves but I miss the dirt. The more use I put my hands to, the more creative I feel. When I was a child my family had a farm where I loved to use a pitchfork to gather hay. I grew and sold flowers and vegetables. I even enjoyed cleaning the chicken coop. After gathering eggs,

I'd make omelets for breakfast, filled with tomatoes and peas from my own garden. We also made our own jelly from the grapes in our arbor. We did so much by hand. Back then I was moved by watching my father make a ceremony of slicing the roast beef at the table. He looked so capable standing at the head of the table, tools in hand, sharpening the knife. During those moments when I'd sit watching him I'd feel a sense of grace in this silent ritual. The simple act of slicing the roast on a cutting board at the center of the table filled my heart with appreciation and my life with a sense of meaning.

I know of no more encouraging fact than the unquestionable ability of man to elevate his life by a conscious endeavor.

—HENRY DAVID
THOREAU

Ever since those often lovely childhood days when I spent hours upon hours working in my mother's garden digging, pruning, watering, and fertilizing, I have depended on my hands to work for me. My heart connects through touch. I've learned the joys of involvement and participation, preferring to use my hands rather than to watch others work. When I learned how to pick flowers for myself I also learned how to arrange them in beautiful bouquets. Today, I find picking strawberries or blueberries is more fun than buying them in the grocery store; growing them myself would be better still. I continue to love arranging flowers. Nature constantly inspires me to remain earthy. I remember going to a wedding when I was a teenager wearing white gloves, hiding my gardener's hands. Look at your hands and think of them as your finest tools to create something useful as well as beautiful.

I do everything I can with my hands. I love washing dishes. I love the direct contact with dish water and lemon soap. I don't wear gloves because I love playing with the sparkly, bubbly, sudsy water. I love to iron. I iron like the wind blows, effortlessly. I love to set a table, to lay down colors and patterns that delight my eye. I'm always puttering around the house, cleaning, polishing floors, brass, and silver, anything I can get my hands on. I love to hand-wash linens and hang them up on a clothesline to dry. There is something thrilling about using old-fashioned wooden clothespins, the kind we painted and made into dolls when we were children. The sight of fresh blue-white linens on the clothesline animated by a breeze is graceful and moving. Sometimes I wish I could wash laundry on an old nickel corrugated washboard, the way wash was done before washing machines were available to the general public. Now you find these in antique shops. I get a kick out of hand-washing my colorful stockings, bras, and underpants. When I rinse them out, I always use my favorite almond soap to please me and subtly perfume my intimate items.

Our own interests are still an exquisite means for dazzling our eyes agreeably.
—Blaise Pascal

I also delight in cleaning out a horse barn and brushing a horse's mane and rubbing saddle soap on the leather saddle. I love chopping firewood and laying the fire. When we do something by hand, we connect directly to the task and become one with it, aware of the value of concentrating our attention fully on what we're doing. I appreciate being able to hear the noises of the task at hand, rather than being irritated by the grating, buzzing noise of an electric machine. I enjoy raking leaves, sweeping the bluestone and brick terrace, weeding the garden, heading the geraniums in the window boxes, watering the grass, hosing off the outdoor furniture, and scrubbing the mildew off the white picket fence. I'm quick to pick up a paint brush and repaint the window boxes if they seem dingy because I love pure, brilliant white surfaces. I move terra-cotta pots around from sun to shade, placing them where the plants will thrive. Whenever I engage my two hands in manual labor, I receive instantaneous satisfaction. Whether I'm washing windows or pruning the lilac tree, I'm fully present and completely self-contained. And when I have no interest in performing rugged tasks, I still love to climb trees.

He alone is an artist whose hands can execute perfectly what his mind has conceived.

—MICHELANGELO

I love using hand-held tools: hammers, screwdrivers, shovels, and spades. Their basic, simple forms look eloquent to me. I don't mean to romanticize primitive tools and methods, but often these rustic tools are beautiful in themselves, and they do so much for us. When things go wrong I feel less of a sense of frustration when I know I can repair a problem myself with a hammer and a nail. When we and our tools work well together we're a team. It's true we have been afforded

Industry keeps the whole body healthy.

—WILLIAM J. BENNETT

many advantages to be grateful for in our modern instruments and new technology, but there is an undeniable satisfaction in using our own sheer animal power and energy. We feel a deep sense of satisfaction when we alone are the engine that makes something happen. When we work with our hands we know that when something gets done it's because we did it.

Our ability to find grace in daily living depends upon how much we participate in finding it. When we work with our hands, we find grace in the process—and a surge of energy.

What differentiates human beings from computers, no matter how clever, is that computers can do anything but enjoy nothing. I can get a computer to play Beethoven, but I can't program it to enjoy it.

—George Dennis O'Brien

Letting Our Legs Do the Walking

For a price we can buy any modern service. We can hire people to do our cooking, our cleaning, even our clothes shopping. We can order our groceries over the phone and have them delivered. If we're really hooked into technology we can do all our grocery shopping and banking from a keyboard and a computer screen. But electronic errands don't appeal to me. I'd miss banking because our cottage is just a few blocks away from the stately colonial bank building, and I enjoy our friendly exchanges with Tina and Debby. Our local bank will count jars of change for us, free of charge, and deposit the amount into our checking accounts. But I actually prefer rolling my own coins, and always have a supply of paper wrappers for quarters, nickels, dimes, and even pennies. (The rolling process reminds me of a trip to France and Italy in 1962 that began with change gathered in a mayonnaise jar.) And as for shopping by phone, I would surely miss looking at all the fresh fruit and vegetables at the farm stand or in the grocery store. I'd miss those beautiful piles of red tomatoes, radishes, and peppers, shiny dark purple eggplants, plums and blueberries, bright oranges, yellow lemons; I'd miss the green limes, grapes, and variety of greens, including spinach. I'd miss all the different shapes and colors of potatoes, apples, and pears. I'd miss experiencing the sheer bounty of nature on a daily basis. I'd miss the sensory experience of wandering around a great market where there might be an inspiring array of cheeses, sauces, and freshly squeezed juices. And breads! I can spend days looking at breads. I've photographed markets in France for over thirty years, and have some spectacular pictures of baked goods. How creative we human beings are in finding ways to feed and enrich ourselves. Even when I'm staying in a hotel, I go to the Paris markets as religiously as I go to museums. We don't need to consume in order to appreciate an experience. When I was seven and had my own vegetable, fruit, and flower garden at our farm, my mother took me to the Museum of Fine Arts in Boston with my godmother Mitzi,

I'm getting on. Time to cultivate my own garden.

—Claude Monet

also an avid gardener and artist. We saw many beautiful Impressionist paintings, including several Cézanne still lifes of fruits. Nearly forty years later I discovered Gustave Caillebotte's painting *Fruit Displayed on a Stand,* painted in 1881 and owned by the Boston Museum of Fine Arts. Peter and I have gone more than a dozen times together to gaze at this picture, and when I made my final selections for *The Postcard As Art,* I included this masterpiece. Whenever I pass a Korean market in New York, I have to pause and experience the wonder of the lush, vivid displays of edible colors.

There are people, though, who believe that doing the shopping or the laundry, or doing errands and labor of any kind is beneath them. Some people have become so accustomed to letting others do everything for them that they've grown bored with life and with themselves. It's sad, because there are so many daily tasks that are actually relaxing and enjoyable, that put a rhythm in your day. If I hired someone to sweep the floor or shop in the market every time I needed to do these tasks, I would be handing over to someone else a valuable part of my life. I remember one exhilarating afternoon when, after writing all morning, I spent four hours mending a broken plate, polishing brass, fixing a broken wooden bucket, cleaning the gunk out of a clogged drain, changing sheets, and anticipating the arrival of the children for the weekend. I was lost in a joyous trance. There are so many

> *Enthusiasm is grounded in play. Your creative work is actually your inner playmate.*
>
> —JULIA CAMERON

opportunities for us to become engrossed in the healing rhythm of productive work. When you cut yourself off from this pace of life, you lose your energy for life. Being physically immersed in daily life is rich and creative. This is, in part, what we were meant to do.

The tendency of man's nature to good is like the tendency of water to flow downward.

—MENCIUS

Today, many people can press a button and turn on all their entertainment. I have been in homes where the owners have an elaborate remote control device in every room that controls a music system whose sound is piped into all corners of the house. The video telephone is coming. There is a CD-ROM that lists all the names and telephone numbers in the country. These devices can be invaluable resources. But what if the big fuse—the generator behind all these machines—were to blow?

Maybe blowing a few big fuses wouldn't be so bad; maybe it would be a blessing in disguise. I remember both blackouts in New York City, both how panicked and helpless everyone felt and yet how exhilarated they were by having to suddenly step in to take the situation literally in hand. Some people took it upon themselves to direct traffic; others brought candles for their neighbors. We all gathered outside to share the evening's event, laughing, smiling, and discovering who our neighbors were. There wasn't anywhere to go. Where we were was just fine.

During the writing of *Mothers: A Celebration,* I was faced with a modern-day technological "catastrophe" that forced me to stop and reevaluate our dependency on machines. My assistant Julie and I had been steadily working on the first draft of the book and the deadline was approaching. I was writing the text longhand and Julie was inputting my writing into the computer and printing it out. One day, while we were hard at work, Julie's computer suddenly conked out, forcing us to be computerless for nine days while the machine was being repaired. I was scared at first. How would we be able to meet our deadline? We couldn't rent a computer, and Julie and I needed to work side by side at this stage, so she couldn't work elsewhere. In retrospect, though I had difficulty at first, I now view those nine computerless days as a lucky break. Forced to pause and figure out how to work with a single hard copy rather than a new and improved one daily, I saw what I had written in a new way.

Slowly, as I began reworking it, the book actually improved. I grappled with every sentence in what I had thought was a solid and worthy first draft. Looking at the page in front of me, I could see what was happening between the words and sentences. *Mothers* was an extremely intense book to write, and now I can't imagine what would have happened without that unexpected opportunity to slow down and really think about what I wanted my book to say.

> *I love tools. They are so beautiful, so simple and plain. They have not been* made *beautiful,* they *are* beautiful.
>
> —Robert Henri

I have to add, at this point, that I have a healthy appreciation for machines. I could never give up my camera, my Bose radio, the telephone, fax, or Xerox machine or my washer or dryer, or the office computer used by Julie, for that matter. I also happily plug in the coffee machine (though I equally enjoy dripping water through the filter by hand).

All the modern inconveniences.

—Mark Twain

Using the machine gives me time to go out and sit in my Zen garden while the coffee is brewing. Or I can retreat to my desk, listen to soft music—including the chirping of birds outside my open window—and write a letter on attractive stationery with a fountain pen. I even enjoy pasting my favorite flowered stamps on the envelope. But when I fool myself into thinking that machines can do everything for me, I end up frustrated and feel hollow. One summer Peter wore out our fax machine with his legal work and we felt we couldn't function until we had a new one FedExed to us the next day. I felt embarrassed having to call my editor at *McCall's* and tell her about our burned-out machine. I felt guilty, as though I had done something wrong. In the humidity of August, the paper crinkles up and gets stuck inside and we have to call Bob, the repairman, to come fix it. When you run low on toilet paper your self-interests are obvious, but I often forget to stock the tray of the fax with paper. When I'd promised to send work to New York and our Xerox machine broke down, I had to go to the local library and pay twenty-five cents per copy, which amounted to a lot of money and irritation. We tend to overpromise, never allowing enough grace time for a malfunctioning machine.

When I think I can be more efficient by using labor-saving devices, I'm usually disappointed. I never really save that much time. Perhaps more critical than not saving much time is that I lose contact with the energizing spirit I derive from working with my hands, which propels me toward exhilaration. The concept of an electric knife or toothbrush seems ridiculous. Americans tend to be gimmick-happy, inventing ways to save time that end up atrophying our bodies and dampening our spirits. Golfers used to get exercise walking the course, and caddies enjoyed their job, but now the ubiquitous golf cart has greatly contributed to the paunch. I can dictate a letter to a secretary, but my pen moves at the same rate as my lips. Before the computer, the typewriter was considered proper for business letters and contracts. When I opened my own firm on March 9, 1977, I went to see Walter Hoving at Tiffany and designed stationery with beautiful engraved lettering in geranium red. The size is unconventional, slightly smaller than the usual eight-by-ten-inch paper, and I made it a policy to handwrite estimates and invoices so my clients would know I had done so personally. Whenever someone dashes off to me a quick handwritten note, I am touched far more than when I receive a formal letter printed out on a computer.

All that in this delightful garden grows,
Should happy be, and have immortal bliss.

—EDMUND SPENSER

I save all the longhand drafts of my books because they document my creative process. All art is a process, imperfect by definition, which is reassuring to those of us struggling to express ourselves creatively. The New York Public Library periodically has exhibits that show early drafts of famous writers' manuscripts—T. S. Eliot, Charles Dickens, William Faulkner, Ernest Hemingway, Victor Hugo, and Ralph Waldo Emerson. I've always been fascinated by the edits they scribble in the margins and the deletions, and find it very instructive to see the artist's thinking process on paper. This always makes me feel connected to the heart and spirit of the author. Observing the guts of the creative process also teaches me more about what the author intended—it's illuminating to see why something was added or deleted. With the advent of computers, who keeps the rough drafts of their work? In a way, the computer enables people to erase their mistakes, erasing history.

Every art and every inquiry, as well as every practical pursuit, seems to aim at some good . . . at which all things aim.

—ARISTOTLE

Many designers use CAD, computer-aided design, which saves time but lacks the soul that can come only from the hands of an artist. We need to remind ourselves that we can lift our hearts and spirits to higher realms and get in closer touch with ourselves and life when we do things by hand. We are now in the position of having to be disciplined not to overuse and overdepend on technology. We should not fool ourselves into being expedient at the expense of creative passion. Alfred North Whitehead said, "The process itself is the actuality." We must always try to stay in touch with the process and not just the result. One of the great blessings of my life is how much I love the work itself. Beginnings and endings are not nearly as en-joyable as being in the flow of the task at hand. When we are creating, we are most alive, and most grace-filled. We must never lose sight of the joy of the process. Com-puters save time, which is wonderful, but a poet enjoys the feel of a fountain pen and paper just as an artist relishes the smell of the pigment on canvas. We should never feel we are wasting time when we take the long way to accomplish a task, or when we choose to use our own two hands over a machine.

One always has time enough, if only one applies it well.

—JOHANN WOLFGANG VON GOETHE

For us computer-enhanced beings, gracious living re-quires that we walk away from all the charged batteries every once in a while and do without the machines. Call me quaint, but I find that this works wonders. Every now and then, in order to retrieve and recharge ourselves, we need to take a step back to a slower, more natural path. When we live a simpler, more hands-on life we enrich our days.

WITH OUR OWN TWO HANDS

I've always loved the image of people wearing aprons. One of my favorite paintings by French Impressionist painter Pierre Auguste Renoir is of a waitress at a restaurant wear-ing a long soft white apron. One hand is on her hip. She has a dreamy look, but the apron says she is working, nevertheless.

I love to wear aprons; I wear them to add color and texture to my life. I have an apron collection rich with memories and meaning. Just as carpenters put their overalls to such good use, when I put on my apron, I'm ready for some serious action. So is my friend George, who often greets us at the door wearing an apron designed to hold his delicate carving tools. We affectionately call George "Mr. Chippendale," because he made all the elegant mahogany furniture in his living and dining room. No doubt his furniture will become priceless heirlooms someday.

My friend Roger loves to garden, cook, drive his car and his tractor, and build things in his house and garden. He's a strong guy; equally strong is his love of life. His clearest expression of that love is in the work of his hands.

So many of our friends do carpentry work around their houses not merely to save money, but for the love of driving a nail into a piece of lumber. Whether it's a bookcase, a gazebo, or a deck overlooking a lake, having fashioned such solid things out of wood, hammer, and nails feels deeply satisfying. The simple relationship between a worker and his or her tools is energizing. Mowing the lawn, pruning the trees, trimming

A natural discipline and intrinsic rhythm establishes itself, free from the strains and tensions of clock-watching. You have a sense of abiding by broad universal laws rather than of being bound by narrow and arbitrary rules.

—LOUISE
DICKINSON RICH

the hedges, watering the vegetable garden, plowing our own land, all engage us in spiritual renewal. There is meaning and grace in this harmony between man and nature in the work, too.

Last year I gave a talk in Madison, Connecticut, at a decorators' showhouse to benefit the Shoreline Foundation, a local charity group. I spoke under a giant white tent by the water's edge, where a hot fuchsia silk banner undulated in the wind and the

One of the greatest necessities in America is to discover creative solitude.

—CARL SANDBURG

summer sea sparkled. A young woman, who had waited patiently on line to have her book autographed, greeted me with open arms and danced a little pirouette. "I made this sundress just for this garden party today, Alexandra. Do you like it?" "Like it?" I replied. "I wish I were wearing your sundress," and with that I gave her a big hug. It was such a lovely dress with flowers in soft shades of blue and green. It was so lovingly made. What a joy to behold.

The pleasure this young woman took in working with her own hands to fashion this dress was apparent. Many of us never consider the joy of making a piece of our own clothing, even if we might have the ability. However simple, making things for ourselves gives us a thrilling sense of our own competence and creativity. Some people take deep pleasure in sewing, knitting, designing their own patterns. I have a friend who designs rugs. First, he paints a watercolor on paper, then mixes yarns in vegetable dyes and hangs the wool skeins—lengths of yarn wound in a long, loose coils—on a clothesline in his garden. At the final stage, he sits at his loom and weaves these fine yarns into beautiful rugs. His work is famous among weavers around the world.

God is the integration of life.

—ERIC BUTTERWORTH

Peter's daughter Andrée, a jewelry designer and sculptress, begins her creations by sketching her design on paper, then making models in wax before they're cast. Her work shows the marks from her manual carving, giving her pieces a unique energy. Mark Pescatello, our village master mason, takes such pride in his work that one feels he has created living monuments for future generations to appreciate. Roger Mühl begins his sun-soaked, vibrantly clear-colored oil paintings on small square sheets of paper with quick strokes of charcoal. He determines what size the canvas should be when he applies his oil paint. I've seen Brooke retreat to her studio, inspired by a pitcher of peonies or a walk, where, with brush in hand, she creates and recreates the energy and beauty that led to her inspiration.

Once we understand that our hands are connected to our heart, mind, and soul, we're able to trust the muse, and let creation flow through us. Often when I'm preparing a family celebration, I'm unaware of my movements, becoming one with the materials, a conductor bringing all the elements together. Whether I'm rearranging objects on the top of a table, arranging flowers, setting a table, or preparing a meal, the more I become one with the elements at hand, the more I lose my self-consciousness and move into a deeper contemplative state, so calm, and so full of grace.

W I T H   H E A R T   A N D   H A N D

I think of hands not only as the tools we use to prepare, build, and fix things, the implements that human beings—unique among all animals—have to work with in the world, but I also think of hands as the instruments of our love and creativity. With our hands we put our heart, spirit, and thoughts into action.

Christmas afternoon last year we invited friends over for tea. We'd had a late family luncheon, lingering at the dining room table, cozy by the fire, sipping wine and then coffee. The girls then went for a walk, and Peter and I decided to bake for the tea. Because no one was watching us, we agreed to mix all the ingredients with our hands. (Julia Child's great success comes in part from her love of using her hands.) In the privacy of our own kitchen, we squeezed the eggs and oil into the flour. Before we knew it, we had concocted a chocolate cake and a batch of delicious cookies filled with nuts, chocolate, and orange rind. While an electric mixer would have worked just as well and would have taken less time, we opted not to plug it in. Using our hands, we were the creators of edible art. We won't forget

On action alone be thy interest, never on its fruits. Let not the fruits of action be thy motive, nor be thy attachment to inaction.

—B H A G A V A D G I T A

our experience of the cake's rich dark brown color, the strong smell of sweet chocolate, and licking our fingers after scooping the batter into the cake pan.

There were eleven of us for tea that afternoon, seated around the dining room table. The group seemed bathed in a glow of affection and pleasure because of our baked goodies—an atmosphere we could never have achieved with packaged cakes and cookies. If I fold clothes, or give Peter a neck rub or a hand massage, or create a handmade card for a special occasion, or write invitations by hand, I am expressing love.

I love writing letters by hand; this is a wonderful tradition to revitalize. Somehow, pen in hand, I can express things that I would otherwise not have access to. These thoughts come from deep within my heart, and sometimes the only way to reach them is in the time and the stillness afforded by writing. All well-meaning letters are love letters. As I sit down at a table or desk to write to a friend, I have a powerful, satisfying experience, bringing the person I'm writing to into sharp focus. The minister who married Peter and me is a close friend, and ever since John left New York to become the Episcopal bishop of Massachusetts in the late 1970s, we've stayed in touch, mostly through handwritten correspondence. Once I was writing John on a New Year's Day, and what began as a personal letter ended up as a book, *Gift of a Letter*. While I never sent that

Intuition becomes increasingly valuable in the new information society precisely because there is so much data.

—JOHN NAISBITT

exact letter, the experience was astonishing because it awakened in me the knowledge of how close we can be to each other when we reach out in kind, generous, appreciative ways. Letters of thanksgiving, thanking somebody for their presence in our lives, are perhaps some of life's most meaningful exchanges.

I write to connect. If a friend is dying I write to remind that person how important they are to me. If someone has died, I write their loved ones, telling of special memories I have of moments we shared that made a difference in my life. When a letter is emotionally powerful, I try not to reread what I write because I want it to be received fresh from my heart, without editing.

With our hands we hold those we love. I adore holding hands with my grandchildren, my husband, my daughters, and my friends. When we dance we speak with our hands. Their shape, form, and movements are powerful expressions of the inner life that charges them; our hands transmit the messages from our heart and soul. When we dance with others, our arms and our hands form the link that connects us; we need no other instruments but ourselves.

It's as interesting and as difficult to say a thing as well as to paint it. There is the art of lines and colors, but the art of words exists too, and will never be less important.

—Vincent van Gogh

When I took it upon myself to paint our bedroom last winter I used a two-and-a-half-inch trim brush for the walls, ceiling, and woodwork. To a professional house-painter this sounds ludicrously time-consuming, but I wanted to create loving karma in the most intimate space in our life. Why use a roller, spattering paint around, being expedient? I created vertical brush marks, showing personal care. There are wallpapers made to replicate this vertical striation, but I did it by hand with paint on a plaster wall. There's energy in those walls, and I believe it is felt by whoever enters the room. My shoulder may have been sore for a few weeks afterward, but my heart was dancing. Sometimes I hug the walls. Yes! We bonded, and even though it was hard work, the results are inspiring, satisfying me beyond my imagination's scope. When I painted the ceiling Peter held the ladder, saying, "Here goes Michelangelo. Go for it, you angel."

Everything that makes more of you than you have ever been, even in your best hours, is right. Every intensification is good.
—RAINER MARIA RILKE

When we make bread, the way we handle the dough— the skill and sensitivity we put into our hands—determines the texture and the quality of the baked bread. When we slice vegetables, the arrangement determined by how they naturally fall on the cutting board expresses the exhilaration and beauty of the partnership between nature and human effort. The tomatoes I planted and later picked from the garden are now ripening on the window ledge— my hands have played a role in every stage, even now at this final stage when I slice them to make a delicious tomato and basil salad to serve to a friend. When we take life into our own hands we are touching and forming life and those we love.

When we use our hands, we feel a sense of both pride and humility. With them we do what we can. With our hands we can sometimes save a life, other times we cannot and are shown our limitations. Rollo May recommends "taking on a way of life which is rooted in one's own powers." Using our own hands is perhaps the most important way we do so.

THE HAND OF THE CREATOR

When I first stood in front of Rembrandt's *Philosopher in Meditation,* I'd already seen several of his paintings in various museums. But I was awestruck by how, on this particular canvas, he painted people who appeared to be embraced by a heavenly light. I suddenly felt a keen sense that what I was seeing was the hand of the creator, and I was deeply moved. Only Rembrandt, with his own hand, could have painted this painting. Rembrandt experienced the life force behind all things, using his hands and paint to recreate that sense of life. When we look at his work we are reawakened to this life force, making us more aware of our own experience and our humanity.

The poet speaks adequately only when he speaks somewhat wildly . . . not with intellect alone, but with intellect inebriated by nectar.

—HENRY MILLER

When I look at a work of art, I am moved not only by the creation itself, but by my awareness of the life and the vision by which it was created. I look at a painting and marvel at how mere paint on a flat surface can convince me of the presence of a three-dimensional world. When you can see the brushstrokes in a painting, or notice the way in which a rock has been carved, or how the clay has been shaped in a sculpture, you are seeing the hand of the creator. In this creation we experience the human passion to explore life with all of our being: through effort, intelligence, determination, hesitation, confusion, clarity, boldness, restraint, pain, and exaltation. To the extent that we notice these forces in a work of art, we can see the marks of the artist and of his humanity. In *The Art Spirit*, Robert Henri writes of how the artist conveys his humanity through his work: "The things he touches receive his kind of impress, and they afterward bear the trace of his passing." A work of art dramatizes our hunger to explore, to learn the essence of life. This hunger is timeless. The artist reaches both outward and within to take hold of what he can of his experience of living. He enjoys a capacity to wonder about the mysteries of life; a capacity expressed by the work of art itself, which, in turn, inspires wonder in us, the viewers.

It is the chiefest point of happiness that a man is willing to be what he is.

— E R A S M U S

I was lucky enough to see Michelangelo's beautiful Renaissance sculptures in Florence, Italy, in 1961. Among them is the famous statue of David, of the Bible story of David and Goliath. Standing before it I wondered which divine creator could take this cold block of marble from the side of a mountain and turn it into flesh. I knew no god had made this, nor was this marble skin and bones, yet the statue was so alive, so present, that I thought, "Only a divine being could make a rock seem soft and tender." But it was Michelangelo, with his passionate desire to capture the beauty of the life force in the human body, who gave us David to appreciate. He is so big and powerful, yet so tender and gentle and soft. In many of Michelangelo's sculptures we can almost see the form emerging out of uncut rock, reminding us that the artist works to bring something into being with his or her own hands. What is this ability? I ask myself, full of wonder at the sheer physical power of the work, as well as its persuasive emotional power. How could a human hand fashion a work that seems to have been born, not made—a work that seems to have come into being fully formed, without a creator—when in fact so much extraordinary effort went into making it?

The earth is the cup, the sky is the cover, of the immense bounty of nature which is offered us.

—EMERSON

Art is about human growth. Keeping this growth process alive in ourselves both by making art and by looking at art is a wonderful way to keep us alive to life and to deepen its meaning. One of the ways we live with grace in the modern world is by being creative, working with our hands, and keeping fresh our capacity to wonder about life's infinite beauty and variety. There are so many things to learn, to understand; so many things about life we've yet to discover.

To see the life within something is to find meaning in

it; this is a definition of grace. There is grace in art, in the harmony between creator and creation. It is the grace that comes when the hands of an artist, a human being like us, are applied to the raw material of life.

CRACKING OUR OWN EGGS

While working on his novel *Roots,* author Alex Haley developed a writing block. Writing about Haley's problem, journalist Danny Romine Powell, books editor of the *Charlotte Observer,* spoke of her conversation with Haley at the time: "When words failed him, he told me, he would abandon his typewriter for the kitchen. He'd crack eggs, sift flour, pour the batter into a cake pan, and pop the pan into the oven." Powell described how "Haley would perch on a stool in front of the glass-fronted oven and watch as bubbles rose in the batter and congealed into substance, the process moving inexorably toward completion. 'That's what happens,' Haley said, 'with writing. Ingredients bubble and cook. Material becomes substance.' "

Studies serve for delight, for ornament, and for ability.

—FRANCIS BACON

Haley's solution to the problem of being stuck in or overwhelmed by his work offers a wonderful example of how we can regain balance and momentum to get back in step on our own path. When thinking too hard and struggling too much blocked Haley's writing, he switched gears and gave himself over to a simpler, more rhythmic process. Cutting, measuring, pouring, mixing, and watching centered him, reconnecting him to his basic creativity. "When we chop and pare vegetables," wrote Julia Cameron in *The Artist's Way,* her wonderful book about tapping into our own creative process, "we do so with our thoughts as well. Scraping a carrot, peeling an apple—these actions are quite literally food for thought. Regular, repetitive activities tip us from our logic brain into our more creative artist brain. Solutions to sticky creative problems may bubble up through the dishwater. . . ."

I don't really feel my poems are mine at all. I didn't create them out of nothing. I owe them to my relations with other people.
—ROBERT GRAVES

The busyness and mechanization of modern life often put distance between us and our natural need for the creative process, whereby a series of actions brings about change and results. Within that process lies our ability to solve a multitude of problems. Getting back in tune with natural rhythms puts us back on the path to a simple, handmade life—a life where we are the acting agent, fully connected to the process.

Often it is the time and space surrounding my writing that proves the most beneficial. One morning I found my mind wandering as I worked. I was sitting at my desk, fantasizing that I was seated on the floor of our kitchen, painting with chartreuse. I've had a lifelong passion for the color chartreuse, a strong greenish-yellow to yellow-green. It is also the trademark for a type of liqueur. But as much as I adore it, chartreuse is not a good color for room interiors, except in subtle touches. The French linen company Porthault has some floral designs incorporating this acid hue, but usually it is best experienced in small doses, relieved by other colors. My distraction grew to an obsession. I needed more chartreuse in my life. My chartreuse Day-Glo Lucite ball and Slinky are fun, but I craved more. Where could I put this favorite color? I have a suit, several scarves, and stockings in this strange shade of yellow-green. I even use Post-it notes this color. Ink? No, it is too pale. I sipped my coffee and pondered. I could paint the panels inside my blue kitchen cabinets chartreuse. No one had to know. Who would notice? I could sneak into the kitchen and quietly paint the three-quarter-inch depth of the cabinet doors, and feel satisfied.

Nature . . . to the greatest toils it attaches the greatest rewards.

— MONTESQUIEU

I'd worked enough. I needed inspiration. I slipped into my tights, a T-shirt, and ballet slippers and tiptoed into the laundry room to get the pint of paint I'd purchased ''just in case'' I could find an appropriate place for it. I'd already covered the entire can and lid with the chartreuse paint so it would bring me pleasure as I did the laundry or ironed. Ah, now I had a plan. I felt so excited I didn't dare announce my plan to anyone. Why should I? Someone would try to discourage me, and I couldn't risk this. When I'm not thinking with my mind, my heart has a way of working things out when I put my hands to use.

I delved into this can of raw acid pigment. What a

sensual experience. I grabbed a one-inch brush and went at it, thrilled to see and feel this subtle detail add such spunk to my kitchen. Who wouldn't want to reach for a juice glass and see this sassy trim color? The entire project didn't last more than an hour. In the end I'd only dipped into the pint of paint. When we're enthusiastic about whatever we're doing, it is difficult to know when to stop. We tend to overdo. I knew I had to be subtle in order to get away with this. Much to my glee, Peter thinks it is a startling, unexpected burst of color, less surreal than sublime. Alexandra and Brooke came into the kitchen, sat down at the table, and sipped coffee. I joined them. "Mother, no, no. What are you doing with that color?" Smiling, I fudged, "Oh, nothing." When Alexandra opened the cupboards to get out a plate for her English muffin she burst out laughing. "It's really cute, Mom." Of all the decorating I've ever done, this sneaky stripe contrasting against the Brittany blue probably gives me the greatest pleasure because no one is assaulted by it but instead people are pleased when they discover it inadvertently. I was itching to have more chartreuse in my life, and I found a way by using my hands to magically spread it about behind closed cabinet doors.

It is neither wealth nor splendor, but tranquility and occupation, which give happiness.

—THOMAS JEFFERSON

I find that working with my hands is as inspiring and as centering as sitting on my Zen bench. There are few things as effective in bringing us back to ourselves and to our connection to life and creativity as doing something with our own hands. This is the antidote for our modern sense of disconnectedness, fragmentation, and our feeling of being cut off from creation.

Lives based on having are less free than lives based either on doing or on being.

—William James

We can leave our highly sophisticated machines alone for a few hours a day or even a few days a week to allow ourselves to work with our hands. In order to maintain a gracious outlook on life we can keep one foot on the "information superhighway" and the other one barefoot, feeling the grass between our toes.

The busy pace of modern life can obscure the simple pleasures that await us when we get back to basics. Dishwashers need not be altogether abandoned, but every once in a while try washing the dishes by hand and drying them with a cotton towel. See how the process slows you down. Feel how your senses are reawakened by the satisfying softness of the cloth and the meditative quality of washing; it can give you an appealing sense of ritual. It's true that if I had to wash dishes throughout the day,

No true disciple of mine will ever be a Ruskinean; he will follow, not me, but the instincts of his soul.

—John Ruskin

every single day, I would grow tired, and perhaps frustrated. But not infrequently, when the hustle and bustle of my life threatens to leave me frayed, I find that I can best pull myself together by immersing my hands in soapy water.

I also find that sharing dishwashing with family or friends can be a wonderful ritual— a time that allows for casual, intimate talk.

While you both become immersed in the rhythm of the washing and drying, a rhythm that creates a kind of protective space around you, you relax and are able to speak about many things you might otherwise feel uncomfortable with. Working together on something with another person also creates a bridge between you and helps you listen to each other. Think of the times when you've washed dishes after a dinner party with a friend or when you and a child got up early Sunday morning and made breakfast for the family and house guests.

Great is he who uses earthenware as if it were silver; no less great is he who uses silver as if it were earthenware.

— SENECA

Early one morning when our granddaughter Julia saw me tiptoe to the kitchen, she followed me, wanting to get in on the action. Inspired by the fresh berries sitting in the sunlight on the kitchen table, we decided to bake blueberry muffins together. We worked side by side and spoke of friendship and loyalty, love and goodness. During that time together, I felt I was in the presence of an angel as we effortlessly prepared a family feast. She and I discovered we were fire lovers, as we both were drawn to light and stoke the fire, and to keep the candles burning. Kitchens are not ordinary places. Not only do they gather us all together as the center of our homes, but we open up to our true selves and are receptive to others in this loving atmosphere. When Peter is sitting at the kitchen table polishing brass or silver or peeling tomatoes and making

Life is a pure flame, and we live by an invisible sun within us.

— SIR THOMAS BROWNE

salad dressing, while I'm cooking or cleaning glasses at the kitchen sink, he'll ask me questions about my childhood. Recently he wanted to know more about the farm and our horse Comanche Chief. As he was polishing the silver frame of a picture of me when I was four, hugging my giant teddy bear, he lovingly commented, "You held on to your teddy for dear life." And he was right. When Peter and I are alone together, working, our conversations are usually about our pasts, as though we're interweaving all the threads of our youthful interests, bringing us closer and closer as though we were actually together then.

Flowers have an expression of countenance as much as men and animal. Some seem to smile.

—HENRY WARD BEECHER

On Christmas Eve last year, Peter and I went to a pageant in the afternoon to see some of our young friends perform, and to enjoy the ceremony and music. Walking back from church we felt so content, so happy with our lives. Once home we put more logs on the fire and puttered around the living room, arranging the table tops, making everything look festive. As Peter selected a bunch of tapes to play, he said, "You know, this cottage provides and sings all things. And if there were a disaster and a fire burned it to the ground, you and I would build it back, exactly the same."

An art in which the artist by means of rhythm and great sincerity can convey to others the sentiment which he feels about life.

—JOHN MASEFIELD

One evening after work, I met Brooke at her office and we went downtown to a studio where we designed and painted some dinner and dessert plates for a friend who was getting married. We were having a shower for Elisabeth and wanted to give her something we created with our hands. Sitting at a table together, talking out our designs, playing with colors, Brooke and I were so close we were beyond words. We both understood the mysterious power in the physical act of creation, and we naturally complemented each other on each different design, so her dinner plates were compatible with my dessert dishes. We were absorbed in the flow of creation and love.

Humanity comes not from the machine but from the heart.

—JOSEPH CAMPBELL

My friend Eleanor and I were painting clementine crates in our basement studio recently when she told me of her desire to do more writing. "Have you always been a writer, Alexandra?" I told her I used to paint before I began to write and now that we have the studio, I intend to paint again. Working with our hands awakens us to deep yearnings and desires.

I hope with all my heart there will be painting in heaven.

—JEAN BAPTISTE COROT

Getting your hands dirty can relieve the stress and strain of modern life. Our cheerful studio is a great place to make a colorful mess. Since we put a huge white drop cloth down in the center of the floor, the place now looks as colorful as an Impressionist's palette. We paint everything, even our T-shirts.

Busy hands can be both soothing and productive. Instead of turning on the television, try taking out some sewing. Which relaxes you more? I have a place reserved on a shelf in our sitting room for sewing. Whether it's something as simple as putting a button back on Peter's pajama top or a baby's pillowcase that needs repair, the projects are there, waiting for me. I love fabric and buttons, and sewing, like ironing, allows me to rest my mind and use my hands to tap into deeper reserves of love and appreciation.

Whenever I work with my hands to improve our cottage, to mend something broken, to touch up some paint,

The gloom of the world is but a shadow; behind it, yet within our reach, is joy. Take joy.

—FRA GIOVANNI

or to sand down a table top, I feel blessed to have a home I love so dearly and to be able to participate in loving ways to decorate and maintain it. My mother was a strong role model of how our hands are capable of great acts of both artistry and practicality. If there was a dent in the lacquer coffee table, I'd observe her applying wood filler. She wasn't afraid of hard work, and all these years later I realize her hands were expressing herself, often when she couldn't express the same warm feelings of affection verbally. Whenever we tend to something in need, or see a way to improve our surroundings, or are inspired to make a set of kitchen curtains, or build a bookcase, essentially what we're doing is giving of ourselves, which is the essence of grace. Whenever we thread a needle, mend a broken teacup, repair a leg on a chair, remove a spot from a tablecloth, wash out the cocktail napkins in the sink, paint a basket, or make a quilt, we are concentrating our energies in positive ways. Doing this calls forth our best, most loving efforts, and in this spirit, our days are elevated into the art of living.

In an article about career women in *Working Woman* magazine, I was quoted as saying, "If something isn't fun I don't do it." I shudder to think of all the wrong ideas readers might get from that statement. Now, upon reflection, I laugh at my lack of guile. What I meant was that I so enjoy doing work of any kind that there are few things I don't like to do. There are so many tasks, large and small "chores" that I love doing, there's little I won't do. "Joy is the affect that comes when you use your own powers," wrote Rollo May. There is hardly a more immediate or greater use of our human powers than in the use of our hands. Once you have become aware of the simple pleasure you derive by using your own two hands to work, to create, and to help, you will never be without resources for finding peace and joy. For joy in living is not necessarily about being happy; it is about the meaning we derive from our existence, the care we take in the quality of our experience.

> *To insure good health, eat lightly, breathe deeply, live moderately, cultivate cheerfulness, and maintain an interest in life.*
>
> —WILLIAM LOUDEN

A GARDENER'S HANDS

Peter never does things in half measures. He pores over our garden catalogs with the same keen interest I do, but he tends to be more extravagant. The Saturday before Mother's Day a large box arrived from White Flower Farms in Litchfield, Connecticut. The box was filled with lily bulbs. Inside was a sweet note, "Beauty for beauty and hooray for spring. I love you. Peter." A nearby nursery had delivered several flats of ivy I'd intended to plant around our brick Zen circular area where we have a round table and chairs. What a happy coincidence. To top it off, for his birthday, I'd given Peter a set of beautiful Zen garden tools from Felissimo in New York, which he handed me with a wink and a smile: "We'll share these gems."

Enjoy the simple, the natural and the plain. Along with that comes the ability to do things spontaneously and have them work.

—BENJAMIN HOFF

The entire day unfolded in the garden. We planted the ivy and by late afternoon we'd placed all fifty lilies in the ground. I was filthy and sweaty and my back ached, but I had never felt more beautiful. I visualized the growth of the ivy, how the sun and water would make it spread, and how we'd enjoy the lilies all summer. When we took a break, I plucked a few sprigs of mint and brought out a pitcher of iced tea with some ginger snaps. We sat together, kissed, and, clinking glasses, sipped the deliciously refreshing cold tea. What an exhilarating day. I commented on how cool the white lilies would look against the rich dark green ivy, reflecting the white trellis. Holding my hand, grinning, Peter announced, "The lilies I bought are a variety, ranging in color from white and yellow to orange and red." I burst into laughter. I assumed they'd be white. How wonderful not to know where the color will sprout. We just have to enjoy all the surprises. We kissed again, clinked our glasses, and, as I poured more iced tea, I looked at my fingers and hands. The more we use our hands, the more beautiful they become. I couldn't stop smiling. I thought of Henry Wadsworth Longfellow's words, "I shall answer and thank you again / For the gift and the *grace* of the gift."

I love to plant, plunk in, prune, and water. I consider myself a gardener of life, my way to appreciate the sunshine while it lasts, but also to be grateful for the rain. My brother Powell told me when I was about eleven, "Sandie, the reason you have such a sunny disposition is because you know the rain is just as important as the sun." When I was a little girl my passion for gardening taught me acceptance and understanding. I had a vivid sense of the rhythms of the four seasons, and of the comparable flow of gain and loss in life. When it is no longer time to garden, because of the cold and snow, it's time to pore

A spark of fire is infinitely deep, but a mass of fire reaching from earth into heaven, this is the sign of the robust, united, burning, radiant soul.

—EMERSON

over seed catalogs. I love the optimism implicit in planting seeds. Inwardly we can continue to plant seeds throughout our life passages.

Advances in science, machines, and medicine can give us the illusion that we have ultimate control over our lives. But nature reminds me that though our ultimate fate is out of our hands, we can take hold of our own life, by taking it into our hands. Our hands connect our spirit to nature, to the earth below us and heaven above. I have a friend Jerry who calls me "Talking Hands." We dig them deep down and stretch them high into the sky. We lend a hand, we guide and assist. Our hands are ultimately extensions of our soul, speaking through our acts and affording us a true sense of fulfillment. When our hearts seek joyful activities, we express ourselves through our hands.

Four

❖

Working with Grace

GETTING OUT OF THE EFFICIENCY TRAP

For me, the human connection is at the root of all satisfying work. None of us works in isolation, no matter
what work we accomplish. The people we work with not
only affect the quality of our accomplishments; they can
greatly enhance our pleasure in the process. I feel strongly
about the people I work with and not only value and appreciate them, I love them. Just as I can't stick with my
work without becoming passionate, it is extremely impor-

tant to me to deeply care about the people I work with, no matter what part they play.

More than thirty-five years ago, a wealthy Texas lady hired me to decorate the family ranch. When we discussed a date for me to fly down from New York and back, she invited me for the weekend to her house in town before heading to the ranch Monday morning. "This way we can get to know each other, and you can meet my boys and our friends. We'll have a party for you." We had a glorious time, never discussing why I was there. The work was to begin Monday morning, not a moment before. At five o'clock on Sunday afternoon, after a weekend filled with family and friends, laughter, storytelling, warmth, and lots of flowers, good food, wine, and music, the party was over and it was time to drive to the ranch so we could get to work the next morning. While this homestead was hardly servantless, my client herself appeared with a breakfast tray. "I hope you slept well, Sandie. I forgot to ask you last night what you like for breakfast so I guessed." And with a giggle, she added, "I made a Mexican omelet. Watch out, dear, the jalapeño sauce is a bit on the hot side." I quickly knew why a large silver pitcher filled with ice water was next to the glass of orange juice.

This beautiful lady made my breakfast, setting a pretty tray with a small bouquet of roses she'd picked from her

Do continue to believe that with your feeling and your work you are taking part in the greatest; the more strongly you cultivate in yourself this belief, the more will reality and the world go forth from it.

—RAINER MARIA RILKE

garden. While the work was hard out at the ranch, this relationship we'd established at the beginning led to a lovely friendship. What Estelle intuitively knows is how intimate all work is, and how essential it is for everyone to feel the significance of their contribution. By being taken into the family, I was able to do a far better job than if I were a stranger from New York, a "foreigner" going to an enormous Texas ranch. She taught me that time spent "not working" is a vital part of productivity.

While my work has ever been before me, my reward has always been with me.

—Shaker Saying

The value we place on efficiency, which is largely a result of our greater ability to be efficient thanks to modern technology, too often overshadows the value of people in the workplace. Too much technology, too many buttons to press makes us frantic, and not necessarily more effective. It's our humanity that determines how graciously we live at home, in our community, and at work today.

The pace of the modern workplace is decidedly speedy. "Efficiency is fondly regarded in the American mind as the greatest contribution of this age to civilization," observed Percival White in a retrospective piece in the *Atlantic Monthly* entitled "Seventy-five Years Ago." He went on, "It is deemed an agency for good, a thing one cannot have too much of." Indeed, in most work environments, work time spent on anything that isn't highly focused, strategic, goal-oriented, and deal-closing is regarded as unproductive. Inviting a colleague to have a long leisurely lunch, inquiring how the weekend was, bringing a bouquet of flowers to someone on their birthday, buying a present for a newborn child, writing a friendly card to let a special person you work with know how much you appreciate him, having colorful file folders and desk accessories to delight you as well as others as you work, always having flowers on your desk, all may seem unimportant or frivolous, but if we don't live this way, we're not in touch with our spirit.

Within the limits of mortal existence, we can work, we can exercise our powers, we can arrange ourselves to labor happily, rest quietly and live peaceably.

—LIN YUTANG

When speed and efficiency are our elixirs, we become irritable and impatient when we don't achieve them. Why wait for the mail, when you can fax a document? Why take the time to meet with someone in person when you can call them, E-mail them, or hire an intermediary to take care of the "soft" work of interpersonal relations?

Striving for efficiency is a lot like striving for perfection: It's always just beyond our reach. Real life has a tendency to interfere with our drive to be efficient: Your child catches a cold and you must leave work to take him to the doctor; a coworker gets sick and you can't complete a job without her; you've been working so hard for so long that you finally cast productivity to the winds and take a vacation, even though you have deadlines coming up. I'm efficient by nature, to an extent. But I've learned that you pay a spiritual price for needing, more than anything else, to be efficient.

Working all the time isn't efficient. It certainly uses up more time, but that doesn't mean it produces results. Driving ourselves to work harder and harder, beyond the point of productivity, saps us of creative and physical energy. We may feel like we're getting things done when we work long hours, but when we look at the quality of the work we've produced, we're disappointed. We need downtime—lots of it, and regularly. When I slow down and quiet down, I get in touch with my inner strength. We can enjoy our work better when we appreciate that it's the *process* of work, not merely the results, that gives us satisfaction.

If the *doing* of work is not enjoyable, we are in a serious trap, because most of us do work hard and long hours. The little ways we bring refreshment to ourselves as we work renew our energy and help us carry on without discouragement or burnout. I've seen many examples of people who pushed too hard, whose identity was wrapped up in their achievements. They drove themselves crazy as well as everyone who worked with them. I have tremendous capacity for hard work, but I sustain my energy by creating regular diversions. A journalist in North Carolina always leaves the newsroom at lunch time to take a walk. If you don't physically leave, you'll risk doing the same work over and over and becoming stale.

One day a client noticed my hair was wet when I met her in the afternoon. She couldn't believe I'd swum fifty laps just

If you are too busy to develop your talents, you are too busy.

—Julia Cameron

minutes before our meeting. I've learned the hard way never to allow a client to prevent me from having a proper lunch. I not only need nourishment, but I also need a break. Some of my best ideas come in my free time, when I'm the most relaxed.

We are involved in a life that passes understanding and our highest business is our daily life.

—JOHN CAGE

Abraham Lincoln would stretch out on a bench and a couple of chairs and take a nap in his office. Thomas Edison took naps at his desk. Winston Churchill got undressed in the late afternoon, went to bed naked, and slept for several hours before bathing and dressing for dinner. He often worked late into the evening. General Eisenhower took ten-minute naps in the back of his car. Even Napoleon closed his eyes during wartime in the back of the carriage that he specially designed as his office. I take a few hours off for a midday break seven days a week. Without this time, I would become a robot, half-alive.

The sun has stood still, but time never did.

—THOMAS FULLER

While I think best with a pen in my hand, often a fork works just as well. Often I find myself jotting down ideas formulated in my mind during these pleasant interludes. I am reliable and almost always get my work done on schedule, but I try to take time to tend to my emotional and physical needs as well as my aesthetic and spiritual expansion. I'm certain the work will be better than if I were run-down and burned out, grudgingly doing my duty.

Putting a Human Face on Work

Relying as we do on transmitting messages via E-mail or fax, we may forget that talking to real people, in person, is still one of the most satisfying and productive ways to work. Talking to another person is often the only way to get to the heart of a problem. We've become so oriented to putting things down on paper (or on a computer screen) that we even forget, "Hey, I can call." Talking to people, either on the phone or, better still, in person—sharing lunch or having tea together—not only provides the atmosphere conducive to clarifying a problem but also creates a relationship, which helps everything go more smoothly in the end. The human connection is the foundation on which all productive work is built. Invariably something good results from physically being together. The former art director at Doubleday, Alex Godfried, would call me up and ask me to pop down to see a jacket design. As the person responsible for supervising the creation of four hundred book jackets, Alex was busy. But he understood the human dimension of the process. Instead of having a design messengered to me, he would take a moment to show me the design personally. Over many, many years,

When you can do the common things in an uncommon way, you will command the attention of the world.

—George Washington Carver

we became friends, and he always knew I would drop everything and run right over.

When I visit my editor or the art director of my publisher, I usually end up running into a variety of people, all part of a team. Having these friendly moments together, whether in the reception area or the hall, makes me freshly aware of how we're all connected, doing our separate parts to create something collectively, sharing our time, talent, and energy. Everything starts from people. People still count. I value the importance, whether it is in my design business or in my writing life, of making human connections. It's more effective than efficient, and more richly rewarding.

> *The greatest thing in life is not where you are, but the direction in which you are moving.*
> —OLIVER WENDELL HOLMES

Several years ago I was assigned a new editor by my publisher William Morrow. Getting to know Toni was very important to me. The relationship between author and editor can be intense. It is the editor's job to make sure that the writer expresses her thoughts or tells her stories as clearly as possible; she also helps to shape language and ideas. The authors have final say, but we try to listen and really hear the editor's advice. Therefore the connection is quite intimate, but formal at the same time.

Many times, author and editor are separated by a state or a continent, and it is often the case that author and editor never meet in person. But even when contact is possible, I've learned, personal meetings can be rare. I think this depersonalization is more and more the standard operating procedure in business, where schedules are so tightly booked that there's never a moment to spare for what would be considered a "soft" strategy: human relationships.

When we first met, I invited Toni out to our cottage in Stonington for lunch and a visit. She took the time to come see me and, indeed, it proved to be a bonding day. Toni arrived and as soon as she, Peter, and I walked into the Zen garden for some iced tea, the sky opened and fell upon us. Calling it rain would be like calling a tornado a breeze. The torrents of water attacked us horizontally. By the time our three soggy souls reached the living room, I found water everywhere. Antique tables stood in puddles of water, and the floorboards were immersed in pools. I ran upstairs to get a laundry basket full of towels, only to discover the same situation upstairs. Every window in the house was open. There I was, on all fours, mopping up the water with a rag. It was fun trying to soak up the water from the floor, the tables, and the windowsills.

Toni and Peter continued their conver-

But to ascribe to money these impossible magic qualities, to make it the measure of things or the very goal of life, is to disinherit ourselves from the divine trust fund we all have stored up inside. Our real wealth is our inner resources, which are infinite because the core of our personality is divine.

—EKNATH
EASWARAN

sation, undaunted by the flood. I was having my own drama with the rain; I've always loved going out in the pouring rain. I feel cleansed, almost intoxicated by the freshness that follows afterward. The air was crisp and electric, as if the very earth had stirred.

It turned into a beautiful day. I set up a fresh, dry tray with English biscuits to munch on. We laughed about the storm and enjoyed another glass of iced tea together, the two of us purring in amusement.

No visit to the cottage is complete without sitting at the round farm table in our kitchen. Toni was amused by the dozens of baskets piled high under the butcher-block table and a wooden box filled with old and odd wooden spoons. As she played with this assortment, she was attracted to a potato masher, which I gave her to take home. I learned at the kitchen table that my editor is a writer and had a book coming out in a few months, and she was newly married to an artist. I'm not certain the chemistry would have been the same in an airless conference room with fluorescent lights, and I'm sure there wouldn't have been a potato masher to play with.

An essential part of a happy, healthy life is being of service to others.

—SUE PATTON THOELE

"Hanging out" together enabled Toni and me to get to know one another on a human level, beyond the simple handshake of a professional relationship. It's not possible to really get to know another person, establish a bond, until you both take this pressure-free time together. That day, Toni and I discovered that we shared many interests, and there is no doubt that knowing each other better will enrich our work together. It already has!

WORKING WITH COMMITMENT
AND COMPASSION

The milkman has stopped delivering glass bottles to our doorstep, the grocer who knew our name has gotten lost in the huge food emporium, and the shoe salesman who always knew our size has disappeared into the department store stockroom. The flower shop that used to call us when the first lilies of the valley arrived in the store couldn't compete with the Korean market that opened next door. A friend who worked at a nearby bookstore who would call us when a book came in she thought we would like to read, left to work at a giant bookstore chain. The woman who ran a local Chinese restaurant (and helped me incorporate some of her dishes when I entertained) has retired. I miss them all because I welcome every opportunity to show my appreciation and respect for the good work of others. After all, we depend on each other. I shudder to think of a day when I might become so preoccupied with my own achievements and needs, that I lose sight of my feelings of warmth and sense of responsibility for others.

I don't believe in failure. It is not failure if you enjoyed the process.

— OPRAH WINFREY

In his book *The Seven Spiritual Laws of Success,* Dr. Deepak

Chopra instructs us to "Discover your divinity, find your unique talent, serve humanity with it." The people who make the trains run (mostly) on time, the coworkers whose effectiveness makes possible your own, are all equal partners in creating a gracious life for all of us. In addition to using our unique talents, we can keep in mind serving and helping other people whenever we work, by being kind, appreciative, and considerate. When we do this, not only are we sharing our talents with the world, doing work that is satisfying to us,

You have been entrusted with a life that's yours to care for, enjoy, and learn from.

—CHARLOTTE DAVIS KASL

but we are also sharing positive energy for people in meaningful, satisfying ways. We are repaid for this tremendously.

There are many simple, but profoundly effective ways to achieve this divinity, this grace in our work. When I was hired to renovate an actress friend's apartment, I often found myself holding a broom at eight o'clock in the morning, cleaning up after the many workmen. The painters never threw out their own garbage, the electricians never carted away all the plaster, and the carpenters never swept up all the shavings and sawdust. One day I arrived at the apartment to find the air clouded with gnats. They were everywhere, even stuck on the freshly painted but now gnat-speckled walls. On closer inspection I realized that the gnats were actually flying into the wet buckets of paint that was being applied to the walls—they were interred in the paint—shades of Edgar Allan Poe! Noticing this, I sprang into action. I cleared out the paint cans, brushes, and other painting paraphernalia, put down fresh drop cloths, and suggested that the workers take a lunch break on the terrace while I sprayed the whole apartment, exterminating these little flying creatures for good. There I was, wielding a spray gun, dressed in an elegant summer suit which I had worn to meet a friend for lunch in the garden of a favorite restaurant. So much for elegance.

After I completed the assault, feeling dirty, dusty, and sticky, I went into the bathroom, splashed my face and neck with cold water, straightened my stockings, dusted off my suit, reapplied a little lipstick and a little powder, and voilà! I was revived. Actually, I did feel great; I'd been committed to getting this apartment done right and it had been done, finally.

As I relaxed in the taxi on the way to meet my friend for lunch, I felt productive, and glad that I had shown respect and restraint with the workmen. The idea of working with grace has become more and more important to me as the years go by. I felt useful and very much alive that day. I was also glad that we all had performed our special magic for my friend. The paint job was terrific. When the walls were finished they were as smooth as glass and as soft as velvet. I was also proud of my design for a graceful bullnosed ledge for the raised

There is a persuasion in the soul of man that he is here for cause, that he was put down in this place by the Creator to do the work for which He inspires him.

— EMERSON

dining room floor. I was happy to be able to make such a concrete contribution to someone else's life.

It was a gracious morning, and although I assure you when I arrived at lunch I didn't smell of Chanel No. 5, my companion had no hint that I'd been chasing and killing gnats all morning. I arrived at the table refreshed, and with an added twinkle in my eye, knowing how much good work we all had completed that morning.

The test of a vocation, someone once said, is the love of the drudgery it involves. I've never had a problem with drudgery. When we do our work with commitment and dedication, we take pride in everything we do, down to the last chore. No matter what we do, when we are eager and passionate about getting it done right, every single thing we do is important, including how we get along with other people who work with us. I love being part of a team of talented people.

Work does more than get us our living; it gets us our life.

—Henry Ford

Becoming mindful of our relationships to the people with whom, for whom, and above whom we work is a powerful way to live graciously at work. I am always moved when I witness acts of kindness and generosity, particularly in the pressured environment where we work today; such acts humanize the workplace and make us all happier.

When I met Tony Gonzales, the cameraman for *Homes Across America,* the television show I host periodically, I instantly recognized that he was a man of grace. After several days of shooting, we'd been through a lot of tense moments together. We were surrounded by people, working under the gun all the time. But Tony's gentleness and calmness eased my tension. On Sunday night, the last night of a full weekend of shooting, I was doing some voiceovers in our New York apartment. It was nearly ten o'clock, and I had been working since seven that morning. To protect the shoot from the noises of the city, I was placed under a black flannel tent. Throat raw, muscles tight, and mind scattered, I ducked into the tent to get away from it all.

It is human nature always to want a little more. People spend their lives honestly believing that they have almost enough of whatever they want. Just a little more will pull them over the top; then they will be contented forever.

—TIMOTHY MILLER

I knew this was the end of the filming. I needed to concentrate completely and get this last bit finished so everyone could go home. I also knew that every time I made an error, the entire crew would be delayed, and overtime is costly. Suddenly, there on a wicker table in front of the chair, I saw a bouquet of flowers. Tony had placed it there with a note that said, "You're doing great. We're all rooting for you. Tony." That small, thoughtful gesture made a big difference. I sailed through the filming and went out to a bistro with some of the crew, Peter, and our daughter Brooke, to celebrate.

On another occasion, while I was filming with a different crew for the same show, Peter and two helpers prepared a delicious lunch—lobster salad, tomatoes and basil with mozzarella, chicken salad, cole slaw, French bread, and a platter of cheese. In his inimitable, charming style, as soon as he heard the director yell out "Lunch break!"

> *You simply cannot develop your brain or be a total person without work.*
>
> —Joan Gauz Cooney

Peter announced "Lunch is now being served in the dining room." We were brain dead and bleary-eyed, tired, and tense. Turning the corner to this feast was such a boost to our morale. Peter and I had planned this lunch the day before, preparing as much ahead of time as possible, including setting the table. Being on camera requires single-mindedness, and worrying about eight empty stomachs would not have been constructive.

Without skipping a beat or wasting precious time, Peter toasted the crew and cracked a few jokes. Then we all settled into the beautiful banquet. It didn't take one second more for us to have a gracious luncheon than to have a grubby one out of brown paper bags.

Getting Back to Basics

A number of years ago, at an author luncheon, a writer told me that I was a masochist because I wrote all my books longhand with a fountain pen. I laughed and recalled with great fondness writing my first published book, *Style for Living,* twenty-two years ago. I remember using a portable

Olympic typewriter for the first draft of the book, believing that I had to use the more modern typewriter, not a pen, if I wanted to become a serious writer. I typed on the back of a rainbow of Pantone colored paper which I still keep as a reminder of my first attempt at putting some soul into something mechanical and colorless. I quickly discovered how I dread machines. I put the typewriter away permanently and picked up my fountain pen.

We have to rethink our relationship to computers. We need to see what we give up when we come to depend upon machines. When our daughter Alexandra, a journalist, first got her computer, she traveled with it wherever she went. She even brought her printer along. She felt she couldn't even consider putting pen to paper anymore. My assistant Julie is equally infatuated with her laptop. She carries it lovingly in a small chintz-covered tote bag, tosses it over her shoulder, and takes it with her wherever she goes. She even sets it up in bed and works on it in the evening. For Julie, the computer is a miracle-worker, allowing her to catch up on work and do things she says she would otherwise not be able to do, such as making complicated changes in copy and developing ideas without having to think through every word in advance.

A hundred times every day I remind myself that my inner and outer life depends on the labors of other men, living and dead, and that I must exert myself in order to give in the same measure as I have received.

—ALBERT EINSTEIN

One Saturday morning, Julie and I were working under deadline when all of a sudden the computer screen froze. Julie was enraged. We had two days to complete a draft of a manuscript which I had written in longhand and which Julie was typing into the computer. But there was nothing to do but turn the computer off, which erased two hours of work. Julie giggled nervously and started yelling at the computer screen, "Why are you doing this to me? How dare you do this to me at the worst possible time?" She had become so dependent on the machine that she felt deeply betrayed by its failure to be unfailingly reliable. But the real frustration Julie felt was that there was no one to explain the problem or apologize for it.

When a great poet has lived, certain things have been done one for all, and cannot be achieved again.

—T. S. Eliot

This brings up, once again, the persistent importance of people in the workplace and the reasons why machines can never replace people. Only people can empathize, understand, and care about the consequences of their actions. Computers are no more "miraculous" than the people who create and operate them. Even with computers, there is no perfect efficiency, no infallibility. Computers can no more prevent us from failure or from coming up against our own limitations, than we can. Luckily, we were able to reconstruct the lost work because I had the handwritten copy. Several weeks later a part broke on that same computer. While he was repairing it, the repairman found a virus. We had to work without our computer for nine agonizing days. But no longer did we depend solely upon its unfailing reliability.

When I lamented to a friend about this computer failure and the delay it caused, she suggested I buy an old manual Underwood or Smith Corona typewriter. In the future, then, in the event of computer problems, business wouldn't have to come to a standstill. Of course, there was a time when even typewriters were too high-tech for my comfort!

The Shakers wanted everyone in their sect to be able to put their hands to multiple uses. Though they did not have the same technological options that we have today, the importance of being able to perform tasks manually remains. Machines are not infallible and we should not be rendered helpless if they break down. If your computer breaks down, bring out that old typewriter that sits in your closet collecting dust, or put pen to paper. If the paper gets caught in the fax machine, don't become paralyzed until someone comes along to fix it. Pick up the phone and relay the information verbally or move on to something else. If the coffeemaker fails to create your perfect cup of coffee, know that there are alternative ways to brew a fresh mug without a state-of-the-art machine. We were managing quite well before the high-tech office became the norm; why should we let it control us now?

> *Out of every fruition of success, no matter what, comes forth something to make a new effort necessary.*
>
> —WALT WHITMAN

THE GRACIOUS WORKPLACE

Whenever we take time to reconnect with ourselves, away from machines, away from rushing, and away from anxiety, our perspective about how we live becomes clearer. When we are in touch with our essential nature, we need less and less outside stimulation to inspire our best, most authentic, true work. Returning to basics from time to time calms us into clarity. How do we want to spend our time? What is the ideal, gracious atmosphere where we can most fully enjoy our time working?

Life is ours to be spent, not to be saved.

—D. H. LAWRENCE

In the past, we generally were self-conscious about our workplace, wanting an impressive old-style office to show off to our clients and associates. Fancy offices were a status symbol of our having "arrived" at a high level of success. Recently, there's been a switch in attitude. Walls have been lowered, the open plan has emerged and small spaces are now lighter and more airy. Now an office can look more as though we're in a comfortable, attractive living room. This change from trying to impress others to creating a workplace where we love to spend productive time is refreshing.

Our interests, the kind of work we do, will determine our office needs. If you're a secretary, you need to sit at your desk. If you're an artist, you need to go to your studio, and if you're an editor, you need an office where you can work, have meetings, and be available to an array of people throughout the day. The atmosphere where we work affects our energy level, mood, and concentration. Not everyone needs an office. Edith Wharton never had one, but I trust her secretary did. Many of my clients don't have an office, but there's always a room or space for files, bookshelves, and the necessary technology. Many of us do have rooms that are specifically set up as an office, but we'd rather not spend all our working time in this one place. I've learned I maintain a high level of energy, for example, when my work settings vary, which has a way of stimulating my senses. Sometimes I do my best writing barefoot at the kitchen table, with all my papers spread before me.

If one advances confidently in the direction of his dreams, and endeavors to live the life which he has imagined, he will meet with a success unexpected in common hours.

—Henry David
Thoreau

As soon as you lose your self-consciousness about having an office, you'll find inventive ways to seize and decorate a gracious workplace. Several years ago, Peter and I gave up our expensive midtown high-rise offices, preferring to work at desks in our living room. I've been in lots of offices, but I've never enjoyed the atmosphere more for work than this open, spacious, cheerful, comfortable room where we turn on the light switch and music and get to work.

The best place to work is one where you are surrounded

by personally meaningful objects, things that provide emotional comfort and inspiration. Claim your favorite room and use *it* as a workplace. What a pity to save a lovely room for entertaining family and friends when you're relegated to a dark space with no charm for a large part of the day. Women always complain to me about their husbands' mess in the living room or study, but I have a practical, relaxed attitude about this—when we're gracious,

One's eyes are what one is, one's mouth what one becomes.

—JOHN GALSWORTHY

we want those we love to be happy, and to experience as much beauty as possible. The messy surface can be tidied when necessary, but a reasonable amount of natural clutter in *any* room can be charming, lending a sense of your presence to the room.

Labels are limiting. Don't get stuck feeling you should work only in designated areas and not claim all your spaces as potential gracious work spaces. My most recent folly, one I adore, is our bedroom in our New York City apartment, where I spend hours each day working in the morning, afternoon, and evening. I've renamed it "the garden."

The garden room is like a fresh breeze, full of color and verve. Painted brilliant white, it feels luminous, and because the surfaces are high gloss, they glow. Twelve months a year in an apartment in a crowded city, I'm able to have a garden in full bloom. The colors of lilacs, hydrangeas, hyacinths, daffodils, cherry blossoms, and anemones are in the art, the fabrics, the quilts, the objects, and we always have fresh flowers. When we love gardens, why wouldn't we recreate this mood in a room where we can work?

On either side of our windows under a wall-to-wall shelf, I have books, colorful storage boxes, notebooks, and binders, as well as several dozen pastel marbleized file boxes. What's wonderful is how organized I can be without having to leave this heavenly space. I'm self-contained because I write with a fountain pen on smooth white paper attached to a colorful clipboard. I have the option of writing in bed, at my large antique wicker table, at a sweet French provincial painted desk, in an old wicker rocking chair, or a love seat. I've even sat at my mother's dressing table, pulled out the ledge in the middle, and written a note or postcard.

You may delay, but time will not.
—BEN FRANKLIN

Not only do I feel comfortable spending time working alone in this luminous room, but I also love to invite people in for a meeting. One day last winter, this happened accidentally—whenever something is natural and spontaneous, chances are grace follows. Peter had a client coming for an informal meeting, and I had invited two people to come for tea at the same time. Peter's client went to sit on the love seat by the fire, and my guests joined me in the garden room, at a seating area set up with white antique wicker chairs and a table.

An attractive work space doesn't have to show any effort. Just as a pretty dining room is a door away from the kitchen and pantry, there are times to be in beautiful places where we can accomplish our objectives in an easy, relaxed way. I have a client who has created two home offices from closets in bedrooms, hiding the equipment and clutter from sight when not in use.

Having meetings in my garden room is joyful because this room is sensual, refreshingly simple, and happy. Everywhere my eye looks it sees things I love: pictures of our children, a favorite baby picture of me, plants, flowers, paintings, pottery, and postcards. Each object is meaningful, and when everything is together, I feel this room's energy. I have hand-painted pastel marbles in a bowl, some old porcelain dishes, crystal objects that reflect light, colorful paperweights to add sparkle, and good white light from halogen lamps. Walking down the small bedroom hall, looking at the walls hung with botanicals, interspersed with Wedgwood pearlware—pink, yellow, and apple-green porcelain dessert dishes—I feel as though I've entered into a secret garden through a gate, and by shutting the latch of the door, the rest of the world is hushed, and I am in the privacy of my own dreams and wishes, free to be and to work.

There is nothing noble about being superior to some other men. The true nobility is in being superior to your previous self.

—HINDUSTANI
PROVERB

Besides making your office or workplace physically beautiful, there are little things you can do to make a significant difference. Select a few symbols of the places you love when you're *not* at your place of work. I have a friend who has a dish of sand on his end table from a favorite beach in the Caribbean to remind him of the rhythms of the waves. Use a piece of mica as a paper-weight, or a stone from a mountain you've climbed. The objects you can touch and fondle on your desk while talking on the telephone or play with while you're working are important and can bring good vibrations and karma.

If you have a copper cup holding your pens, pencils (or crayons!), keep it polished because it will give you energy as well as reflect light. I always keep my silver meat skewer polished so I'll enjoy using it to open my mail each day.

It's all right to shut the world out for a brief break, and you shouldn't have to go to a stall in an institutional bathroom to be unavailable. Either lie on the floor and have a five-minute meditation break or lean forward at your desk, rest your head on your arms, and empty your mind. Do nothing but breathe. I take minibreaks from my work to read a magazine article or dip into an inspirational book. Have a shelf or ledge where you keep a dozen or so books you've read and love and could open to any page and find refreshment. Even if you have no door to close, make a DO NOT DISTURB sign, put it on the floor or tape it on the wall, switch the telephone ringer off, and just sit, eyes open, and don't do anything except look around. Stare at your desk without touching anything, look at the walls, the floor. Realize that work is a process, and you will only be more creative by not overdoing.

Happiness comes when your work and words are of benefit to yourself and others.

—BUDDHA

Working Graciously at Home

One of the most profound ways that modern technology has changed the working world in the last two decades is by making the workplace mobile. Today, we can set up an office with nothing more than an electrical outlet. The advent of personal computers, faxes, modems, on-line services for research, voice mail services, cellular phones, and Xerox machines has given many people the freedom of flexibility. Whether we relocate our office entirely to our homes or are enabled to leave work early, carrying our office over our shoulders, we certainly have more options for where and how we want to work than ever before.

My poetry doesn't change from place to place—it changes with the years. It's very important to be one's age. You get ideas you have to turn down—"I'm sorry, no longer;" "I'm sorry, not yet."

—W. H. Auden

Because of his fax machine, Peter can choose to conduct business with his New York office, even China, if need be, all from the tiny village of Stonington. I can run my office long distance, from New York or Connecticut. My assistant Elisabeth can forward any packages and relay any urgent information to me from my New York office to my Stonington office within a day. If I'm working on a manuscript for a book, I can fax it to Julie, page by page, and she then transfers it to the computer. I've grown so accustomed to this luxury, it has become a necessity.

I can't imagine how I ever lived through those late nights at the office, when that was the only place where my files could be accessed. It wasn't really *me* to go to a midtown office in the morning, robbing myself of my Zen time of working in my nightgown in solitude. Now I get up early and work for several hours before I talk to anyone on the telephone or do any office work. Those late nights were work-oriented, but now when I read or write letters, or write in the evenings at home, I feel I'm having a moment's peace. I can enjoy my paintings and feel the comfort that only home brings us. I can be at my workplace at five o'clock in the morning if I wish. One of the most successful businessmen in America walks into his office in a white terry cloth robe, bare feet, coffee in hand. He works in a room next to his dressing room. A woman who has her own public relations firm in North Carolina turned her garden room into her workplace. The magic of working at home is that we are allowed to be ourselves. No one has to see us or our space as we pad around, doing our work in the privacy of our own home.

> *True happiness comes to him who does his work well, followed by a relaxing and refreshing period of rest.*
>
> —LIN YUTANG

Now, as never before, we can work at home, or wherever we need to be. Indeed, more and more people are doing so for a number of reasons. Interior decorators need a space to store samples, floor plans, and files, but clients rarely come to us. We go to their house or office or ranch to work. I did everything I could to create a living-room environment in my office on the twenty-sixth floor of a high-rise office building, but I dreaded pushing my way through rush hour and having the expense of rent, when I was leaving empty all day a large, attractive apartment, filled with my favorite things. I loved my office, and did everything but eat and sleep there, but that chapter is closed and I have no regrets. Not only do I save money on rent and the commute, but I also spend less on clothes. Working at home is more relaxed, more flexible. I can schedule certain days when I dress up and have appointments, and other times when I'm in at home, in casual attire, only doing local, neighborhood errands.

Wisdom is principally a sense of proportion, more often a sense of our human limitations.

—Lin Yutang

Many people I know have turned their lives around by being able to work at their own pace, in the environment they love, feeling exhilarated by this nourishing atmosphere. The basic components of a personally nourishing atmosphere are the colors you love that stimulate you, designated spaces where you want to sit, other places where you store your necessities, lots of books, flowers, and time to be there. At home we have familiar objects around us, we can be with loved ones around the kitchen table, and we have access to the great luxury of having a leisurely bath, taking time getting dressed, and savoring our lives, as though we are artists in our studio. After all, we are.

If I keep my good character, I shall be rich enough.

—Platonicus

One of my former editors and friends works from her

computer in the corner of her charming living room. Here she is most at ease. Sally can get right to work without distraction, and she feels settled because she doesn't have to tote work back and forth. Everything is in one place, ready for her to come and go without any transition periods of starting and stopping the flow of work. She can take breaks whenever the spirit moves her, peacefully. By turning off her computer, she can walk away from her work. And, after a break, all she needs to do is turn it back on, and she's there, ready. She has the luxury of being able to listen to her favorite music on her stereo and adjust the volume to suit her. She is surrounded by graciousness because she can work in an environment that is totally her own. Everywhere she looks she sees something she loves. She gazes at a painting of Oklahoma and daydreams of her childhood, and the French provincial furniture she's collected over many years brings her a great deal of joy.

By virtue of being born to humanity, every human being has a right to the development and fulfillment of his potentialities as a human being.

—ASHLEY MONTAGU

If children are still living at home you can adjust your work schedule around them. Even the most active children exhaust themselves and have to take their naps. By setting a policy where your children rest every day in their rooms at specific times, you can use these breaks productively. Even a good twenty minutes is valuable. Your pen, computer, or paintbrush is right there. My mother was an amazing example for me when I was raising wildly energetic children. While she was baby-sitting, she was always in the same room with them but never skipped a beat. She continued to work as they played. Her secret was always to provide so many stimulating projects for them, they were fully engaged. If one project didn't click, she had a dozen backups, including sorting fabric swatches by color or pasting color schemes into a scrapbook. Remove the paper wrappings on a sixty-four-color pack of Crayolas and provide a big pad of white paper. I guarantee you'll be free to do your work for another twenty minutes. Time and results accumulate.

If our children are already out of the nest, rather than downsize our home, we can rearrange the space to incorporate work spaces. You don't have to hire an architect or be otherwise extravagant. But be sure your children give you their blessing as you transform their still life of a bedroom into a useful workspace. All you really need to do is remove all the furniture—take out the beds, the bulletin boards; paint the room and rearrange the furniture; put a sitting area where the beds were and your desk on a long wall where you can hang bookcases above you. Stores and catalogs offer attractive office items that are more conducive to home life than a downtown office. I often help clients who are making career transitions design a home office—by walking down a hall, they're CEOs again. Peter and I are now in the process of turning our dry basement into a studio with spaces and rooms to use

Lost time is never found again, and what we call time enough always proves little enough.

—Ben Franklin

as we wish in the years ahead. We're not in a hurry to define all the spaces, but we anticipate putting bookcases up, and perhaps having a wine cellar. We already have a wet sink so we're free to explore all kinds of creativity and be messy.

There are some dangers to working at home. The big one: There's no leaving. Sometimes we can't prevent ourselves from calling just one more client, or revising a letter just one more time. Both Peter and I confront these temptations at times, and I admit, there are occasions when we have to rely on lunch or dinner reservations to force us to take a break or call it a night. Discipline yourself to always leave your desk or workplace for lunch and dinner. Try not to work after dinner, if possible. I save all the fun reading and often even personal mail until after dinner so I can savor it with some herbal tea or grapefruit juice in the comfort of our bed. Set a timer for sixty minutes and when the buzzer goes off, take a stretch break. After you do this for several days, you'll be able to incorporate these minibreaks naturally until they're habitual.

Working at home can be a dangerous thing to someone who has a hard time knowing when it's quitting time. If we're not careful, laptops can become a nightmare, with our fingers seemingly glued to the machine. Working graciously with modern technology requires that we ward off the new temptation to work even more. We really need

When you work you are a flute through whose heart the whispering of the hours turns to music.

—KAHLIL GIBRAN

tools to help us make a deliberate effort to say no to work at the appropriate time, even if it means not writing the last two pages of a proposal or waiting until the following day to send information to the office.

> *Self-trust is the first secret of success, the belief that, if you are here, the authorities of the universe put you here. . . . So long as you work at that you are well and successful.*
>
> —Emerson

Overall, working at home is a positive experience. This setup allows us so much freedom and flexibility, especially for people who are raising children, and for those of us who are not especially geared to the nine to five, Monday through Friday schedule. If I want to pad into the red room, turn on the light box, and work on a slide lecture at three o'clock in the morning, even a few minutes feels exhilarating because I'm so fresh from my dreams. Peter and I find this situation ideal. Because we are both writers, and want to spend as much time together as possible, our lifestyles need freedom to maximize our creative energy, which is continuously replenished in our own private domain.

The Myth of "Time Is Money"

Our orientation toward greater efficiency not only sometimes disturbs our working relationships, it can also wreak havoc with our sense of time. "The computer introduces a time frame in which the nanosecond is ordinary tem-

poral measurement," writes Juliet Schorr in her fascinating book, *The Overworked American.* "The nanosecond is the
billionth of a second, and though it is possible to conceive
theoretically of a nanosecond . . . it is not possible to experience it." We're under the illusion that faster is always
better. But at what speed can we function and still call it
living?

Our ability to do more in less time has put a consid-
erable strain on us; rising expectations of performance
can be punishingly unrealistic. We are in danger of losing
touch with our own needs and a healthy sense of our own
limits. Many of us are losing touch with family life, with
our need to be still and quiet sometimes, to
live in the moment without goals, without
ambition; in short, to reconnect with our
simple, basic selves.

Family life, in particular, is threatened
under the pressures of eighteen-hour days,
which many people are working more and
more. In an article entitled "Goofing Off"
in *Psychology Today,* journalist Paul Roberts reports that
we're headed in the wrong direction: "Despite promises
that technology and automation would shorten our work
week, nearly every study suggests we're actually working
more hours now than even a decade ago, and earning less
real income. We've actually added nine hours of work to
our work week." Says Chris Smith of the American Association for Leisure and Recreation, "People are moon-
lighting, working extra hours. . . . And with dual income

*Kindly words do not
enter so deeply into
men as a reputation
for kindness.*

—MENCIUS

families, neither mom nor dad are there to do the house-work or handle child care." As Juliet Schorr points out in her book, it's so much harder for women because we have to juggle everything: job, marriage, and children, and, last but not least, still find time for ourselves. A woman recently approached me, obviously dis-turbed about the circumstances of her life as a single mother of two children, working as a freelance designer. We talked for a while and I realized that her agitation came from overwork. "Why are you so anxious about your work?" I asked. "Why not ease up a bit and see how you feel? If you walked away from your work for a three-day weekend, do you think you could relax? Could you have fun?" She sighed, "Yes, Alexandra, if I didn't have to come back to so much work."

And the purpose of life is not to accumulate physical tokens of wealth but to mine these deeper resources for the good of all. That is the supreme goal of our existence and the only source of lasting value.

— EKNATH EASWARAN

Clearly, she had too much on her plate. I could sense that she was conscientious and would never cut back so much that the quality of her work would suf-fer. But even if she could cut back as little as 10 percent, perhaps she'd feel her burden lighten.

One of my friends recently told one of her bosses, "I've been at this company for twenty-seven years and I might be old-fashioned, but I like to have dinner in the evenings with my family. When I leave work at eight in the evening, having been here since eight in the morning, people stare at me, as if I were less dedicated than they are." My friend said that her boss replied that the new management team is there to make a profit: "If you love your work, you won't be watching the clock." My friend winced and said, "But I love my husband and children, too." When you work for someone who sets cruel, unyielding standards, how can you continue to contribute in a free spirit? How can you maintain graciousness? People today are often laboring in this kind of pressure-cooker environment.

Another hazard of these excessive expectations is that we're so busy working overtime, we no longer know what we would do with our leisure. We come home exhausted and all we can do in our few moments of relaxation is fall asleep in front of the television. We forget what it's like to make dinner with friends, to read a book for pleasure, to go for a walk, and simply to hang out and do nothing. I've made a habit of taking a two-minute bath

Remember, when life's path is steep, to keep an even mind.

—HORACE

in the evening, squirting in some Vitabath or some other gel, and changing my clothes. This gives me a fresh start and I always emerge restored, invigorated, and ready for a pleasant evening.

Do we have to work so hard? Certainly, for many, basic money issues are a big part of the problem. Unfortunately, for some people, overworking would be a luxury, since many are without jobs due to corporate downsizing. For others, the only alternative to not working at all is to take a job in very inconvenient situations. Many executives now must leave their families on Monday to work at a job in another state, returning on Thursday or Friday to be with their families. We are living in difficult times. Some people must work grueling hours just to put a roof over their heads. But, we have to ask ourselves, does the roof really need to be so big? Before we talk about money, though, let's just talk about time and the value we place on it in our lives today.

I have heard you mentioned as a man whom everybody likes. I think life has little more to give.

—Samuel Johnson

Many of us can afford to step back and ask ourselves if we really need to be working the long hours we are putting in. Many books, articles, and television shows bear witness to the fact that more and more people are feeling stressed and feel they don't have enough time in their lives to enjoy living. There are tragic stories. One of my acquaintances, a partner in a Wall Street investment firm, had been working eighteen-hour days since the year he graduated from college. On his days off, usually only Sundays, he was often on the golf course of his Connecticut country club making business deals with other club members. Though he was married and had two sons and a daughter, he rarely spent more than a few minutes at a time with them except on holidays. Two weeks shy of his forty-fifth birthday, he died of a heart attack aboard a plane return-ing from a business trip. I spoke with his wife, who confided in me a year later that he had started out simply wanting to provide well for a future family but ultimately became caught up in making more and more money. He had convinced himself that the only security in life was an extensive financial portfolio. He achieved it, but at the price of not knowing his children and losing his closeness to his wife.

Many of us must work overtime in order to fill our basic needs, but how many more of us are working to have more than we need? Perhaps some people crave more possessions because having more gives them a sense of identity; material goods sometimes fill the gaping hole left by low self-esteem. Perhaps it's a new set of values we need. There's nothing gracious about living like a jumping bean, chasing after more prosperity and more possessions which only imprison us in time-money consciousness; always running to catch up, never getting to really live.

We can learn to be more selective in how we give away our time, even when we can use the extra money. We can live more simply, and by so doing discover what really matters. We can back off a bit so we don't get so caught up in all the events going on around us. Pretend you're going away for a week. If you're not available, everyone will understand. Often we have to change our daily rhythms, doing things differently in order to readjust our priorities. We need more time alone than we have because free time awakens our inner yearnings. When we spend more time at home, appreciating what we already have, it costs nothing. Last

'Tis not important how the hero does this or this, but what he is. What he is will appear in every gesture and syllable. In this way the moment and the character are one.

— EMERSON

winter Peter and I spent a magical day alone at home. We puttered around the house, enjoying all the rooms, feeling the sweetness of freedom from obligations, appointments, and expectations. We escaped from the world successfully, doing what we wanted to do, quietly, on our own terms. As we undressed to go to bed at the end of this sublime experience, I asked Peter why we feel greater contentment and love now than when we were younger. His answer didn't surprise me. He said, "We're more free to do what's important and we pick and choose; we sublimate less. Now, finally, we're free spirits." And we were, and as a result, we were supremely happy.

To cultivate kindness is a valuable part of the business of life.

—SAMUEL JOHNSON

I've met a great many restless, breathless, rushed people in my work life. One client who made millions on Wall Street couldn't take the time to look at the furniture he was spending a small fortune to buy because he was always in too great a hurry. Time was money; it was in his body language. He left all the decorating decisions to me and his wife, even though these designs would have a great effect on the quality of his life—after all, this was his home we were shaping. When the furniture we selected finally arrived, he complained that he didn't like it, it wasn't his taste.

One of the great joys of living is taking time to enjoy the everyday things in your immediate surroundings. Recently I rested on a love seat in our living room in front of a warm fire, feeling cozy, my head leaning on several pillows, nestled under a yellow mohair throw, with a book in my lap. I enjoyed looking at the peach-colored tulips in a shiny hand-hammered pitcher and at the teal-green candle, flickering in the soft light. Gazing up at the painting over the mantel opened up moments of lovely contemplation. My eye traveled down to the beautiful carving on the French mantel. Peter told me later what time it was, and I was surprised to discover I'd been in reverie for well over an hour. We'd moved several of our paintings around in the living room, which made everything look different. When we're free to appreciate the details and beauty in our midst, we feel contentment.

I'd like to thank everyone I've met in my life.

—MAUREEN
STAPLETON

Whenever I'm not in a rush, I'm open to absorb the energy of my favorite things. I never tire of appreciating our collection of tinted bubbly-glass pitchers from Le Biot, France, or our paper-weight collection from Murano, Italy, or our paintings, porcelain, and quilts. Our possessions are bits and pieces of our personality, and collectively they have powerful meaning to us, but we have to be present and conscious in order to be aware of their importance to us.

I remember looking at an issue of *Architectural Digest* which featured the home of a client of a famous decorating firm. In one of the pictures a work of Chinese calligraphy was hung upside down on a wall behind a sofa. How sad that no one was enjoying the art to know enough to hang it right side up. What a waste of a beautiful piece of art. Do we value the trappings of success more than the life we are living because of them?

We all have to make compromises. Chances are there will be periods, even years, when the primary goal of our work life is to put bread on the table, not to fulfill our personal passions. For some the two may never overlap. But if we can look at our situation realistically, we see that in many cases we have, indeed, given away too much of ourselves to work, and have lost the ability to enjoy our lives.

TIME IS PRICELESS

Time can be so rich, so rewarding to us. We can be totally carefree, expressing truly what is inside us. I've always been able to amuse myself, and appreciate the freedom to let my spirit move me. When I'm not sched-uled I'm able to transform time into an ar-tistic, ephemeral experience where I'm in no hurry to come down to earth. When we can become absorbed in what we're doing, we're living fully. But whenever we attempt to do more than we're capable of in less time, we become anxious and lose our state of grace. Time, looked at broadly, is all we have. It provides us our space on earth. We don't need to fill it in order to live it.

We should aim rather at leveling down our desires than leveling up our means.

—ARISTOTLE

However, we often make the mistake of equating time

with money; when we do, time loses real meaning to us. Having spent thirty-five years designing home interiors, I've come to realize the unfortunate con-
nection so many people make between time and money. Because their job often "prices" them at a per-hour dollar amount, people will put this same price tag on their nonwork hours. They begin to question everything, asking themselves, Is this worth my time? As a result many people hire workers to do the household chores that they might actually enjoy doing, chores that might relax and inspire them.

He had a sense of well-being, knowing that he had improved both house and garden these past few years, added the hot house, purchased the second studio next door, and each season gave him the opportunity to improve every inch of ground.

—EVA FIGES

"Efficiency is a lightning calculator, by which you may convert time into anything you like, and read the answer in percent-ages, to the third decimal place," continues Percival White, in the *Atlantic* article referred to earlier. "Money is a tangible thing. The more you save, the more you have. But time is far more subtle stuff. Saving it does not imply having it. As soon as a man seriously starts saving time, make up your mind that he will no longer have a moment to spare."

I'm not interested in living so efficient a work life that I have to cut out the simple pleasures of living. If I make a salad that takes an hour to prepare, allowing me to won-der and reflect as I enjoy the sensory and satisfying pleas-ures of chopping and dicing, delighting in the natural colors, textures, and smells of all these gifts from the garden, why should I rush and diminish my pleasure in the experience, or delegate the task to someone else? I could be working, but one is no replacement for the other. I lose more when I lose my earthiness—my contact with the real stuff of daily life. While I've never equated time with money, I have at times lost sight of the priceless importance of this earthly connection. Last winter, partially because of all the snow, and also because I was doing some decorating as well as a lot of writing, we abandoned our village cottage for several months. We were both so busy we kept putting off our plans to go to Stonington. We finally settled on a date to go, and while dressing that morning Peter said, "It's time." On the train, as we approached Old Saybrook, the Connecticut River on one side and the Long Island Sound on the other, I realized how I had been starving myself of nature's beauty. When we finally got to our lovely cottage, I realized I should have been there all the time. I do my best work there, and I'm most content living simply. My clients, as it turned out, didn't need my supervision, and if there had been a problem, my assistant could have worked things out.

"Don't you want a vacation, Mr. Gandhi?"

"I'm always on vacation."

A few years ago a young man offered his services to cut our lawn and trim around the picket fence. We travel a great deal, so this seemed like a good idea. The only problem was, I love to mow the lawn. One day last August, after a heavy rainstorm, I looked down at the lawn from our bedroom window and was overcome by the brilliance of the new light that dawned at the end of the storm. What better way to enjoy the clean, light air than to mow the lawn? Besides, one of my absolutely favorite smells is the smell of freshly cut grass. I was in heaven. Outside, delighted by the deep shadows cast from the picket fence onto the grass by the sharpness of the new light, I felt intoxicated by the crisp, fresh air. I went to fetch the lawn mower, put on some hot-pink rubber boots I had bought in a department store in Paris, grabbed a straw hat, and off I went.

When Peter saw me he smiled and said, "You know, don't you, Alexandra, that you're taking a job away from someone?" But we have the smallest lawn in the world— so small that we had to order a special tiny red lawn mower. A five-year-old child could mow our lawn in the blink of an eye. I love this "chore." I don't love it all the time, but when the spirit moves me, I move. If I had been thinking about the dollar value of this time I would have hired someone else to do the work, but I would be giving away something I really enjoy doing. Peter is paid substantially for his time serving clients as their lawyer. If he were to apply his hourly rate to his free time, he'd never do any gardening. He'd be sitting at his desk working nonstop. He'd lose all the simple ways he enjoys living every day. He loves to spend time with his children and grandchildren. When he goes to the

One machine can do the work of fifty ordinary men. No machine can do the work of one extraordinary man.
—ELBERT HUBBARD

village to get a haircut, he takes the long way home, browsing in a used-book store and several antique shops, wandering around in a contented trance, absorbing the sights, sounds, and textures of village life. He loves to read and take long bike rides and walks, and he spends hours polishing brass or rubbing beeswax into wood. We always have long, leisurely lunches, celebrating the moment, and he enjoys the ritual of preparing a meal, another opportunity for celebration. Peter, a close friend observed recently, makes moments into ceremonies. Every moment is full of curiosity, whimsy, and wonder. Peter is essentially playful, so his free time is passed in pleasant ways. If he sets a tea tray he puts some fruit on it for color. He loves adding a finishing touch to whatever he does. To take pleasure in life, you have to take time. This fact is not always clear when we're working hard, and it's not always so easy to do, but when we start giving our personal time priority, we like it so much that somehow we do find a way. The next time you give away your free time to work, realize that you may be losing an opportunity to cook, if you like to cook; garden, if you like to garden; decorate, if you like to decorate; read, if you like to read; write, if you like to write. If we don't hold fast to the ways we can live more vitally, more intensely, and with more passion, we have given our lives away to a busy day.

> An hour's industry will do more to produce cheerfulness, suppress evil humors and retrieve your affairs than a month's moaning.
>
> —BEN FRANKLIN

Getting a helping hand now and then when we really need it is a blessing. But we don't need someone to arrange flowers in a pitcher for us. All we need is a pitcher, some cutting shears, some water, and a moment's peace.

Seeing time as only a moneymaking opportunity deprives us of what makes our time truly valuable: the possibilities for meaning and grace that only time can provide. When we take time, we appreciate and savor life by valuing the beauty of nature, the warmth of our home, our love of people, the wisdom of others we learn from through literature, poetry, music, art, and architecture. Taking time to have tea with a student you want to help advise on a career decision, or to give a talk at a local high school, or to go to auctions to learn more about the decorative arts, are ways to use time in rewarding ways. When we walk to do an errand rather than driving, or bake bread or refinish a table, we are actively participating in the grace of the moment. When you give your best time to work you lose time to enjoy your life— even the pleasure of doing simple daily chores turns into grace notes. Time, unlike money, cannot be accumulated: once you've exchanged it for money, you may have more money, but you've lost the time in which to enjoy it. Time is irreplaceable because it expires just as we do. Time is not money. Time is priceless.

What are we working for, after all?

I am born a poet, of a low class without doubt yet a poet. That is my nature and vocation.

—Emerson

Enjoying the Fruits of Our Labor

Juliet Schorr suggests in *The Overworked American* that a shorter work schedule can actually raise productivity because it boosts morale, giving people time to enjoy life so that when they go to work they perform at their optimum level. She recommends shortening the workday by offering people the option of taking less money for less work time, instead of the reverse, which is what we generally do: work longer hours for more money, leaving us less time to actually enjoy the fruits of our labor. It's an interesting idea, and one that places value on our neglected need for personal time.

Every now and then a man's mind is stretched by a new idea and never shrinks back to its original proportion.
— Oliver Wendell Holmes

There's a wealth of possibilities available to us when we work fewer hours. We can't work all the time without robbing ourselves, our families and loved ones of cherished, shared, loving moments. A wealthy Texas deal-maker told me with an ironic chuckle, "Sandie, all business is bad business." What Tom meant is there is more to life than making a deal and making money. Without time to reflect on what you're working toward, and the kind of work you do, you'll be blinded to a vaster awareness of your human potential for generosity of spirit, kindness, and contentment. Our job and how much money we make cannot define us. We must ultimately cherish our spirit and nourish our essential nature, which is not material. To live life fully, first we have to cherish it abundantly.

What do we do with this new free time? First, all we need to do is be present, to listen to our spirit, and deliberately make a more concerted effort to meditate, contemplate, and value the gifts we receive when we step away from a busy, frantic lifestyle. Value also the spiritual experiences available to us all the time if we only become more receptive. Start to switch your energy toward deepening your appreciations of all things good and beautiful, and in this broadening of your lens, you will have boundless, timeless vastness of things to cherish.

The biggest mistake many people make is to immediately rush into filling the empty cup. Your free time must be unrestricted until you've taken time to sort what's true from what's false, and by reevaluating how you want to use your resources of time and talent, then you will be able to make thoughtful decisions about the future. If the spirit moves you to involve yourself in more activities, take an art class, do a community project, teach Sunday school, or start a cooking class. Coach a local sports team, but make sure you do it with a glad heart. Whenever we push too hard or are pushed by others, we experience a sense of resistance and regret.

Only learn to seize good fortune,
For good fortune's always here.

—JOHANN WOLFGANG VON GOETHE

Once we've thought things through, then we can calmly and confidently decide that taking a language course to

Cultivate . . . peace of mind which does not separate one's self from one's sur- roundings. When that is done success- fully, then everything else follows natu- rally. Peace of mind produces right val- ues, right values produce right thoughts. Right thoughts produce right actions and right actions produce work which will be a material reflection for others to see of the serenity at the center of it all.

—ROBERT M. PIRSIG

become fluent in French or traveling more to broaden our exposure is a positive use of our free time. We may discover that participating in community theater, seriously taking up a sport or musical instrument, getting involved with a church, synagogue, or community or- ganization, taking a course, studying painting or drawing, can add dimensions to our life. We will find there are many ways to be paid in life, and not only with currency.

By setting some boundaries with our work schedule in order to be with our children and nourish our inner selves, we begin to discover a whole new world. The rewards are heartening, and accumulate over the years. A successful television host, recently sepa- rated from her boyfriend, has taken in and unofficially adopted a teenage boy who is the product of a troubled family. A woman who volunteered two hours a week at an abused woman's shelter in Brooklyn counseled a family—a mother and her five children—and now, eight years later, the family has a stable home, is financially secure, and has become a second family to Susan. She now spends time every week with one or more of the children, ages ten to seventeen, not out of charity but friendship.

You don't have to do things with time off

that cost money. You can go hiking or bird watching, or do a research project at the local historical association, or make a reading list and begin taking out books more regularly from the library. When you think about how to reclaim leisure, think of summer, think of the unstructured time we're allowed during our vacations, when we enjoy the simple unfolding of the rhythms of each day. This is a treat we treasure after having our lives planned up to the minute all year through. Being able to float, to pursue projects of interest freely and dabble in home improvements gives a pleasant balance to our days.

Even if our efforts of attention seem for years to be producing no result, one day a light that is in exact proportion to them will flood the soul.
—SIMONE WEIL

By slowing down and stepping back, we can look with more clarity at the contribution we want to make with the time we're given on earth. Remember Rainer Maria Rilke's sage advice in *Letters to a Young Poet:* "If your daily life seems poor, do not blame it, blame yourself, for you are not poet enough to call forth its riches." Our time is *now* to assess what we can do to leave this earth a little better because of our existence. Is the work we're doing making a difference to the welfare of others? When we do take time to reflect, do we like what we see? If not, chances are you're missing the point by not looking at the big picture. Are you really spending your time, your most valuable asset, wisely? It's not the actual work we do, but the person we are behind the work. How we get along with our coworkers, how we treat our employees, is our essential nature, not how efficient we are or how rich and powerful.

We all work hard, but we need to look beyond the results and examine the process. Do we ever feel superior to those under us in our work or in life in general? At the end of a long, tiring day of work, are we pleased we've done our best to be as kind, open, and fair as humanly possible? Do we appreciate the help we receive, and are we friendly to others, no matter who they are or what their work is? And do we feel that sense of grace and contentment that comes from being in the flow of love, and doing our part to make the whole more grace-filled? As we work things out, we'll move toward being our most authentic self, which will greatly improve the process of work as well as the result of our labors of love.

Five

✳

Gracious Solitude

TIME FOR SOLITUDE

We need solitude in order to draw ourselves inward for renewal. We miss our solitude, though we hardly know it. What we do know is that we often feel splintered, confused, stretched too thin to feel comfortable in our own skin. If we realized that these feelings could be remedied by solitude, we would all feel a lot more hopeful about having enough time to enjoy life.

"Words cannot convey the almost voluptuous sweetness

of the feelings experienced in solitude. . . ." wrote adventurer Alexandra David-Neel. "Mind and sense develop their sensibility in this contemplative life made up of continual observations and reflections. Does one become a visionary or, rather, is it not that one has been blind until then?" Many of us are blinded by our busy lives so that we cannot always see what life is about.

Several summers ago I increased my time alone—I call it my "Zen time"—to last from sunrise, when I naturally awake, until noon. I did this for three months, six days a week, and experienced one of the most heart-melting summers in memory. I remained by myself until the sun was at its zenith. I had never before allowed myself this much contiguous free time. I wasn't able to since there were children to raise and a home to support. I also had my work, and often I was paid to be on construction sites at eight o'clock in the morning, leaving me little opportunity for sunrise solitude.

I learned the interior of life was as rewarding as the exterior life, and that my richest moments occurred when I was absolutely still.

—R I C H A R D   B O D E

My absolute contentment must have been noticeable that summer—perhaps people recognized some mystical aura or power about me—because before that summer, no matter how clear I had ever been about my need for free, solitary time, I was constantly interrupted and my peaceful solitude was regularly broken.

That summer, with the children already grown, I finally had the freedom to take the time I'd longed for. It was a treat I gave myself for thirty years of being too available to the many demands of others. It was an experiment. I took what I suspected was the time I deeply needed, and it worked! It was transformative. I became truly aware of myself and my aliveness to life. Most of our time is spent living with and caring for others, but it is only when we are alone that we have the opportunity to fully emerge, to become ourselves.

I'd had free days or weekends before this, but this extended time was metamorphic. I felt a spiritual transformation and vitality I had never known before. I was able to relax enough, to remain quiet long enough, to allow new and deeper observations and reflections to rise up in me. I took my time every step of the way. Because I knew I had the freedom of this time and the guarantee

One can see time flow sometimes; one does not have to do something to pass the time; time can pass by itself.
—LIN YUTANG

of privacy, I relaxed into the morning. Once, when a journalist interviewed Peter, inquiring, "What is she *really* like?" he chuckled, "I get her coffee, juice, and a slice of a muffin, and she goes." If Peter is awake, he enjoys getting me breakfast in bed, a ritual he began after Brooke went off to college. By the time he arrives with the tray, I'm either reading or writing. My bedside table has a stack of books, magazine articles, newspaper clippings, as well as my clipboard, pen, and glasses. I'm ready immediately to be in the flow.

Before I write, usually I read—or "research" as Peter and I call it. We fill our well before emptying it. In solitude, we're liberated to be the persons we truly are, and I love being alone to read, write, and contemplate. Our four-poster bed is high off the floor, and when I sit up straight, comforted by several pillows, I'm free to gaze out at the water. Only in solitude are we able to daydream. As I sip freshly ground and brewed French roast coffee, I'm able to meditate, reflect on my dreams, and begin to weave together my thoughts before I write. Once I begin, soon I'm able to go along unselfconsciously, and, without being aware of it, I move to a writing table by the window, or go into the Zen room, or downstairs and out into the garden.

Every morning is fresh and different in the specific ways I ritualize this solitary time but, without exception, I am always quiet and private. If I'm up earlier than Peter, I'll get coffee and juice and tour the garden, checking to see if anything needs watering. As I listen to the birds chirping, I muse about many things. I never bathe and dress until I've had several hours of quiet time.

I have no idea how I've grown into this habit of writing in my nightgown. I began my first book in 1966, when I was pregnant with Alexandra, and it wasn't published until 1974. Even then I found the early morning the most peaceful and productive because I was protected from the telephone ringing and other disturbances that occur later in the day. Now, almost thirty years later, I've merely extended this time from two hours to the entire morning. I've come to count on this solitude, and

He has the gift of quiet.

—JOHN LE CARRÉ

find it more valuable than sleep. My deepened awareness
of myself in both mind and body allows me to experience
the fullness of the moment. At times I simply sit still and
notice the air and my own breathing:
"Awareness of breathing provides a unique
opportunity for one to integrate time into
the self experience," explains psychothera-
pist Mark Epstein in his groundbreaking
book, *Thoughts Without a Thinker,* which de-
scribes our sense of connectedness to our
life force in these meditative moments.

*Silence is the
perfectest herald of
joy. I were but little
happy if I could say
how much.*

—WILLIAM
SHAKESPEARE

These summer months convinced me
that it is essential to take time alone (not
necessarily this much time) to experience the grace of living. They allowed me to become more conscious of what
I have control over and what I don't. I was awakened to
what really matters and guided to look beyond temporary
distractions and annoyances in order to carry out my own
intentions. I was in a good place and enjoyed dwelling
there, free to be fully myself. I also learned to avoid negative distractions by letting them enter me and float away,
without becoming overly disturbed by anything. Wherever
we live there are noises that can be annoying, but in our
village I enjoy the sounds of others at work, hammering
or sawing wood or mowing the lawn. Because I cherish
this time, I refuse to allow anything to interfere. How can
I answer the door in a see-through nightgown? I rarely
even answer the telephone until I've completed my morning's quiet time. Peter is protective of me, understand-

ing how essential this is. He answers the door and phone, taking messages when necessary.

SOLITUDE: SELFISH OR SELF-SUSTAINING?

Gracious living requires the sense of balance that solitude brings. I used to get up predawn and go to my writing table, in order to be alone. I would sit by the open window listening to classical music or to the birds singing, enjoy

Life was resumed, and anxious living blew away as if it had not been. I could not breathe deep enough or long enough. It was a return to happiness.

—SARAH ORNE JEWETT

seeing the English ivy and a white French faience cachepot on my desk or looking out at the water, free to be totally absorbed in the here and now. I find that I am more grace-conscious when I am in this state where I feel all of me is integrated—mind, body, and soul are all connected. I feel I'm not just one individual human being, but a life force like air, water, sky—only I also have consciousness. This experience fills me with a thrilling sense of wonder, often rapture. I feel enlarged in a cosmic, limitless, sense of expansion—difficult to convey.

Every moment of grace I experience emanates from this still inner space where I live as if in a quiet garden that I tend and nurture.

I shudder to remember how tired and anxious I often was before I discovered this place of stillness within myself. How much more splintered and fragmented I would have been had I not given myself at least some time and space to gather myself together. No matter what schedule I have had, I have always taken advantage of early morning hours to be alone, to begin each day by giving myself some moments to be inward before facing the momentum of the day. These hours guarantee graciousness. I'm able to clear my head and nourish my own needs so I'm then prepared to focus on the demands of the day and be more effective because I approach everything with a sense of calm. I'm mentally prepared to handle the day's problem solving, including clients' demands, family issues, and any other unexpected occurrences.

Because my mornings are so precious to me, I almost always wait until lunch time before inviting guests over. When we're in Stonington, I inform guests which trains they can take from New York so that I can eagerly greet them at the front door when they arrive. I never answer the phone or pick up a fax before noon. People sometimes knock at the door or walk right in when it's open, shouting, "Hello! Hello? Are you home?" I try not to feel odd not responding, even though I may physically be in the cottage. When I'm in my solitude, I'm not available even though I'm at home. I might as well be on a deserted island where no one can reach me.

It takes discipline to hold fast to time for yourself and

But your solitude will be a support and a home for you, even in the midst of very unfamiliar circumstances, and from it you will find all your paths.

—RAINER MARIA RILKE

your family and colleagues. People question how we do what we do, but there is no mystery. The key is consistency and perseverance. By not answering the telephone, not paying attention to the knock at the door, I carry on without interruption. I'm adamant about my need to be undisturbed. I don't feel guilty about wanting this solitude because I've accepted that it is a crucial part of my life. And because I prefer to meditate and work at home, I refuse to be forced out of my own home because other people don't live this way.

I've had to learn not to worry about hurting someone's feelings. This is my time. I've claimed it, and I'm territorial about it. I've discovered what works for me and I'm receptive to this knowledge. Only when I'm unavailable to others am I fully in touch and in tune with myself. I require large chunks of time, space, and calm during and around my actual writing. Without making time for this time, time simply slips away and I lose my chance to recharge. Time is not retrievable.

Your feelings, and the thoughts that created them, are your own responsibility, nobody else's. Change your thoughts if you want to change your feelings. . . . Imagine your mind as a garden. Which thoughts will you plant in it?

—SUE PATTON THOELE

On one particular morning a few years ago, I was sitting in my writing room in the cottage, deep into my Zen time, when friends who were driving down from Bangor, Maine, for the weekend called to say that they had arrived early, at ten o'clock in the morning. They were not expected until lunchtime. I was in the middle of writing, very much in the flow of it. I couldn't afford to lose this precious time. Once I allow one interruption (unless it's a life or death matter), many more tend to follow and before I know it I have given away an important piece of my writing life. "An artist requires the upkeep of creative solitude," writes Julia Cameron. "An artist requires the healing of time alone. Without this period of recharging, our artist becomes depleted. Until we experience the freedom of solitude, we cannot connect authentically. We may be enmeshed, but we are not encountered. Art lies in the moment of encounter: We meet our truth and we meet ourselves; we meet ourselves and we meet our self-expression."

I heard Peter on the telephone downstairs graciously inviting our friends over, "Sure. We can't wait to see you." It was lovely of Peter, but I just couldn't break away. I felt pangs of guilt: Would it be "ungracious" of me not to come down or must I stop what I was doing to greet them and begin our weekend earlier than I could? I love these people and value their friendship beyond measure. I felt torn. My arms became tight and I could feel myself gritting my teeth anxiously.

Nothing can ever happen to you that you can't handle if you prepare yourself psychologically and emotionally.

—DR. GERALD LOREN FISHKIN

Is this need for solitude selfish? Or is it simply self-sustaining? It's a need I wouldn't hesitate to respect in another person. As artists spend countless hours alone in their studio working, there is something we can learn from their need for solitude: Time alone gives us time to ourselves to regroup, renew, and refresh ourselves, whether we're painting, writing in a diary, listening to a piece of music, or writing a letter to a friend. Any of these are solitary actions that, in the end, reconnect us to our life force and to others.

Peace is not an absence of war, it is a virtue, a state of mind, a disposition for benevolence, confidence, justice.

—SPINOZA

With that thought, I decided to stick it out, well aware that the good energy I would take away from this morning Zen time would be released during the remainder of the day, and we would all enjoy each other's company that much more. I would be the generous host I wanted to be and that would be a blessing to us all. Peter told our friends, "Alexandra is upstairs working, under deadline, and she'll be down when she's finished." Peter understands my need for quiet when I'm in the flow of writing, and felt no need to explain or apologize to our guests. And with the help of some good classical music, I drowned out most of the laughter and the lively sounds coming from downstairs, and finished my writing, satisfied with and renewed by my efforts.

Apparently, being interrupted is a timeless problem, not just a hazard of our overcrowded, speeded-up modern life. In an article in *The New York Times* entitled AFTER 150 YEARS WALDEN IS STILL YIELDING SECRETS, writer Suzanne Hamlin described the invasion of privacy even as it affected Henry David Thoreau: "Trying to live simply 150 years ago, the 28-year-old refugee from convention who

was seeking solitude appears to have had the same problems as many country-house owners: a stream of guests,
meal-planning, curious neighbors, a garden
needing constant tending and decorating
decisions." Even Thoreau at his retreat had
lots of "unreckoned guests." He built his
modest ten-by-fifteen-foot cabin on land
that Ralph Waldo Emerson had lent him.
Emerson lived a mile away and was a friend
of the family. The whole reason for
"roughing it in the woods" was to get "quiet
and time to think, away from the masses
leading lives of quiet desperation. Instead,
he became a captive host."

*Language has
created the word
"loneliness" to
express the pain of
being alone, and the
word "solitude" to
express the glory of
being alone.*

—PAUL TILLICH

I cannot say this enough: This time alone is irretrievable
and nothing can substitute for it. No matter how brief it is,
be sure to build time for yourself into your day.

TIME ALONE HEALS

The essential reason I'm such an advocate of gracious living
is that I see in it a way to emancipate ourselves from the
frowning friction, the discord in our mind, the dissatisfac-
tions and disappointments of modern life. When we learn
the attributes of gracious living we feel a sweetness, a tenderness, a light shining through that cleanses us.

Spending adequate time in solitude is an essential in-
gredient of gracious living. It is no more self-indulgent

than prayer or meditation. "Without this period of re-charging," wrote Julia Cameron, "we become depleted and over time we become anxious and out of sorts."

Deep, lasting behavioral changes cannot be imposed from the outside. They are internal battles.

—JANICE M. HOROWITZ

I owe my ability to maintain a semblance of grace under pressure to the freedom and time I've carefully guarded ever since I started writing in the early sixties. Start by claiming just five minutes every morning so you can create a space for solitude. Any time you take for this inner awakening will be restorative. For people with a busy schedule, especially those with young children, get up earlier than anyone else. We all need a sanctuary, a place where we feel comfortable. Whether you can be alone in your own thoughts at the kitchen table, the sink, in the bath, in bed, at a coffee shop, in the library, in a garden, or at a museum, your soul is nudging you toward taking this time. The only way to know how to integrate your life is to have these moments of reflection, and they will always, without exception, be healing. We begin to become whole when we recognize our fragmentation. Who we really are is only revealed to us in these quiet times. The compellingly thoughtful philosopher Joseph Campbell believed, "We're seeking the experience of being alive." The best things, he claimed, can't be told. We dwell not in our mind but in our soul, and the rapture comes from connecting to our center.

"More than anything else," urges Julia Cameron, "experiment with solitude. You will need to make a commitment to quiet time. Try to acquire the habit of checking in with yourself. Several times a day, just take a beat, and ask yourself how you are feeling. Listen to your answer. Respond kindly. If you are doing something very hard, promise yourself a break and a treat afterward."

We're able to face crises with Zen calm when we're centered in this inner nourishment. When we're caught off guard, we're better able to handle confrontation with grace because we are internally healed, wanting to assist others rather than contribute to the problem. Whether we have to face a difficult client, a household disaster, or something more serious such as sickness or death, we're mentally and spiritually equipped to be a positive presence. Rather than judging what is happening, we open up to it. Even when I was in Chicago, where my brother had open heart surgery and died without coming out of a coma, I got up early every day. When I had a date with his surgeon at six o'clock, I got up at four o'clock so I could be present and fully conscious of the situation.

> *Suddenly all my ancestors are behind me. Be still, they say. Watch and listen. You are the result of the love of thousands.*
>
> —LINDA HOGAN

❋

INVENTING WAYS TO BUILD SOLITUDE INTO YOUR DAY

You don't necessarily have to be entirely alone to create a sense of solitude; you can do so even in the company of another person or in a crowd. When Peter and I are together in the morning hour we don't necessarily speak. We each do our separate reading and writing, and feel a nice sense of comfort in the respect we each create for the other's sacred spiritual space. We're compatible partners in our solitude. One of my favorite columns in *McCall's* was "Solitude for Two." I wrote about time alone together, where Peter and I are aware of each other's presence, but feel completely free to be in our own worlds, making no demands on each other. Neither one of us is needy for attention from the other, and we both seek time and space to deepen our inner journey.

Any good thought you have is a prayer.

Rather than feel defeated or drained by being together too much, we feel excited. We then connect with kisses or with words. After we've both fed our well, we're ready to be together again.

I enjoy being with loved ones but not necessarily always talking to them. The closer I feel to someone, the fewer words are needed. Brooke and I can go for a walk, hold hands, or wrap our arms around each other, never uttering a word. We feel a telepathic connection in each other's gentle presence. We don't need to say that we see the rambling roses on the trellis, or the beautiful old stone walls covered with ivy, or the secret gardens behind the gates, or the sun dancing on the water, or the hollyhocks, the sailboats, and the children, while walking together in the park. "Isn't it pretty?" is superfluous to the lovely trance we're in together.

A minister in our village, who also writes books, reads to himself as he walks down the street. He recently described to me how every morning he walks from his house to a coffee shop, reading a book along the way. "You look fifty feet ahead, see what you have to watch out for, and you read." Steve laughed as he continued, "Alexandra, I'm obviously amusing myself, minding my own business. Still, complete strangers go out of their way to speak to me, as if my absorption were some kind of provocation for them to approach me. If I didn't have the book in front of my face I would be left alone." Which is what he actually wants. Once at the coffee shop, Steve writes part of a mystery, glad his walk and read helped him to plot out his characters. But he still wishes he could do so with fewer interruptions en route.

The messages come from within, and transmit cues that tell you what your mind and body need for your well-being moment to moment.

—CHÉREE CARTER-SCOTT

Before I had children, my favorite technique for creating private space among others was to go with my husband to a coffee shop for breakfast. We'd take the bus to our favorite coffee house, Stark's, sit at the counter, eat breakfast, and read the paper. After breakfast, I'd linger for an extra half hour or so to write. Neither of our offices opened before nine o'clock (imagine today the luxury of being locked out of a workplace until a civilized starting hour). I thoroughly enjoyed this time to think, sit alone, and write; even back then morning was my time to meditate, to sit in solitude. I always looked forward to this time.

One feels the spirit of peace as definitely as heat is perceived on a hot summer day.

—WILLIAM JAMES

I once made the mistake of telling a friend about this morning ritual. Thinking it sounded wonderful, my friend asked if she could join me. "I promise I won't say a word," she urged. I had to say no; I knew it would blow my whole morning to have a friend there with me. I would no longer be alone. Even though I said no, she appeared, forcing me to switch coffee shops.

To find solitude in a busy life, we have to train ourselves to walk away from friends, from work, from anything that interrupts the flow of this reconnection to our self. "Only in solitude," wrote the Chinese novelist Han Suyin, "can man learn to know himself, learn to handle his own eternity of aloneness. And love from one being to another can only be that two solitudes come nearer, recognize and protect and comfort each other."

By thought I embrace the universe.

—BLAISE PASCAL

Claiming this inner space requires self-esteem, because

we have to feel worthy of enriching our own spirit. This self-love is essential to being able to participate joyfully in all the experience of living. Life is full of sorrow, pain, and loss, and yet if we're not able to recognize the great gift of the mystery of our own *being* here, we've missed it all. As I've said before, it's all right to shut the world out for a moment's peace. It may be a saving grace at the end of the day to go to a café and be alone for a cup of espresso before going home, or to take a walk by yourself before meeting people for lunch. It's not unloving toward other people to claim space, and to find a private place where you can hear the vibrations of your heart.

If the house is full of family and friends, go to an empty room, shut the door, sit still, and listen. Don't go to a bathroom because someone will find you. If you can't do this because you're watching a child, concentrate on your breathing, look at a favorite painting or picture book or read a poem. Visualize walking barefoot on a beautiful beach, alone, and feel the wet sand under your toes. Be astonished by the beauty of the sky and the waves. With time, we can feel harmony even in chaos or in hectic times.

I often disappear and retreat to the kitchen to cook, or I'll do a load of laundry,

To meditate is to listen with a receptive heart.

—BUDDHA

Perhaps the best way to thank God for the gift of living is to appreciate the present hour, to sit quietly and hear your own breathing and look out on the universe and be content.

—LIN YUTANG

or iron to be alone in my thoughts. People may not even notice you're missing, or will pretend they don't so they don't feel they have to help you with a chore. This frees you to have Zen time.

The Grace of Meditation

Prayer is not asking. It is a longing of the soul.

—Gandhi

More and more people today are learning to turn inward, to quiet down, and be still. They are doing so as I have, in many different ways, including through various forms of meditation. Through meditation we can train our attention to float, not to become trapped or stuck in anxious thoughts. Eknath Easwaran teaches us to become completely absorbed. In his book *Conquest of Mind,* he writes, "In this profound absorption the mind is still, calm, and clear. This is our native state. Once we become established in it, we know once and for all who we are and what life is for."

The revelation of a moment, a solitary note heard in a symphony thundering through debatable existences of time.

—Henry Beston

Meditation is a state of being when our self-consciousness temporarily disappears, and, according to Mark Epstein, we learn a new way to be with our feelings. "Stripped of pride or shame," Epstein says, "stray thoughts lose their charge and are seen as 'just thoughts' or just feelings. Meditation offers a refuge. Our thoughts move from a narrow focus on the content of experience to a focus on the process." Most of the time we are so busy being productive and efficient in getting things done that the end becomes everything, even though the means may make us suffer too much. But life is lived in the *process* of living. When we lose our appreciation for the process of life, we lose our ability to live. We also lose our resilience, because when we focus on ends and not means, if we fail we've lost everything.

Fill what's empty.
Empty what's full.
—ALICE
ROOSEVELT
LONGWORTH

All too often we are out of sync with ourselves, lost in thoughts of past or future and unable simply to be with our immediate experience. When I learned to become still, I became aware of the most elemental things, including my connection to the earth, my lack of control over what *is,* and the state of constant change that governs our existence.

GRACEFUL SOLITUDE

Graceful solitude is not easy to accomplish. I have my own blind spots when I become distracted and irritated by something small. Even when I concentrate on being mindful, unaffected by distractions, I am not always gracious. Just as an Impressionist painter may paint an idealized version of reality, I try to remain focused on what is true, redemptive, kind, and loving. But there are times when

The only Zen you
find on the tops of
mountains is the Zen
you bring up there.
—ROBERT M.
PIRSIG

this can be a real challenge. Even so, we can learn the necessary skills for "effortless grace."

The great man is he who in the midst of the crowd keeps with perfect sweetness the independence of solitude.

—Emerson

How can we turn our attention away from anxiety and worry toward exuberance and calm? Dante suggests, "Don't reason about it, but give a glance and pass beyond." And the Buddha said, "All that we are is the result of what we have thought." If we have thought fear we shall fear, if we have thought calm, we shall be calm. It is not selfish to carve out whatever time it takes to feel rapture in the mere reality that we're here. By claiming and taking solitude regularly, however you manage it, whatever your circumstances, you're awakened to inner grace. This nourished spirit is essentially what we pass on to others, whether family, friends, coworkers, or strangers. Through our appreciation of a deep, rich, inner reality, we're there, aware, awake, and receptive to fully participating in the sorrows as well as the joys of life.

In solitude, be a multitude to thyself.

—Tibullus

Six

❋

Family Graces

The Nourishment of Family

It's no secret that I love family life. I treasure the sense of connection, being part of this generational flow of continuity. The children are all, without exception, devoted to Peter, looking up to him, asking his advice and wanting to hear more of his vivid stories of his childhood as well as his memories of the stories his parents told him of their younger days. We're able to show the fullness of our love for each other in the warm privacy of our family's companionship. We're able to collectively honor our combined histories, while also recognizing individual personality traits, that make each family member unique.

I value this delicious home feeling as one of the choicest gifts a parent can bestow.
—Washington Irving

Family is the source of life's most profound blessings. The loving kindness I receive from family can ease life's frustrations and soften the cruel blows of fate, providing us with the nourishment we need to face each day.

When I'm with my family I'm myself, and I'm truly at home. Where else but in our family are we safe to sing along with the radio off-key at the top of our lungs, dance around our rooms, lounge around in bed half the morning, pad around in our pajamas, with bare feet, bad breath, and hair unbrushed? We can parade around immodestly in our underwear, say strange, ridiculous things and not be questioned because no matter how odd we are, our family knows where we're coming from, allowing us to speak in code. We intuitively understand and accept one another's quirkiness. Anyone else would respond, "Excuse me. What did you say?" or just give you a bewildered look. With family there's such a fortress of love and affection, we can safely tease each other in good humor and fun with no undercurrent of meanness. We can watch a sappy, romantic movie together and cry our hearts out. Certain things strike us as funny, and we can have aching, cathartic belly laughs. When Peter walked into the kitchen recently wearing his bathrobe and his black patent leather dancing shoes, the girls ended up in tears of laughter and love. No matter how many times they see Peter in his pajamas, bathrobe, and black, shiny pumps, there's only one "Sweet Pete" and he never fails to break them up. We can be our silliest when we try on old clothes, hysterically aware how dated and dowdy we look. "Mother, Mother, out, out. Mother, Mother, *noooo.*" I hate parting with anything and the only way I ever can is when the girls insist on a "de-thugging."

We can express frustration at the turn of an event, we can admit to wrongdoing where we didn't communicate well enough or acted awkwardly. But there's an underbelly of acceptance, where we trust each other in times of disappointment and sadness, and delight in all the happy times, celebrating each other all the way.

Our family is a powerful force field of emotions. All of our most basic needs are played out among family: the need to be taken care of, the need for independence, and the need for love. Sometimes the needs of one clash with the needs of another. In a family we are constantly negotiating that balance of giving and taking. Given the normal intensity of family life, our ability to provide each other with love and support is sometimes a challenge.

Only friendship which can stand occasional plain speaking is worth having.

—Lin Yutang

As the shapes and styles of family life change—two working parents, single parents, stepfamilies, extended families—we face the still greater challenge of discovering how to achieve this balance under a whole new set of cir-

cumstances. Families today have less and less time together, and often no one is home to tend the hearth. We
feel more pressure about our work, both because our jobs

*One of the oldest
human needs is
having someone to
wonder where you
are when you don't
come home at night.*

—Mᴀʀɢᴀʀᴇᴛ Mᴇᴀᴅ

seemd to demand more of our time, and
because downsizing and a shrinking job
market make us afraid of losing the job we
have. We have more decisions to make about
who takes on which family responsibilities.
Does mother continue working while father
stays home with the baby, or does father go
to work while mom stays home? Do they
both go to work? Though the straightfor-
wardness of family roles in earlier genera-
tions was restrictive and certainly not preferable, today we
do have the added burden, and freedom, to negotiate new
family roles that work for us individually. But, regardless
of the style of family life, a family is ultimately defined by
the energy and life force it generates toward love, support,
acceptance, strength, understanding, and communion.
The basic things hold. It's up to us to decide how to bring
what is best about family to any arrangement we call by
that name.

When we get all the parts to work in synchrony, a family
is like a well-orchestrated symphony that gently guides us
forward along life's path—with lots of stops for nurturing
love and connection along the way. And even when the
road forks from time to time, as it does, we find each
other again and again.

A DAY IN THE LIFE OF FAMILY

One of my great joys in family life is the wonderful way that we slip in and out of each other's days with grace, respect, and pleasure in each other's company. This ease in moving together and apart throughout a day, a week, months, and a lifetime is something I've worked very hard to achieve. It's been well worth it. Last summer, I was freshly reminded of all my joy in family life when we spent a long family reunion weekend together with the cottage bursting at the seams with grandchildren, their parents, and Alexandra and Brooke. That weekend, there was such a feeling of mutual affection and appreciation for each other in the air that everyone felt totally comfortable doing what was natural to each of them. Alex, who is Peter's daughter Blair's husband, got up at sunrise, went for a walk, made coffee, and sat at the kitchen table absorbed in a book. Andrée, Peter's younger daughter, who also got up at the crack of dawn, went down to a coffee house in the village to meet with a friend. All the children slept late, exhausted from playing with water bal-

True happiness is of a retired nature and an enemy to pomp and noise; it arises, in the first place, from the enjoyment of one's self; and, in the next, from the friendship and conversations of a few select companions.

—JOSEPH ADDISON

loons until midnight under the dim light of a lantern in the backyard.

Everyone has daily rituals, moorings which help provide structure and comfort to each day. It's important that we respect each other's individual needs, whatever they may be. Some people want to be alone first thing in the morning, others enjoy eating breakfast and having a conversation at the table. Some people dress, others don't. Peter and I have our coffee and juice in bed, while our children prefer to be up and about during the morning hours. We're all different. I like to read and write first thing, before I meet and greet, whether I'm alone, or with Peter, family or friends. Regardless of who's in the house, I tend to stay upstairs in our bedroom for a few hours every day, to catch some privacy. The bedroom is also the prettiest room in the house and I enjoy spending as much time there as I can.

On that particular weekend, on Saturday morning Brooke came into the bedroom to show me some tag sale finds she planned to paint and decorate. Hillary, Peter's rambunctious five-year-old granddaughter, ran in and jumped on our bed. She really loves the chartreuse bed cover and the white flowered chintz "Joy" bed hangings. Then came Alexandra, giving me a kiss en route to the shower after her morning power walk. I could smell the rocks, sea, sand, and sun on her skin from her walk.

Kindness is contagious. The spirit of harmony trickles down by a thousand secret channels into the inmost recesses of household life.

—Henry Van Dyke

Later, it felt so good sitting alone in my room listening to my family downstairs filling the cottage with their exuberant sounds.

That weekend, everything felt right. In the morning when I bathed I lingered in the dappling light, breathing in the sea air perfumed by a huge pot of pale pink lilies placed on an old wicker table at the end of the tub in front of an open window in the bathroom. I could almost see the buds unfold as they reached for the sunshine and the warmth.

Walking down our stairs I remembered that we had had a sleepover in the living room—three grandchildren and Darcy, my eight-year-old friend from across the street. She had offered her bed at home to my friend Andreas from London, who had spent two days photographing the cottage for the Australian *Vogue*. Darcy brought over her exercise mat and joined the others on our living room floor under a quilt she selected from a pile. I found her the next morning with her head resting on several baby pillows, clutching her ratty, worn-out, but obviously well-loved Teddy. Four exercise mats, eleven pillows, four patchwork quilts, three balloons and one water balloon, twenty-eight Day-Glo beads, three books, a flashlight, a pair of size-two sandals, and a T-shirt covered the living room's raspberry-and-white-striped rug. Together we rolled up the mats, folded the quilts, put the baby pillows in a huge basket and gathered the unstrung beads in a Ziploc bag.

Friendship always benefits.

—SENECA

The rhythm of family life flowed harmoniously from morning into midday, with drinks in the Zen garden, rides for "the young" in the wheelbarrow, more balloons to pop on the rose thorns, climbs up the lilac-colored ladders to perch in a maple tree. I quietly read William James's *The Varieties of Religious Experience* while others read the paper, and others magazines and catalogs. We picked mint for our iced tea, which was brewing in the sun, and basil for our tomatoes, which were ripening on the kitchen window ledge. Everything looked gorgeous against the French blue and white paint inside. My mouth watered in anticipation of the boiled lobsters, steamers, mussels, corn on the cob, new potatoes dripping in butter, fried parsley, and a salad of avocado, Bermuda onions, mozzarella, tomatoes, and basil that we would be eating for lunch.

We all know that to sit on how we're feeling, and to not be able to be who we are in the world, is intrinsically less satisfying than being who we are.

—MICHAEL LERNER

When we sat down to lunch my blessed granddaughter Julia, age ten, insisted on sitting next to me at the meal (she also sits on my lap in church, reminding me of Alexandra and Brooke when they were little). Hillary and Andrée's son James wanted to use my blue-handled forks to eat their peanut butter sandwiches, which had been cut into amusing shapes with cookie cutters. We then had "hands around" where everyone holds hands with the people to their left and right, and, one by one, squeezing each other's hands as if for dear life, there is a chain reaction that binds us together in spirit, thanksgiving, and blessing, a nonverbal grace. *Mmmmm*s filled the air as lips smacked with the rich taste of lobster. These groans of delight were punctuated by lively conversation. I jumped up to get us finger bowls for all the drippy butter and our feast continued.

Now the smell of blueberry pie mixed with sea air wafts through the room, reminding me of the blueberry patch of my childhood when we had a farm in New York State. Mother used to put the warm pies on the kitchen table and cover them with gauze. The fly-paper that covered the screen doors would protect the pies from the hungry flies. I wonder if the sleepy lumberyard down the road still carries this old-fashioned flypaper, a very practical item.

I get up from the table and try not to trip over Hillary and James, who are now lying on their tummies on the floor in front of the kitchen door, painting a watercolor together. I serve pie à la mode at the table. Julia helps by laying a spoonful of fresh blueberries on the side of each plate. More yums, more stories, more laughter, more toasts, more love, and more family life. How simply delicious it can all be.

The endearing elegance of female friendship.

—SAMUEL JOHNSON

At the end of the meal Julia and I pretend that the dishwasher is broken just so we can spend some time together washing the dishes in the sink and hand-drying them with a variety of colorful plaid, striped, and checked cotton kitchen towels. We continue our conversation from the table in the kitchen, interrupted by Hillary's squeals of delight when she realizes that the chartreuse of the watercolor set is the same color as my bed covers. Children open our eyes to the simple pleasure of observing with passion everything around us.

The brilliant sun dappled the maple trees that day, and shone like a spotlight on the rose bushes. We had some Day-Glo chartreuse thread and a bucket of vibrantly colored beads, which we strung up in the Zen garden as group project. I remember taking a deep breath, inhaling all the joy I experience in being able to share life with the people I love. This is gracious living.

I wish that every human life might be pure transparent freedom.

—SIMONE DE BEAUVOIR

TRANSCENDING TIME THROUGH RITUALS

Families today are terribly pressed for time together. Rituals can create a sense of continuity, and are an important way to connect, in a limited amount of time. The importance of family rituals cannot be underestimated. Cooking together, doing art projects, building things, reading to each other, watching home videos and old movies together, shopping, going to museums, painting a room, going out to a movie or to a tea house, all the things you share, when ritualized, create transcendent moments that sustain a rich sense of family.

Julia and I like to make play dates together. On a Saturday morning last winter, in a snowstorm, Peter and I picked up Julia and her friend Laura at their art class. (Since school had been closed for several days because of a blizzard, they were both making up a class.) We all walked to a nearby paint store and bought some white paint, spackle, sandpaper, and a few brushes. Off we went to a French bistro for chicken salads for fuel before beginning our project of painting the front hall closet. After lunch, Peter and I took them to the Emilio Pucci boutique. As we walked around the displays, I told them, "This place is a contemporary museum. The colors are so vibrant and the designs so bold, I just want you to absorb all this energy before we paint the front hall closet." I let them each select an inexpensive cotton handkerchief they could wear as bandannas or around their necks. They took their time studying the nuances of each pattern and color combination. After they'd made their selections I had them individually gift-wrapped, and each of them left with a glossy blue shopping bag bearing the designer's name.

To be objective is possible only if we respect the things we observe; that is, if we are capable of seeing them in their uniqueness and their interconnectedness.

—ERICH FROMM

The three of us got to work as soon as we returned to the apartment, and by the time Laura's mother came at six to pick up the girls, we'd finished the project. Mission accomplished. Paint as white as snow in our hair and on our cheeks and hands, we felt like heroes. During the project, we were able to laugh, talk, and paint as a team, giving our work and each other our undivided attention.

One of the best ways to persuade others is with your ears—by listening to them.

—DEAN RUSK

When Julia's parents came for dinner a few weeks later, Julia brought her mother over to the closet, opened it, and proudly had her look. Her father was equally fascinated. Ritualizing an experience makes the memory of even household chores a lasting one.

Peter was my chief plasterer, spackler, and ladder holder when I decided to paint our New York bedroom myself, aided only by a great deal of sandpaper, a two-and-a-half-inch trim brush, six gallons of white paint, a gallon of blue for the ceiling, and Peter's and my companionship. When you do a project with a spouse, whether it's painting a room, preparing a family meal, or refinishing a table, the undivided attention you give and receive can be full of grace. Helping Brooke paint her apartment is one of our greatest memories together. As she was building her future life, she loved talking and reminiscing with me about her childhood.

Rituals are a wonderful way to build a sense of continuity.

RITUALS AND REUNIONS

Staying in touch with our parents, our siblings, and our children, sharing joy, and maintaining respect for one another is the core of sustaining family as we move in different directions over the course of our lives. Though our needs will change over the years—sometimes we will be closer than at other times—and though we may find ourselves living far away from each other, when we reconnect for a family weekend, a day, or even a dinner, or through the mail or over the telephone, we are reminded of the love and support we have for each other. Peter enjoys sending his family clippings from magazine articles and the newspaper, as well as a bunch of postcards from a museum. He also sends books to his family which enlarges their frame of reference and communication.

For Peter and me, with the children all grown and having families of their own, family life often takes place on the telephone, in letters, on stolen visits, and during celebrations at turning points in our lives. Celebrating milestones together brings a sense of grace that transcends any one event. That's why I love to hold family reunions, where everybody can enjoy being themselves, show their appreciation for one another, and be a family again.

I had a joyous reunion with my family at the publication party of *The Art of the Possible.* I was happier than a storybook bride with the publication of my fifteenth book, this one dealing with the crucial issue of creating balance in our lives. I love everything about this book, including its lovely colors and its Zen-calm design; it also

> *In my opinion, the close emotional ties of an all-round good family provide the strongest stimulus to mental development.*
>
> —DR. BENJAMIN SPOCK

received some complimentary reviews. I couldn't have been more delighted with this event except to have Alexandra and my whole family there to celebrate with me. I was bursting with excitement. Alexandra had taken the shuttle up from Washington, D.C., to join me, Peter, Brooke, and some friends to celebrate. When I asked Alexandra if she had plans to be with friends after the party, she exclaimed, "Oh, no, Mommy. I want to go out to dinner with you, Peter, and Brooke." My joy was complete. To cap off this wonderful day we went to our favorite Italian restaurant. Being at this restaurant that we have enjoyed together throughout the years was just the right place to punctuate all the joy that my writing has also brought me.

If you want to find the rainbow we have to stand some rain.

—Old Adage

The owners of this restaurant have known our family for more than ten years. We've always gone there for special family celebrations; the waiters make a fuss over us— which we love. Evenings there have a wonderful sense of event; dinner always feels like a party. Being there with my family again was the icing on the cake of this great day. Having the ones I love most dearly sitting next to me at a small round table chattering excitedly to each other was almost too sweet to bear; it was as intimate and exciting as a huddle before the beginning of a football game. Certain occasions call for this privacy when we speak in code and thrive in the safe haven of the people who know and accept us. On this particular evening we lost all track of time and place as we were overtaken by love.

Some of our favorite times together as a family have been spent celebrating in intimate restaurants. We've enjoyed going out together as a family since Alexandra and Brooke were old enough to hold their own spoons. Now that the children are no longer living at home, whenever we all get together, it's such a treat to go to a special place, particularly one that holds such treasured memories. We sometimes bring each other presents and gushy notes that make us cry. We tend to say things more beautifully in these settings than we otherwise would at home. We make goopy toasts where we let each other know, without reservation, just how much we love them, and how proud we are of them.

At the end of that evening Brooke kissed us good-bye and went up to her new apartment. Alexandra, Peter, and I took a taxi home; I was delighted that Alexandra would be spending the night with us. As Peter and I changed our clothes for bed, and rested ourselves on our firm, cozy mattress and soft down pillows, we felt such a deep sense of grace. We always feel this aura when one of our babies is in the nest. We looked around the room at the purple flowers, the English grape ivy, and the paintings on the bedroom walls, and reminded each other of the sweet satisfactions of family, friends, and this poignant day. We kissed and hugged good-night. "Sweet dreams, darling." "Sweet dreams, darling."

I came home forever!
— C H A R L E S   L A M B

The next morning, at five o'clock, I padded into Alexandra's pink room to wake her up for her six-thirty shuttle back to Washington. I crawled into bed with her, where we talked and talked about her new job, her boyfriend, how happy her sister seemed in her new apartment, and how much it means to her to be able to come back and be with us and sleep in her room so rich with childhood memories and a pink glow. We had such a good time that she missed her shuttle back to Washington. She caught the next shuttle. A half hour isn't a significant period of time, but if you are with someone you love, these extra moments are precious.

Even when we're not together, my family makes me feel complete.

After Alexandra left, I slipped contentedly back to bed and fell asleep for two more delicious hours. When I awoke, I had a powerful awareness of the deep importance of family in my life. Celebrating this milestone would have had less meaning without Peter, Alexandra, and Brooke beside me. That morning I realized that marking these passages in our lives together is a powerful way of sustaining our love and our connection, keeping us in touch with who we are as we grow and change.

ABSORBING STRESS AND SHOCK TOGETHER

Those wondrous family days, when we move in and out of each other's lives gracefully, effortlessly, are a great gift. They are also the result of the effort we put into making a rich family connection possible. When people are in such intimate contact as they are in a family there are always plenty of problems that can threaten the peace. Achieving this expansive energy and acceptance in a family is among our greatest challenges, but it also offers some of life's richest rewards. When family life achieves balance it provides the deepest love, the greatest support we can ever know. With family we are our essential self, stripped of all pretense.

Our family is usually the first to take the brunt of our emotional difficulties; they feel our frustration and anxiety. If we've had a particularly bad day or week at work, we can, unfortunately, bring the office home, and our problems with it. When we do, the first sign of our arrival may be the sound of a door slamming. Some of us leave a mess everywhere in the house as a clear sign that we are having a hard time. Short tempers can make everyone tense, as can a scowling silence at the dinner table.

Friendship ought to be a gratuitous joy, like the joys afforded by art, or life . . .
—SIMONE WEIL

We all wear different faces at times. We know we can be wonderful, yet at other times, we can be equally impossible. We can be generous, yet we are as surely capable of being withholding and selfish. We can be endlessly patient, yet later become intolerant and demanding. We can shine with effervescence, then stomp around in grumpiness. We can be especially lighthearted, yet at other times have absolutely no sense of humor. Even if we don't say or do anything, no one can better sense how we're feeling than our family. When we notice a family member is off their beam, sometimes the most we can do is to look for silent ways to be helpful and provide a comforting, stress-free and calming atmosphere. Bring your loved ones something to drink, offer to put a plate of dinner aside for them to eat whenever they get hungry, or simply let them know you'll be around if they need you.

We have to learn not to feel rejected when someone needs some time alone. We need not to take it personally, but to give that person space. We have to learn how to get past the anger in a nondestructive way, preventing unnecessary rage or unpredictable explosions. We have to know when to respond to another's anger and when to just let them blow off steam. Sometimes you'll be able to talk things through, but often you just have to let the tension pass until the air is clear, and then talk if necessary. It's hardly ever helpful to ask, "What's *wrong* with *you*?" Accept that the person is upset, be patient, and let them come to you when they're ready to talk about it. Remember, it probably has nothing to do with you, and digging for information may only exacerbate the situation, making you part of the problem.

To some extent these daily shocks have to be absorbed by other family members. There should be some safety in releasing our tension at home where we are supported and loved. There's just no other place to let it all hang out.

If a man does not keep peace with his companions, perhaps it is because he hears a different drummer. Let him step to the music which he hears, however measured or far away.

—HENRY DAVID
THOREAU

It's not always easy for families to withstand this tension. We do have to consider the consequences of our behavior, particularly when our way of speaking to each other is unnecessarily harsh or angry. We also have to be mindful not to take advantage of one family member's readiness and willingness to do all the caring. If we don't keep this in mind we risk putting too great a strain on one another, possibly to the breaking point. No one can expect us to give more than we have, but *we* have to know when to back off, separate ourselves from the situation, and have faith that "this too will pass." Nobody, even family, has a right to take advantage of us, but sometimes we need to draw that line for the other person. This doesn't mean we lack understanding and sympathy, but that we know when enough is enough. When a spouse has a problem with a coworker and cannot stop talking about it, or a sibling is fighting with a boyfriend, telling us the same story over and over but never doing anything about the problem, eventually we have to ask them to stop, or else their problem will begin to affect us in damaging ways. Our work and personal life may begin to suffer from their neediness, and we have to pull back.

The opinions which we hold of one another, our relations with friends . . . are in no sense permanent, save in appearance, but are as eternally fluid as the sea itself.

—MARCEL PROUST

The strain of seriously destructive behavior on the part of one family member can become destructive to all. The rest of the family begins to feel stretched to the limit, causing individuals to retreat from one another. Robert Wright, in his book *The Moral Animal,* warns us that patience within a family is not unlimited. "To define the degree of commitment to any relative is to define the degree of indifference and, potentially, antagonism; the cup of common interest between siblings is half empty as well as half full. While it makes genetic sense to help a brother or sister, even at great expense, the expense is not unlimited." Just because someone is a blood relation doesn't mean we have a separate reservoir of patience and giving for them. We all have limits to how much we can help a family member in need. In every case, we need to remind ourselves that we're doing the best we can under less than graceful circumstances.

There may also come a time when one of us in our family develops a chronic problem of some kind, or an addiction, possibly to smoking, alcohol, or drugs. It's then that the power of family, of what we are willing and capable of doing for each other, can become truly inspiring. When Peter and I left to be with my brother Powell in Chicago while he faced open heart surgery, our entire extended family was there for us emotionally and, if we wanted, physically. Alexandra and Brooke gave me a pastel bathrobe and love notes before we left. Peter's daughter Blair included us in Sunday night's supper, so we could play with the grandchildren and feel the sacredness of life.

A family's ability to pull together and buoy each other

Without friends no one would choose to live, though he had all other goods.

—ARISTOTLE

up through the stresses and strains of living can teach us some of the most profound lessons about the possibilities for redemption in our lives. Perhaps it's when we pull each other up from our lowest points that we see the power of family grace at its most luminous.

BUILDING BRIDGES TO EACH OTHER

That is my home of love: if I have rang'd,
Like him that travels, I return again.

—WILLIAM SHAKESPEARE

The world has changed a great deal since we were young. Our children are faced with a whole new set of challenges. But though the particulars have changed, living graciously with our children, young or grown, still takes the things that it has always required: love and understanding.

In a close family we run up against the tensions and confusions that result from our individual growth and change. Because of this we have to know when and how to give each other room. Respect for each other is at the heart of maintaining balance in a family. If we cannot accept each other's ways we risk losing each other entirely. We have to learn when it is right to reach out and when it's better to pull back. We have to know how to listen to each other and try to be understanding even if our ways are very different, even when we don't always agree. There will be times when our instinct will be not to support a family member's decision. Whether it concerns a career move or a fiancé we don't approve of, unless we're asked for our opinion, we need to keep our feelings to ourselves. We have to step back, be ourselves, and let them live their lives.

It's not always easy. There are generation gaps to overcome. Our children aren't growing up in the same world as we did; there are cultural differences, some we may find outrageous. The world has changed so radically. Children explore more after college, taking more time to study their options. Older generations, who came of age in wartime or during the Depression, sometimes view younger family members as spoiled and lazy. We are all products of our upbringings to varying degrees, but in order to remain in touch with the new generations, we all need to listen and learn. What was once scandalous is now more common. Your daughter may live with her boyfriend whether you approve or not. Younger-generation parents may not set the same disciplinary boundaries our parents enforced with us. Some young adults choose to have children out of wedlock. Surprise pregnancies certainly happened in past decades, but they were very hushed, and usually led to a sudden wedding.

In my own very self, I am part of my family.
—D. H. LAWRENCE

The cultural differences that exist today are an opportunity for the older and younger generations to learn from each other. The younger can respect the wisdom of the older, while the older can learn from the openness of the younger. The continuity is refreshing, and the best, most effective way of teaching is to hand down and hand up truths to create a mutually broader perspective and life experience.

ACCENTUATE THE POSITIVE

No matter what strains my family has endured, every time we pull through it's because of our desire and our ability to remain flexible and optimistic. Rather than resist a problem because it disturbs us, when we face it, we accept it, and are already on the positive road to its solution. A few years ago I was scheduled to be in Dallas to give a lecture on my birthday. The commitment was made so far in advance that I forgot to mention to my family that I would be gone until two weeks before, when I learned Alexandra and Brooke were planning a big

I used to think if I love someone, they feel it. Now, I've come to discover, no one feels loved enough. By telling someone you love them, over and over, this has an accumulative power.

birthday bash for me in New York City. When I apologized to them, explaining that I could not back out of a lecture on such short notice, they exclaimed, "How could you plan not to be with your family on your birthday? Didn't you know that we'd want to celebrate with you? We already invited everybody and made reservations." Their anger and hurt caught me off guard, but once the initial confrontation died down, we were able to talk sensibly and come up with a solution. We would celebrate my birthday in full force the following weekend, and in the future I would be more sensitive about being with my family on my birthday.

Many of us, even Peter, who is generally a cheerful person, can lapse into negativity and woe. Just the other day I was surprised to hear him say, "If something can go wrong, it does." He probably doesn't even remember saying it. We do indeed suffer pain and disappointment in our lives. It's a natural aspect of living. But so too is optimism and joy. Life will always throw us curve balls, but we are more likely to catch them if our arms are open.

Life's short and we never have enough time for the hearts of those who travel the way with us. O, be swift to love! Make haste to be kind.

—HENRI-FRÉDÉRIC AMIEL

One weekend after we had all been feeling slightly off center during the week and we had gotten to the point where we were all getting on each other's nerves, we agreed to have a "positive day" in Stonington. We had all been suffering from colds, hadn't slept well in days, and were exhausted. Our morning conversation consisted of "What? There's no milk in the entire house?" "Who took my *New Yorker*?" "Who used up the Tabasco?" "Why is my face all broken out?" "How could I have scorched my favorite pink blouse?" Peter grumbled about going out in the slush to retrieve his *New York Times*.

We suddenly all broke out laughing at our collective disgruntled behavior, being excessively hard on ourselves

and the household. We all agreed we wouldn't allow ourselves to entertain or express any negative thoughts.
Though in the normal course of things we're all entitled
to complain and grumble, this time it had gone too far,
and we needed to rise above the dark cloud
that was hanging over us.

We made a deliberate effort to think
good thoughts about everything that happened during the day, including the
weather. It was a kind of meditation, with
our mantra being "Unless it's positive, let
it pass." We decided that by literally trying
to draw our thinking from our higher
selves, we would be freed of the burden of
our conditioned behavior, which might
keep us finding problems everywhere we
turn. Alexandra, Peter, and I laughed often
as we went on several nature walks, ate de-

*We are not the same
persons this year as
last; nor are those
we love. It is a
happy chance if we,
changing, continue
to love a changed
person.*

—W. SOMERSET
MAUGHAM

licious food, and sat out in the sunlight of the afternoon.
Brooke painted as Alexandra wrote letters and called some
friends. I worked on scrapbooks, we all baked muffins,
Peter clipped newspaper articles and read books. After the
sun set, we moved furniture around and rehung some
paintings. The positive attitude encouraged our appreciation and we saw things in a more uplifting way. All day
we worked at remaining in this grateful, peaceful trance.

We weren't allowed to complain if there was no milk
for the coffee. Brooke laughed, "Peter, darling, would

you like me to buy the newspaper while I get milk? Is there anything else we need?" I couldn't complain about my pink blouse. "Well, thank heavens for Clorox II!" "I'll put some water on for chamomile tea," exclaimed Alexandra. "Let's all have honey," added Peter. It was a beautiful, dazzling day, but the afternoon weather prediction was for showers. "Oh good," I exclaimed, "we won't have to water the lawn and flowers. Nature will do it for us." Though at first our perky, positive attitude was forced, over the course of the day it gradually changed. We did actually become happier. The forced optimism set off a spark that emancipated our good spirits. No one whined or complained, even about some of the real problems we each were facing. None of us can always control our workload, and we were all facing deadlines with no letup in sight. We became acutely aware of how much we actually can control our feelings by exercising our free will. In doing so we were free to be okay, even if circumstances weren't necessarily so. "Freedom," said Rollo May, "is man's capacity to take a hand in his own development." On our positive day, we took ourselves in hand.

Almost one hundred years ago the spiritual writer R. W. Trine wrote in *In Tune with Infinitude,* "The great central fact in human life is the coming into a conscious vital realization of our oneness with this Infinite Life, and the opening of ourselves fully to this divine inflow. . . . We

And, incredible wonder of love! there is the house, there is the Beloved.

—CHARLES WILLIAMS

make ourselves channels through which the Infinite Intelligence and Power can work. In just the degree in which you realize your oneness with the Infinite Spirit, you will exchange dis-ease for ease, inharmony for harmony, suffering and pain for abounding health and strength. . . . One need remain in hell no longer than one chooses to; we can rise to any heaven we ourselves choose: and when we choose so to rise, all the higher powers of the Universe combine to help us heavenward.''

The day after our positive day, we all agreed we'd shared a heavenly time together. We had the sense that there was a deeper significance to the day. We felt a certain sweetness about our shared purpose. Agreeing to try this experiment, which we entered with hope and optimism, showed us that behaving positively was possible, if we make the effort. It was an illuminating experience: If we could feel this good after only one day, what might we feel like if we did this on a regular basis? This was but a crumb; how might the whole cookie taste? The affirmation that flowed through us because of this day gave us a taste of the divine possibilities within ourselves. This feeling was both tender and strong, at once terribly simple and enormously complex.

The philosopher William James held that ''in many persons, happiness is congenital and irreclaimable. Cosmic emotion inevitably takes in them the form of enthusiasm and freedom. I speak not only of those who are animally happy. I mean

If I insist that another person adjusts to me, I am not taking him as a person.

—ROLLO MAY

those who, when unhappiness is offered or proposed to them, positively refuse to feel it, as if it were something mean and wrong. We find such persons in every age, passionately flinging themselves upon their sense of the goodness of life, in spite of the hardships of their condition. . . ."

One day of optimism is a start. A day can be a microcosm, a tiny representation of all our days, of our whole life. There is no reason why the lessons of our one positive day could not stand for what we need each and every day of our lives, as a family and for ourselves.

It is in men as in soils, where sometimes there is a vein of gold which the owner knows not of.

—JONATHAN SWIFT

THE EXPANDING DEFINITION OF FAMILY

Modern life is rich and complex. We have so many more choices today about how to live. With this freedom comes a depth of experience and a greater understanding of life and love. Social and economic changes have altered so much: Today, women are in the workplace in every capacity. Both husband and wife can have a career. Or women can work and men can stay home. Divorce is also an easier, though still wrenching, option because of greater economic flexibility; and because of divorce there are more and more stepfamilies. More of us are living in stepfamilies, which ideally can teach us how to connect intimately to new people in our lives. There are also many more single parent families. Delayed childbirth allows older women and men to start families, which can both limit and expand the possibilities of family life. Children are growing up with more people around them, including baby-sitters. The old rules about what flies and what doesn't fly in the family are being questioned, and the intolerance arising from some of those old rules is being whittled away. By necessity, the family has become a more flexible, more encompassing organism.

Type of the wise who soon, but never roam,
True to the kindred prints of heaven and home!

—WILLIAM WORDSWORTH

When Peter and I joined each of our families together we were combining the histories of three previous marriages, not to mention our separate immediate families. I can't imagine the loss it would have been for Alexandra and Brooke not to have had Peter as a second father. Peter's presence in no way detracted from their love of their biological father, but rather added breadth and depth and love to their everyday lives. The story of Cinderella paints stepmothers as stepmonsters, but from my experience, despite the difficulties, there are also many rewards. I got off to a tough start because I was so much younger than Peter, and closer to his children's age than to those of his older siblings. His brother and sisters treated me as though I was another of Peter's children. The difficulty is always the same for stepmothers—where *do* we fit in? It took a lot of time for mutual understanding and friendship to develop with

Peter's children. Peter was happy I came into his life wanting to join our families and carry on together. Yet no arrangement works ideally. We learned along the way how to deal with complicated family situations and develop a new understanding of family.

We all must be patient, and try not to be critical of one another. We have to be careful not to judge a stepchild in front of our spouse because we will likely meet resistance, a "blood runs thicker than water" mentality.

We live in others,
and they in us.

—Freud

Families become very defensive of their blood relations, even to an irrational point, and criticisms may cause a heated discussion to escalate into an argument or full-blown fight. If a stepchild is especially difficult, don't force the relationship. Give space, be open, let *them* come to you.

Before marrying Peter, I was a single mother for two years, an experience that also broadened my definition of family. I am especially empathetic to women who are the single head of a household, and I have experienced first-hand the outside criticisms that accompany single parenting. People who are single parents in most cases did not set out to raise their children alone. They may be widowed or divorced, and women who unintentionally become pregnant and choose to keep their baby may not want to marry until they are confident their marriage will be a lasting one. In all these cases, families can play a very helpful, loving role. When a friend's unmarried sister became pregnant unexpectedly and decided to keep the baby, her family at first strongly encouraged her to accept the marriage proposal from her boyfriend. Her father especially had a problem facing the prospect of his daughter having an illegitimate child. But by the time her baby was born, the whole family was excited, eager to help, and confident that she'd be a wonderful mother. Though some still wish she would marry the father, they do not push her because they know it is a decision between her and her boyfriend.

A lovely aspect of our changing relationships is that marriages today, being less and less based on economic needs, are more about love and the joys of companionship. Marriages that work well are built on relationships where there is greater freedom to feel more deeply. Peter and I both brought our family histories "to the table" of marriage, but always rose, and continue to rise, above family dynamics that lead to tension, because it is understood that the wholeness of our union is greater than its parts. If you join a large family, there will always be concerns and challenges that need to be faced. Peter and I feel a great deal of freedom in our equal partnership, and it is worth whatever we both had to overcome to get here. When you do what you intuitively believe is right, you own your freedom and it gives you strength.

Freedom also brings difficulty. Overcoming that difficulty and seeing that not only are other options viable but that they can provide us great blessings in themselves

The dinner hour should be more than eating. It should be about teaching, listening and loving.
—WILLIAM J. BRATTON

expands our understanding and appreciation for life. Gracious living within the modern family today can indeed become a challenge when we find ourselves stretched thin by divorce, single parenting, and remarriage. But because of what we have learned in breaking down barriers, generations to come will begin their lives at a better and more tolerant point. We pass these blessings on with generosity. No doubt, our children and our children's children will have to deal with a whole new, unimagined set of choices about how to live. So they, too, will have the opportunity to encounter the struggles and the rewards of living a gracious life. Though the outward shapes of the family may change, inside we're all looking for the same thing: love, meaning, and joy.

> *I always felt that the great high privilege, relief and comfort of friendship was that one had to explain nothing.*
>
> —KATHERINE MANSFIELD

THE GRACE OF ACCEPTANCE

Families fight, sometimes in horrible ways. I have felt some of this pain in my own life in my broken relationship with my one sister, who is fifteen months older than I am. In *The Art of the Possible,* I talked briefly about this sad story in my life. We have different lifestyles and beliefs that make it impossible to spend time together at this point in our lives. Now we've let go and moved beyond this pain and loss. Ours is an example of family members who, after years and years of trying, tragically cannot retain a friendship, despite our biological ties.

We learn that we can never control someone else's behavior, and when people want us not to be true to ourselves and push us to engage in their anger, all we can do is remain calm. There are no prescriptions that we can hand out that will appease the other person. But we can stop in our tracks, take deep breaths, and listen to become better informed. Do not indulge poor behavior by yelling back, even though this may be your immediate, self-protective instinct. Try to keep the other person's best interest near and dear to your heart, love that person, but never give up your own grace. We should be careful never to issue an ultimatum that might sever our relationship or make reestablishing a basis of respect difficult. Always remember we cannot be someone else's savior. If they're over twenty-one, they make their own decisions and they're responsible for their own actions.

It is that my friends have made the story of my life. In a thousand ways they have turned my limitations into beautiful privileges, and enabled me to walk serene and happy in the shadow cast by my deprivation.

—HELEN KELLER

Family members never want to give up on each other, and there seems to be an endless reservoir of hope even in the most extreme cases, such as a sibling who is a drug addict who only calls when he or she wants money for drugs, or an uncle who is mentally ill and refuses any treatment despite psychotic episodes that take place even at family gatherings. As much as it may hurt, sometimes the best you can do is nothing but remain loving and wait for that person to come to a realization on their own. We cannot let ourselves be destroyed in the process, but we can always give love.

I have been joyfully surprised to see genuine reconciliations take place among battling family members. Often, these reunions come when there is an illness or death in the family. Life forces bring us back together. When my friend Brenda received a telephone call that her mother had died of a heart attack, her automatic response was to call her older sister, Catherine, whom she hadn't spoken with for nine years. She'd had difficulty getting along with Catherine, who had a bossy personality, and had decided nine years earlier that it would be healthier for her and her family to sever contact. But after learning of her mother's death over the phone, Catherine at first became silent until she cried, "I love you. I'm sorry for all the pain I've caused you. I miss you and want to see you. How are Dan and the children?" Later that week, at their mother's funeral, there was a real sense of forgiveness, and Catherine seemed to truly rediscover her appreciation for her family. She, who had previously thought herself superior to her sister, was genuinely glad to be reunited.

Do they miss me at home—do they miss me?
'Twould be an assurance most dear,
To know that this moment some loved one Were saying, "I wish he were here."

—CAROLINE ATHERTON BRIGGS MASON

Another friend told me a story recently about her husband's family that also involved a period of separation followed by a successful effort to become family again. When Geoffrey's sister, Megan, married, she and her new husband gradually drifted further and further away from her family to the point where they'd miss important family gatherings, such as weddings and holiday celebrations, and never return phone calls. Nobody knew for sure what was making Megan feel compelled to push her family away;

In choosing a course of action, it's best to take the tack of kindness.

—PETER MEGARGEE BROWN

they knew her husband, Greg, came from a broken family and didn't like to talk about it, but they couldn't understand why they both didn't embrace the strong sense of family that was available to them. Five years passed where there was no contact except a few rare and brief telephone conversations. Finally, when Megan became pregnant with her first child, she called her mother with the news. Before she could finish telling her, she burst into tears. "I miss you. I want my child to know you and Dad, and to grow up with their cousins. Can we come home for Thanksgiving?" The family was ecstatic, and suddenly it didn't matter why Megan and Greg had put distance between

Friendship makes prosperity brighter.

—CICERO

them. The family reunited the following November, and though it was a bit awkward at first, the barriers of discomfort gradually melted away and were replaced by family grace.

Grace opens the door to the light of love. Grace is always possible. When we love someone, we understand what my minister friend John Coburn says: "Grace never pressures, grace invites." Two people who were stuck can now move forward in optimism and empathy. When we treat someone else in the caring tender ways we wish to be treated, we have all it takes to reconcile.

Thanksgiving Day: A Symbol of Graciousness

Thanksgiving is my favorite holiday. I love the whole idea of gathering together to share life's blessings. Thanksgiving is nothing less than an offering of grace and gratitude for our family and for our life. On Thanksgiving we give thanks for the gift of having people to love and the great bounty of life to share.

'Mid pleasures and palaces though we may roam,
Be it ever so humble, there's no place like home.
—John Howard Payne

At our Thanksgiving everyone helps in the preparation of the feast. Turkey is stuffed, pumpkin pie is baked, and onions are creamed. We still serve dishes that were our grandparents' and parents' favorite recipes. My grandmother's mince pie, my mother's herb stuffing, and a vegetable casserole we invented over the years, rich with layers of cheese and bread crumbs, would be award-winning fare at any four-star restaurant.

We hum hymns as we cook. The table is set with five generations of dishes, silver, and large white linen monogrammed napkins, generously draped over the edge of the dining room table. A cornucopia of autumn fruit, vegetables, nuts, and flowers is strewn over the waxed fruitwood surface like rose petals at a bride's wedding. Our farm table usually seats eight, but leaves can be pulled out at each end, doubling its size. Some years we have to bring in our kitchen table because we invite stray friends who are always welcome as part of our extended family. At Thanksgiving, we know that the true expanse of family extends well beyond our front door.

To forgive but not forget. To forgive and forget means to throw valuable experiences out the window.

—SCHOPENHAUER

As the turkey is being carved, the vegetable dishes are brought out. Lots of candles are lit to help brighten up the dark corners of the world. There is a spiritual reality felt in the room that transforms it into a sacred place. Our souls become more beautifully illuminated because of our collective presence.

Thanksgiving Day is devoted to the creation and enjoyment of the feast, so we never rush. When everything is complete, we sit at the table with family and friends, holding hands with whomever is seated to our right and to our left, squeezing our fingers tight to express our deep affection and love. Someone recites the Twenty-third Psalm, "The Lord is my shepherd," and

One of the hardest things in this world to do is to admit you are wrong. And nothing is more helpful in resolving a situation than its frank admission.

—DISRAELI

Peter says grace. At this moment we do indeed feel all the grace that is within and around us.

> We pardon to the extent that we love.
>
> —Dᴜᴄ ᴅᴇ Lᴀ Rᴏᴄʜᴇꜰᴏᴜᴄᴀᴜʟᴅ

Whenever we work at being a family and help each other make an event special, our pleasure and appreciation for each other increase. On Thanksgiving we anticipate the deliciousness of the sweet potatoes, the ones we mashed and whipped with honey, cinnamon, and butter. We share our delight, talking about the food, its preparation, and all our pleasure in feasting together with each other.

I remember going to Wilmington, Delaware, as a child, to be with my grandparents on my father's side for Thanksgiving. My sister and I would always set the table together and arrange a variety of fruit in a bowl for a centerpiece. I remember struggling with the nutcracker, trying to retrieve a nut from its shell in one piece. And as much as I loved turkey and stuffing, I couldn't wait for the pumpkin pie with sweet whipped cream that would be our dessert.

> Love can never be understood on a purely biological level but depends upon such factors as personal decision and commitment to the other person.
>
> —Rᴏʟʟᴏ Mᴀʏ

The shape and size of our Thanksgiving table have shifted over the years; so, too, have the people who were seated around it. After I married Peter, I loved having my mother come to our home, joining Peter's mother, my friend and mentor, Eleanor Brown, usually an assistant minister from the church, and a large gathering of our combined families. One year artist friends from England, Anne and Alistair Gordon and their daughter, joined us "at table" as our friend Ruth Noble Groom likes to say in her Alabama accent. "At table," we are a family. After thirty years of marriage my parents divorced and my father remarried and moved to Naples, Florida, so he wasn't able to be with us on Thanksgiving Day. But extended family and friends always fill all the empty seats. When she was in her eighties, Eleanor Brown came to our house for Thanksgiving because her son's home in Concord, Massachusetts, was too far for her to travel to alone. In addition, since she ran her own design firm, she needed to be back at the office on Monday morning. My siblings had their own Thanksgiving Day in their own homes. Their seats were taken by my own and Peter's children. And now, blessedly, we have the "grands," Peter's children's children. My mother died, his mother died, and eventually Mrs. Brown died—but the poignancy of both the continuity and the disruption of that continuity of family life is marked on Thanksgiving Day. We accept the flux and change of life and collectively we are strengthened by this acceptance.

Keep the home fires burning,
While your hearts are yearning;
Though your lads are far away
They dream of home.

— LENA GUILBERT FORD

Families all over America come together; churches and other groups devote their time to preparing the traditional Thanksgiving meal for thousands of homeless and needy people, a meal complete with cranberry sauce and dignity. Many of us cook two turkeys, one for our family and one for others. Thanksgiving Day reminds us that no matter how many problems there are "out there," and in our immediate lives, there is always something we can be grateful for—our health, a peaceful environment, companionship, the wonder of nature, the beauty of music and art, the love we give and receive, life. These things have no material value but have boundless spiritual worth.

> *The greatest thing in family life is to take a hint when a hint is intended—and not to take a hint when a hint isn't intended.*
>
> —ROBERT FROST

How can we keep this kind of appreciation alive? We can love each other for who we are, just as we are. We're a family. We can roar with laughter, cry in joy, nibble with our fingers, and have a second helping of stuffing.

Seven

✳

Celebrating with Grace

REACHING OUT TO OTHERS

Although we need solitude to gather ourselves together
after the push and pull of our busy lives, our solitude
would be a lonely place if it didn't lead us out of ourselves
toward the love and company of other people. Be they
friends, family, or coworkers, other people play an important part in our lives. At a dinner party or while sharing an intimate meal with friends, we have the opportunity

to extend our loving energy to others. We connect, enlarge our joy, and ease our sorrow.

One of my greatest pleasures, on a large or small scale, is to prepare a beautiful dinner, party, or luncheon. All the thought, planning, effort, ingenuity, and creativity that go into such events are my way of showing appreciation for friendship and love. By remaining focused on my good feelings and my pleasureful purpose, things seem to fall into place rather sweetly. Of all the celebrations I've planned and given, including wedding receptions, anniversaries, and birthday parties, parties honoring artists, writers, and anyone I admire and love, parties to celebrate the first day of spring, parties to bring people together, celebrations of the life of a loved one who has passed on, I devote myself to all of these events as a way of celebrating life. Serving wonderful food, setting a beautiful table, thinking about what others would enjoy is a way for me to show that I hold others sacred.

Jubilation is an expansive affection, and all expansive affections are self-forgetful and kindly so long as they endure.

—William James

The Exhilaration of Planning a Celebration

Celebrations enlarge my capacity for joy. I love everything about planning an event. Last year we celebrated a family reunion with guests ranging in age from four to eighty-nine. Hoping for a beautiful, sparkling sunny day, I'd planned for the children to play in the Zen garden while the adults gathered inside in the living and dining rooms. When I began preparing the house for the party, I noticed a blue pitcher filled with indigo-blue delphiniums sitting in the sunlight on my fruitwood desk. The flowers had shed hundreds of gorgeous petals which covered the desk like a blanket. I walked into the study and upon seeing the beauty of this shower of blue petals, I decided to leave them just as they were. I walked away from the still life of delphiniums feeling happy that I hadn't scooped them all up and thrown them in the garbage. I then filled our blue and pink living room with pitchers of magnificent, giant peonies which were grown by a local gardener. The sight of the fallen delphinium petals in my office through a mass of giant peonies was exceptionally beautiful, a brilliant accident of nature.

I love to create a palette for the table by selecting colorful napkins and tablecloths from a collection I have lovingly gathered over the years. I love to slice and dice a bright assortment of fresh, raw vegetables and arrange them in small heaps of red, white, orange, and green on my butcher-block cutting board. Both the food on the menu and its presentation are very important to me in creating an inspiring, celebratory atmosphere.

He is only completely a man when he plays.
—FRIEDRICH VON SCHILLER

A celebration is a wonderful opportunity to let the energy flow wherever it seems most natural. When I wrote

Creating a Beautiful Home, a book about how I decorated our old cottage, I demonstrated how I turned a wreck of a house into a welcoming home. If you can understand how to design one house, you can fix up any house. This same theory holds true for celebrations. If you can be relaxed and gracious having ten people over, having twenty-five or fifty is not much more complicated. I love making celebrations so much that I refuse to make them too complicated for comfort. I wasn't always this way; I went through a round of disasters until I learned to relax. But now I use my energy to have fun in planning. There are always a zillion details, but that's just part of the pleasure. We all have a far greater capacity for arranging the details and making necessary preparations for a gracious celebration than we think. I find I have infinite energy and concentration when I do something I really want to do. I love the way the house feels when it's dressed for company; our cottage seems to smile. Everything shines brightly.

Celebration is the recognition of a moment of joy.

—PETER MEGARGEE BROWN

I always pace myself. Once Peter and I set a date for the gathering, we polish all the brass and wood. We talk over our plans, suggesting different ideas for food, decorations, and guests. We tend to throw out many labor-intensive options and end up with remarkably simple arrangements. As an interior decorator I've learned that the most charming rooms are created with a sense of ease in the details. A relaxed atmosphere increases our sense of pleasure and our guests' comfort.

Planning begins with a guest list. Peter and I use name cards, placing friends where their energies will be most appreciated. We have so much fun during this process. We love using our intuition about seating friends next to one another and then we enjoy watching relationships flower from our lovingly planted seeds. We've introduced two friends over dinner who fell in love while eating my roast lamb. Six months later they were married. It's all in the garlic!

Next, I develop a color scheme. The color of an invitation, the color of the ink, the stamps, napkins, tablecloths, flowers, serving dishes, and even my clothes, are all coordinated to set the tone. I use one fabric generously in a room when I decorate, and I do the same for celebrations. Continuity in the scheme of the decorations is pleasing, so I select a color combination before anything else because color speaks louder than words.

Have one color in abundance. Sometimes we'll use blue as the predominant color with white and pink accents. By repeating blue in water glasses and candles, a simple setting has style. Try yellow as the key color with white and green. Something as simple as using yellow candles with yellow and white plates, yellow and white napkins, green Wedgwood salad plates, and, for the centerpiece, a large bowl of lemons with two smaller bowls of limes, is simple, stylish and festive.

People have the natural capacity to affirm and embrace life in the most difficult of circumstances.

—RACHEL NAOMI REMEN

Cut off some sprigs of English ivy and tuck them inside

the napkins. Have the plates in hand as you plan each course so the food will enhance the look of the plate. The plainer the plate, the more the food will be shown off. If the plate is light in color, then more contrast is pleasing. Celebrating with grace is an art. Sketch the shape of the plate, and actually draw in the blocks of color of the food you're serving with colored pencils so you can visualize just how it will look. When we put our best foot forward, we're often amazed how effortless planning becomes.

I have a client who has made scrapbooks of all her celebrations for more than thirty years, including photographs of her table-top decorations and flower bouquets. Maybe you'll be inspired to do the same, adding your colored-pencil plate drawings. Charles Masson, a famous restaurateur from the family who founded La Grenouille restaurant in New York City, is also an accomplished artist. Some of his best drawings and watercolors are of flower bouquets he's just arranged and tables set with food. Roger Mühl, our artist friend from Provence, gets a great deal of his inspiration from his table as well as his garden. We have a large painting in our cottage of a scene after a three-hour lunch. The wine, grapes, cheese, and bread crusts whet our appetite for the ritual and ceremony that encircle mealtime.

Let us be grateful to people who make us happy; they are the charming gardeners who make our souls blossom.

—MARCEL PROUST

Using pretty dishes and crystal, and sharing laughter and love is, perhaps, "being there" in the fullest sense. And we should remember the great pains Claude Monet went to in order to paint his garden: First he had to create it. Likewise, the celebration begins with our loving preparations. I take the time to iron the tablecloth and napkins. I love setting a pretty table. I do this several days ahead of time in order to extend my joy by lengthening and heightening my sense of anticipation.

I polish the silver and rub the glasses with a cotton dish towel. I scatter some charming porcelain fruits and vegetables around the apartment on the mantel, on shelves, and around the table. Sometimes I even put a rose in a tiny bud vase in front of each place setting, and tie a ribbon around the throat of the vase. After dinner I put the vases out on the console table so everyone can take theirs home. I've saved all the Chanel No. 5 perfume bottles that Peter has given me over the years and use them to hold a rose bud, pansy, or daffodil.

If you can walk you can dance. If you can talk you can sing.

—ZIMBABWE PROVERB

Often, I'll put one inexpensive item in a miniature shopping bag—a bar of soap, hand cream, a small blank book, a small crystal egg, or select a few art postcards and tie them together in a colorful ribbon. Giving a gift to your guest gives you a wonderful feeling. If you have a photograph of yourself and a guest from another time together, frame it and put it in a small shopping bag. Colorful bags, in either silver or gold foil or bright shiny primary colors, can be placed on top of the plates at the dining room table to be opened before the first course.

If you are a whiz on the computer, you can print out

an attractive menu, date it, and save it for a keepsake. Many of us can be very sentimental—particularly in our maturing years—and these mementos can be quite meaningful to us. Peter and I have been known to frame these menus so we can savor the flavors years after our celebrations.

Trifles light as air.

—WILLIAM SHAKESPEARE

When you enjoy doing all the planning and making all the decorations for a colorful event, your body's juices flow and you feel a natural high surging through your whole being, filling you with grace.

When I invite a large group, sometimes I love to seat everyone around a single table, to allow for rich conversation to be shared by all. At the time of one particular dinner, I needed seating for sixteen but could only squeeze in eight, maximum. I pulled out a pair of collapsible sawhorses that I had bought for fifteen dollars back in 1961. I painted them fire-engine red. I had two white lacquer drums fifteen inches in diameter and twenty-eight inches high that I enjoyed using as bases for glorious flower bouquets on either side of our living-room windows. They looked so pretty, creating a kind of still life with the painting on the wall. Could I use these as pedestals with a piece of plywood to create a large table? I mused over this possibility and, after consulting the apartment building's handyman, Pasco, I determined that I could. I used some rubber rug lining on the tops to hold the plywood in place without using nails, which would harm the lacquer.

I selected a long piece of boldly striped white fabric

covered with blue and pink morning glories. I used this to cover the thirty-four-inch-wide by one hundred thirty-inch-long plywood plank that Pasco had cut for me. It looked terrific and was large enough to seat everyone comfortably around the table.

Dinner was delicious but our appetites were in a different place. We were being nourished by warm toasts, beautiful flowers, fascinating conversation, and good friends surrounding the attractive table. The dinner lasted several hours. No one wanted to get up and break the spell. Peter and I actually *couldn't* get up because whenever someone would sit back in their chair in laughter or lean on the table to cross their legs the other way, the top of the table would disengage from the bases, creating a serious risk of collapsing the entire table onto seven unprepared guests. I was at one end holding on for dear life and Peter was at the other end doing the same. We both woke up the next morning feeling as though we'd climbed Mount Everest. Our upper arms ached. We agreed we'd never laughed more or had a happier evening.

> *The most evident token and apparent sign of true wisdom is a constant and unconstrained rejoicing.*
>
> —Michel De Montaigne

Keep It Simple

Though I enjoy doing everything I possibly can to make an evening lovely, my intention is never to overdo it. My philosophy is to always keep it simple. We want our guests to feel at ease in our home. Even when Peter and I throw a formal black-tie party, I take steps to keep the atmosphere as casual as possible; that way people know that *they* are what counts.

To keep decorations simple, I sometimes put two yellow roses in turquoise water glasses and place them in front of my windows, or set a half dozen lemons on a green plate and place them on a table. This can be truly lovely. I simplify the flowers, repeating one color or variety, creating a quietly sweet atmosphere.

For a black-tie dinner I might tell the women I've invited that I will be wearing pants and a tunic, so they'll feel free to wear pants as well. There is no need to wear a long dress, even to formal celebrations, unless that's what makes you comfortable. When Peter and I have a really casual gathering, we often use our best china and linen to elevate the event to a celebration. But when the event is more formal in nature, such as a black-tie fund-raising dinner, rather than use our fanciest porcelain dessert dishes or table linens, we select simple, boldly colored pottery and use kitchen dish towels for napkins to create a more spirited, relaxed mood.

The revelry alone will do.

—EMILY DICKINSON

Peter's class of 1944 at Yale was star-spangled, and he remains in close touch with a large number of his college classmates. A few years ago, we had a black-tie dinner to celebrate their fiftieth reunion. I went to Williams Sonoma, bought packages of blue and white dish towels in plaids, checks, and stripes, and used them as napkins. I laced four-inch-wide ribbon along the length and width of the wooden table, and placed thick cobalt blue candles on white plates. The utter simplicity of the setting with cane-seated folding chairs accentuated the elegance of our being all dressed up.

Recently when I had a large reception and needed a few bartenders, the office inquired if I wanted the men dressed in black or in blue oxfords and khaki pants. I opted for the latter. The waiters were so adorable in their khakis and blue shirts, they added verve to the party's energy.

CELEBRATE WITH FRESH AND SIMPLE FOOD

We're all guilty of overdoing it sometimes, particularly with food; we tend to put too great an emphasis on its extravagance and quantity. Perhaps we do so because we want to be generous providers. Many of us fill our refrigerators to the brim. This is unnecessary. When I plan food portions, I plan to run out of everything. A party should not break your bank.

We all have our classic menus that work every time and keep our family and friends coming back for more. Many of my favorites in my repertoire are so easy, I wonder what the big fuss is all about. When the food is

I felt an earnest and humble desire, and shall do till I die, to increase the stock of harmless cheerfulness.

—CHARLES DICKENS

fresh, there's no necessity for a lot of fancy sauces or garnishes. Nowadays even the most elegant restaurants serve meat loaf, chicken potpie, and baked potatoes. The all-time best meal award is a roast leg of lamb, broiled tomatoes with herbs and melted Brie, snap peas, and brown rice, a meal that has become ritualized in my family due to the dozens of times I have made it with my daughters since their childhoods. The recipe for the lamb is in Julia Child's *Mastering the Art of French Cooking*. Once the butcher prepares your leg of lamb, generously stud it with garlic cloves. You can put toothpicks in the cloves so you can easily locate and remove them before serving. I like to keep them in. (Garlic is good for us; it lowers our cholesterol, and some even say it's an aphrodisiac.) Make a paste of Dijon mustard and Medaglia d'Oro instant espresso. Don't bother measuring the amounts, do it by mood and intuition. Drain a medium-size jar of Spanish olives stuffed with pimentos, and after you've slathered the entire lamb with this rich, chocolate-brown paste, throw the olives in the roasting pan. Place the lamb in a preheated 500-degree oven. Keep the heat on high for twenty minutes, then turn the oven off. Don't fret. Walk away. Don't peek. It's fine.

Any holiday communicates to us its color.

—EMERSON

Serve it up to two hours later. Slice paper thin. The olives will be crispy, and should be put on top of your overlapping slices. An all-green salad served afterward is refreshing and cools the blood. Sourdough bread or rolls with some ripe Brie and Merlot or any smooth red wine is quite wonderful. Dessert can be as simple and delicious as an assortment of fruit sorbets. If I decide to have a first course, it is often a small portion of Maryland crabmeat in a wedge of avocado, garnished with lemon and lime wedges, with a sprig of watercress and a few cherry tomatoes on the side of the plate.

Remember that you ought to behave in life as you would at a banquet.

— EPICTETUS

Another prize-winning dinner is my veal specialty, and it takes two minutes from pan to plate. When veal is fresh, it doesn't require much cooking. I learned about this dish in 1968 in Basel, Switzerland, when Alexandra was fourteen months old. Our mother's helper came from this Swiss town and was homesick for her family and friends. Rather than losing Margaret, we took a vacation to guess where! I now call this dish Veal Alexandra and have made it on a television news show to illustrate how quick the entire process is.

Have the butcher pound the veal slices (enough for six people) as thin as cardboard and separate the slices with waxed paper. My editor, Toni, can do this with her wooden potato masher. I've known big, grown men to use a clean hammer (over waxed paper). Have a platter, as well as the plates, in a 250-degree preheated oven. (The eccentric turn-of-the-century American interior decorator Elsie de Wolfe was considered quite the hostess both

236 ✳ Gracious Living in a New World

in New York at her brownstone Irving House and outside Paris in her beloved Villa Trianon on the grounds of the château at Versailles. Her dictum was to have drinks cold, cold, cold and her plates hot, hot, hot.)

You live but once, you might as well be amusing.

—Coco Chanel

In a hot frying pan, melt sweet butter until it sizzles. Place each slice of veal in the pan, and as soon as the pink turns beige, turn it over. After a few moments on each side, off it goes onto the heated platter. If you have two ovens, cook on a left-hand burner and use the right-hand oven or vice versa. Atop each slice, add a touch of butter, just enough so the veal won't stick. Work as quickly as possible. Do not answer the telephone during cooking—turn on your answering machine, if you have one, and cook more gracefully!

When you've cooked each slice of veal, squeeze the juice of three lemons through a strainer into the pan and with a wooden spoon or wire whisk, mix the pan juices. One tablespoon at a time, add sour cream, approximately a spoonful per serving, and let this bubble up with the lemon, butter, and veal essence mixture. Add a few tablespoons of cognac, and sprinkle white pepper into the sauce.

Quickly arrange the veal in overlapping slices on the warmed platter, pour this light, thin sauce over the veal, alternate thin rounds of lemon and lime slices over the top, sprinkle finely chopped parsley down the center of the veal only, place lettuce leaves or parsley sprigs on the inner rim of the platter, and serve on the heated plates immediately. Leaf spinach and glazed baby carrots are a wonderful accompaniment to the veal and seven-grain bread or rolls are delicious. This whole meal, including cleaning the greens, peeling carrots, and cooking, takes approximately half an hour, and the veal takes less time to cook than a quick shower.

Warning: The conversation will stop, there will be a hush, and you'll hear lots of *mmmms*. As host, you then are obligated to go back to the kitchen and repeat the whole procedure because, as we learned in Basel in 1968, that's the proper way to serve veal. It should never be cooked ahead of time, but must be savored the moment it is made. Because veal is so delicate, cooked veal will quickly start to dry out and become tough and tasteless. *Bon appétit!*

Do not apologize, friend, when you have come into my field. . . . We will invest our time not in corn, or in cash, but in life.

—DAVID GRAYSON

Pasta, salad, and bread is a wonderful supper to serve. I love to roast a few small free-range chickens, doing nothing to them but rubbing rosemary on the skin and basting often so the meat remains moist. Foil is all right after the skin is brown and crisp, but there's nothing better than a rotisserie, and, short of that, basting. Cooking wild rice on the side while sitting at the kitchen table preparing the salad and vegetables makes the experience seem effortless.

What can be more delicious than a ripe pear, some bread, cheese, and wine? Consider serving fresh ripe pears with Camembert and some good crusty peasant bread. If you are serving dessert, a dollop of ice cream per person and a few cookies is wonderful.

He who sings frightens away his ills.

—CERVANTES

What tastes better than a gooey, hot chocolate-chip cookie, fresh out of the oven, with a dollop of French vanilla ice cream? Even if I haven't made the cookies, heating them up before serving them is a grace note. If this dessert seems too simple, or common, think of it as uncommonly enjoyable, opening up smells, textures, and flavors from early childhood. Or, you can serve fresh strawberries to be dipped in brown sugar and sour cream. If you plan to serve a rich pie or cake, a slender two-and-a-half-inch wedge on an attractive plate will be more elegant than a huge, filling slice. Comfort food like this is grace-filled, provided you don't eat the whole pie or plate of cookies. My weakness is pastry, which I enjoy munching on with espresso once in a while. I savor special treats more when they're celebratory and not an everyday indulgence. Peter's favorite saying when it comes to a sweet is "just a bite," which he always says with a grin.

The most important quality of the food you serve yourself and friends is that it be fresh. In our village, Walter, our chef friend, orders swordfish in the morning from nearby Block Island. The swordfish is delivered to his restaurant at five-thirty P.M. Once you've tasted Walter's swordfish it'll spoil you for frozen fish for good. At one of the finest restaurants in New York City, La Grenouille, the freezer is used only to keep the ice and the fresh sorbet prepared there every day. Obviously, we can't always get the finest fresh fish in the world, but whenever possible, we can go to our nearest fish store and ask the fishmonger what the freshest fish of the day is. We're likely to be in for a treat.

Dr. Deepak Chopra speaks of the importance of cooking with fresh, organic ingredients, explaining that fresh food has life force. It's true that nourishing ourselves and our loved ones with as much fresh, nonchemically-treated food as possible is essential to living healthfully; we must be particularly careful now that there are many unhealthful additives and impurities in our food. Also, relaxed inspection standards further expose us to problematic food. Chopra urges that we avoid packaged foods. It's best to use common sense. I'm reminded of the diet Mrs. Brown followed for more than five years. Every day a chicken was boiled with peppercorns, cloves, onions, potatoes, carrots, celery, and parsley. After she turned one hundred, the recipe was altered somewhat: The chicken was taken off the bone and the stock was put in a blender for soup. This procedure was repeated seven days a week. I believe the freshness of the ingredients gave her essential life-sustaining nutrients.

A good laugh and a long sleep are the two best cures.

—IRISH PROVERB

I certainly appreciate any opportunity to eat truly fresh, wholesome foods. The color and freshness of food can help us to decide what to serve. Choose whatever is in season—that's likely to be the most delicious choice. I love to serve raw vegetables. The less they're cooked, the more nutritious they are. What can possibly compare with the taste of a sun-ripened garden-grown tomato—fresh from our friend's backyard? Whether I'm cooking for a three-star chef or my children, I always try to serve the freshest ingredients.

When we serve guests we can also try to be mindful of the need to cut back on fat. All sauces can be served on the side. If you have questions about your menu—for example, if you want to serve fish and are concerned that some people won't enjoy fish—just make sure that there are plenty of wonderful side dishes; no one will ever go home hungry.

Life is a luminous halo,

a semi-transparent envelope surrounding us from the beginning.

—Virginia Woolf

In any celebration, whether formal or casual, whatever feels good to you is right. When we open ourselves and share our joys with others, nothing can be wrong. When everyone at our home feels at ease, it's because we have made their pleasure our main concern.

Going over the Top Once in a While

Every once in a while, despite my desire for simplicity, I may do something "over the top" for an event. I must admit that I might have gone a little overboard with my preparations for the publication party last fall for my book, *The Art of the Possible*—but it was a very important day for me. Most publication parties are arranged by the book's publisher, usually in a restaurant or in a hotel. But I prefer to host the event myself, in our home. Sharing my home with others is important to me. It's one way I can express my loving feelings to friends.

When you eat, eat slowly and listen to your body. Let your stomach tell you when to stop, not your eyes or your tongue.

—BUDDHA

Peter and I hadn't filled our New York apartment with a large group of friends in months, so we used the publication party as an opportunity to "spruce the place up" to maximize our guests' pleasure in our home. My book tour had already begun; I was literally on the road almost right up to the Tuesday of the party. To get our apartment "party ready" for the celebration, I bought one can of bright white paint and two cans of "Brittany blue," and went to work. By the time I came up for air, I had painted all of the kitchen cabinets blue, touched up most of the white trim throughout the apartment, and even painted the ceiling of Brooke's bathroom—which doubles as the guest bathroom at parties—blue. When I was finished, each room of the apartment sparkled, and I still hadn't even bought the flowers. I was exhilarated. In less than twenty-four hours, I had accomplished the "art of the possible," indeed.

When I asked my literary agent, Carl Brandt, why I was so "over the top" with excitement about the publication of my fifteenth book, he answered, "Publishing fifteen books is very exciting indeed!"

Sometimes you just can't keep yourself from doing it all . . . and then some.

Party Anxiety

Many people I know, myself included, have at one time or another become terribly nervous when they were planning a party. For some people entertaining is always a strain. I guess we're nervous because we feel we're being judged for everything: how we look, what we wear, how the house looks, the flowers, the food—everything, we believe, will be scrupulously examined. We feel we have to be experts in all the social graces to pull it off. We overdo as we try to outdo, and what we originally intended as a joyful gathering becomes clouded with anxiety.

No matter how brilliantly you plan every detail, something you have no control over can still go wrong. Who can predict that there will be a record-breaking heat wave when you plan to throw your parents' fortieth-anniversary surprise party in your garden? Or that your guest of honor comes down with the flu and cannot come? How can you know that the waitress you hired to serve for five hours refuses to put the roast in the oven because she's not the cook? How can you anticipate that the air-conditioner will die when the temperature hits ninety? At one of our parties someone choked on a chicken bone while laughing

When I am dead,
my dearest,
Sing no sad songs
for me.

—Christina G.
Rossetti

at a joke and ended up in the hospital. One night we experienced a total blackout during a dinner party. At this last event, I actually felt that the electricity failure was somehow my fault. We can't control every minute of any event we plan, nor can we guarantee that everyone will have a great time; that's up to forces that are out of our hands. Nevertheless, many of us worry over every detail.

Let us live, laugh, and be merry among friends.

—MICHEL DE MONTAIGNE

Every disaster that can possibly happen at a celebration has already happened to me. When I was a young bride, one evening I invited my mother- and father-in-law for dinner in our new apartment. I had never been so pan-icked in all my life. I was so nervous that I actually forgot to put the roast beef in the oven. When it came time to serve dinner, I suddenly realized that there were no suc-culent aromas wafting over from the kitchen. That same day I had such an attack of nerves that I kept mixing egg whites instead of yolks with the sugar for the lemon soufflé I was making. I did this three times, sprinting back and forth to the deli each time, shaking and incredulous that I'd made the same mistake over and over again.

One large dinner party I planned had to be canceled because I came down with a terrible case of "emotional" flu. I spent the whole day worrying, What if John doesn't like crabmeat? What if the lamb isn't tender? Rather than enjoy a roomful of friends, I wound up in bed by myself, with a fever. On another occasion we had a reception for over a hundred people and in my enthusiasm I got a bit carried away in the preparations. Everyone who knows me—and as you now know—understands that I have strong feelings about brilliant white paint. I keep several cans handy in the laundry room so when the urge hits I can touch up the baseboards, door trim, and the windows. On the afternoon of the day of the party, less than two hours before the guests were to arrive, I decided that the front edge of our bedroom window ledge looked sad from the chipping caused by constant use. So I dragged out the paint, for a quick coat. It would look so clean and bright. I painted the ledge and it looked terrific.

Halfway through the evening my friend Jane asked if she could use the telephone. I suggested she go into our bedroom for some privacy. The telephone is right by the bed, next to the painted window ledge. I was in the library,

If there is a sin against life, it consists perhaps not so much in despairing of life as in hoping for another, and in eluding the implacable grandeur of this life.

—Albert Camus

mindless of the trap I'd just set. Wearing a black leather miniskirt, Jane began pacing up and down in front of the windows enjoying the rosy sunset and the flowers on the ledge. She hadn't a clue that the paint was wet. When she returned to the living room to thank me, there was a four-inch white band of enamel paint across her hip.

Despite the disaster, I couldn't hold back my laughter. "Jane, you poor thing. I'm so sorry. I never dreamed anyone would rub up against that ledge in the bedroom. Stupidly, I painted it this afternoon." Looking in the mirror in the hallway, Jane broke into uncontrollable laughter. "This skirt has never looked more interesting. It has real style now. Alexandra, don't tell anyone. Let's see if someone notices this work of modern art." Jane kept her cool and continued to have fun. Jane and I still share this inside joke. That evening taught me to finish painting the day *before* a party—or find a brilliant white fast-drying paint.

Then there was the time I made a dinner to honor someone and served fresh spinach, which, it turned out, my honored guest hated. Once I was dining at a restaurant with nine friends, each of whom ordered something entirely different. I remember thinking how hard it would be to come up with a menu for a dinner party that would satisfy each one of these people.

Happiness is perfume, you can't pour it on somebody else without getting a few drops on yourself.

—JAMES VAN DER ZEE

In the fall of the publication of my book, *Tea Celebrations: The Way to Serenity,* part of my book tour included a tour of my own kitchen, and would be used to raise money for a local charity. I got the big, but not too bright, idea to serve iced tea and Portuguese bread to everyone who came to our home. The local newspaper announced the event and I became quite excited. I made gallons and gallons of delicious tea, and filled buckets with ice. I asked my friend Donna to make this bread, which tastes better than any cake I've ever had. The tea was lovely; thinly sliced lemons, limes, and oranges floated in the pitchers. I hired a teen-ager to keep replenishing the iced tea and cake. We had cups galore. We had everything we needed. The weather was perfect. But what a poorly thought-through event it turned out to be.

My idea was to enjoy each person's visit by serving tea and this sweet bread. I also planned to be out in the Zen garden autographing books. There was obviously no way I could do both at the same time. I also had no clue as to just how many people would want to tour our kitchen and have tea. After an hour and a half we ran out of ice, tea, cups, napkins, and sweet bread. Huge yellow recycling bags began to appear in the kitchen to dispose of the refuse. When I stood up for a stretch, I noticed these ugly plastic bags were heaping in the very kitchen that was supposed to be the showplace. I cringed, grabbed several bags, and hid them on the landing to the basement. But it was all hopeless; thirteen hundred people showed up for the kitchen tour, and I owe about a thousand of them a glass of iced tea.

Nothing more do I ask than to share with you the ecstasy and sacrament of my life.

—Emily Dickinson

Friends teased me about being in too many places at once. I've finally learned my lesson: I can't be a hostess if I'm not completely available. But even if I'd hired lots of help that day, the kitchen would still have gotten littered, looking like Fifth Avenue after a parade, rather than the perfect kitchen, frozen in time, the way I'd imagined it would be.

We all suffer from party anxiety to different degrees. In any life there's almost always some period when preparing for a party becomes overwhelmingly anxiety-producing. That's normal; but it's easy to learn to overcome this anxiety, realizing that you just have to be yourself. You don't need to be anyone else.

Another aspect of parties about which I'm phobic is making a toast. At times, I've been so afraid of standing up in front of guests that I trembled so much I could hardly speak. Again, as with party anxiety, I was expecting myself to be someone better, someone other than myself who gets very emotional when speaking to an audience. But once I learned to let myself express what my heart wants to say, I relaxed. The most gracious toasts come from the heart. Peter always thinks through what he wants to say, and when he gives the toast he doesn't have to look at a word. Being prepared makes it a lot easier. I, on the other hand, let the spirit move me. My toast is my spontaneous blessing.

Almost every person has something secret he likes to eat.

—M.F.K. FISHER

We can learn to overcome most of the anxiety surrounding celebrations by bringing ourselves to each moment with our own particular energy, our own particular style and sensibility. When we do so, we will not worry about what might go wrong. We know that it's what goes right that counts.

THE SIMPLE GRACE OF BEING YOURSELF

Through all the many years of celebrations, I have never seen myself as much of a star hostess. Whenever I've tried to make an impression on people, I've failed. Whatever the occasion, the greatest gift we have to give anyone is our true self. The more you're able to be yourself, the greater the gift to your guests. I participate with joy when serving family and friends, but I have learned never to try to play any role other than myself.

We may live without poetry, music and art;
We may live without conscience, and live without heart;
We may live without friends; we may live without books;
But civilized man cannot live without cooks.

— Edward Bulwer-Lytton

Everything becomes important when we bring ourselves to our celebrations. The books we read, the art we enjoy, the beautiful things with which we surround ourselves, all come into play. The more we love and feel loved for our individual richness, the more our self-consciousness melts away. What is there then to be nervous about?

Since that first disastrous dinner for my in-laws, I've cooked for a three-star chef from France and entertained total strangers from far-off places whom I've admired. Each time I've remained centered in myself. A celebration from such centeredness always becomes a meaningful, happy, and memorable occasion. This comfort has enabled me to give big parties, as well as special parties in honor of people I admire.

Twenty years ago, Peter and I held a party with Dr. René Dubos, the microbiologist, philosopher, and writer I spoke of in the first chapter of this book, and his wonderful wife as our honored guests. Dr. Dubos has had such a profound impact on me; he changed the way I think about interior design, the home, and what it means to be on our path in life. We were great admirers of his and wanted to celebrate him in our home. When he and Jean accepted my invitation "with delight," I had never felt more honored. That night also happened to be our wedding anniversary, but Peter never mentioned it. We were feeling so extraordinarily blessed that we never thought of mentioning it.

The energy in our apartment was electric that May evening. I remember the joy I felt planning that dinner. I took whatever time was required to do it right, so I never felt rushed. I was as happy that night as I'd ever been. I knew this celebration would be forever imprinted in my heart. I wasn't nervous because I knew that everything I was doing was coming from a genuine, loving place. The more we express that love and respect, the more we receive. The apartment looked so pretty. Our guests were exceptionally receptive to the presence of this noble man and his brilliant wife. Our conversations were fascinating, full of laughter and meaning.

Living graciously is to a great extent a function of our ability to be astonished by life and to celebrate our astonishment. That evening, we were all astonished by Dr. Dubos's words and we celebrated each other for our shared grace. There are so many admirable people whose thoughts and actions fill our lives with grace. In our cot-

> *Fresh is always best.*
> —MARCUS LAUX

tage, Peter and I hang pictures of the people we admire; they are people whose inspiration has helped us to understand and find joy in life, and to share our blessings with others.

Animals feed themselves, men eat; but only wise men know the art of eating.

—Aɴᴛʜᴇʟᴍᴇ Bʀɪʟʟᴀᴛ-Sᴀᴠᴀʀɪɴ

On another memorable occasion, we threw a party for our friends the minister John Coburn and his wife, Ruth. It was a glorious evening, and I remember being a little sad when it ended. John and Ruth came down from Boston for the event, and I felt bittersweet at our parting. I confess, I'm not very good at saying good-bye. I'm often speechless, and so I simply hug. After the Coburns left, Peter and I were sitting in the living room, delighting in the evening and running through some reflections we had about the event, when there was a knock at the door. As if he could read my mind about not wanting the evening to end, the guest of honor had returned. He'd left his umbrella and it was pouring outside. Seeing him again—the practical purpose of his return notwithstanding—gave me a momentary surge of joy. I felt this short moment with John was blessed. Peter and I worked hard preparing for our celebration in honor of the Coburns, but the effort was our way of channeling loving energy.

SPONTANEOUS CELEBRATIONS

Not every occasion of reaching out to others turns into a big celebration. I love small luncheon parties. Some of my most intimate celebrations have taken place over lunch with either my daughters, Peter, or other family or friends. I truly relax in these settings.

One clear, fresh morning in July, apropos of nothing more than the beautiful sunshine and the glory of the day, I suggested to Peter, who was sitting in the sunshine in the Zen garden, that we invite our neigh-bors Diane and Jack over for a spur-of-the-moment lunch. "The tomatoes are perfectly ripe," I pointed out to Peter. "We can fill them with fresh lobster, get a loaf of crisp bread, and lunch can be ready in less than an hour." We were both eager to see Diane and Jack and celebrate the day together. I imagined the four of us, sitting at our French farm table, breaking bread, eating fresh vegetables and lobster, and telling each other stories. I couldn't wait to take out my periwinkle-blue-and-yellow cotton pansy place mats with the white picket fence bor-der. Not only do I enjoy color and design everywhere I see it, but I know my guests take pleasure in these things as well. When people sit down to a beautiful table they feel delighted. There are so many simple ways to express love and to share life's easy pleasures.

The grace that elegance affords.
— MICHAEL DRAYTON

I loved the spontaneity of this little luncheon. When I called Diane she was happy to hear my voice and delighted with the invitation. "Just give me an hour," I said as we made our plan. "We can't wait to see you both. The door is open; meet us in the garden." With that, Peter danced over to Bill's store to pick up some fresh lobster, and we had a lovely day.

Some of my happiest memories are of meetings with friends, arranged on the spur of the moment. Impromptu meetings prevent me from sitting and fidgeting over every detail, distracted by all the things I need do in order to prepare for a planned event. Sometimes, when you invite guests in advance, the simplest meal can become a big to-do. We all tend to get a little more fussy and self-conscious after sending out formal invitations. Rather than worrying about the deadline and all the preparation you have to do, always remain aware that your intention is to celebrate, not to provide the best, most lavish of everything to impress people. Focusing on impressing others defeats the whole purpose of celebration.

Such is the fullness of my heart's content.

—WILLIAM
SHAKESPEARE

TEA IN THE AFTERNOON

The rush and tumble of our busy lives has all but crowded out the potential for the grace and pleasure of just "hanging out." But the tide seems to be turning. We seem to have learned something from the Europeans who know that the afternoon is an ideal time for "hanging out."

When I was decorating a house in Paris, four o'clock in the afternoon was break time. The French have a lovely ritual of taking tea or an espresso in the midafternoon. With all their wonderful cafés, filled with people through-out the day, the French really enjoy the art of taking their time. While sipping their café au lait or hot chocolates, they enjoy the easy pleasure of watching people go by, talking to friends, reading, writing, or just sipping. Since the French tend to dine late, the midafternoon espresso or tea is actually midway between lunch (another meal the Europeans take very seriously) and dinner. After my tea break I'd return to work refreshed, ready to work several more hours before bathing and dressing for dinner.

Fortunately, taking time for tea and cof-fee have finally made their way into the American day. Coffee and tea houses are popping up all over the country. Recently I invited my assistants Elisabeth and Julie to take their tea with me in the garden room at our apartment. As Peter walked into the living room to sit by the fire he asked me

Am I the person who used to wake up in the middle of the night and laugh with the joy of living?

—LOGAN PEARSALL
SMITH

to join him, not knowing we were just about to ask him to come with us to "the garden." Torn, not wanting to miss the cozy fire, he also realized he'd been in the same space all afternoon, at his desk. "Sure," he answered, "I'll be right in." Our little seating area seats five if one person sits on a chintz-covered cushioned stool. Peter followed the ladies into the bedroom, happy for a break, to try out his new, round, vanilla-flavored tea bags, and sat himself on a large, sturdy, white wicker rocking chair. Not only did he purr with glee, but he felt so comfortable he chattered away, telling lively stories. A rocking chair is as soothing to the body as tea is to the spirit. A rocking chair is a grace note, and livens up tea-time conversation. This is a time to philosophize, to enjoy lighthearted time together. With children, even if our "tea" is warmed-up apple juice, when we serve it in china cups and saucers hand-painted with sprigs of flowers and Chinese figures, tea time makes little ones feel grown up. As busy as my grandfather was as a minister in Wilmington, Delaware, he always took time to say grace at tea time with his grandchildren when we went for a visit, and his presence continues to grow in my soul even though he died when I was only seven. Because of his influence, I have tea with children often, and sometimes I forget I'm all grown up.

We ask for long life, but 'tis deep life, or grand moments, that signify.

— EMERSON

SHOW THAT YOU CARE

Whenever we can, and in whatever way we can, it's so fulfilling to give time and thought to friends. I don't reserve my expressions of love for birthdays and special occasions. When I go walking in the village I often pause in a shop or two to say hello to storekeepers who are my friends. I love talking to them and browsing in the store for things that I know friends will appreciate and enjoy. Often I find some modest item to add to a friend's collection; one friend collects 1950s salt and pepper shakers, and I buy them for her whenever I spot choice pieces. I love to buy tea towels and wooden spoons to add to the collections of a friend who loves to cook. Whenever I give these gifts to friends they're so moved and flattered to know that they are in my thoughts. There's hardly any clearer or sweeter expression of love and affection.

A friend of mine shares her friendship by going through old photographs and decorating a small album for friends. Another friend, who cans fruits, gives her friends homemade jellies and jams. For another friend who is often unavailable for a spontaneous visit, as a gift I will suggest she drop her children—whom I adore—at my cottage to free her to catch up on work. There are countless ways to share your time and affection with others. I love to gather a bunch of field flowers, tie them in a ribbon, put them into a mason jar with a note, and carry the bouquet over to a friend to brighten her day.

There is always plenty of life to enjoy for a man who is determined to enjoy it. If men fail to enjoy this earthly existence we have, it is because they do not love life sufficiently.

—LIN YUTANG

Whenever someone comes to the cottage for lunch, we enjoy sending them away with a treat. Even if it's just a small thing, when we prepare delights for someone, we're telling them that we delight in their company and value their friendship. Whether we put some freshly baked cookies in a tin or put together a small flower arrangement, it's a gesture of love. Our friend Harry gives his lunch guests a basket of plump, ripe tomatoes, the best I've ever tasted. Peter enjoys autographing one of his books in anticipation of a friend's arrival; he leaves it out on the hall chair to give to guests when they depart. Whether you've discovered some great cheese sticks that you'd love to share or bought several copies of a book you've enjoyed reading to give to friends, any of these make lovely tokens to show you care. After a memorably delicious lunch, our friend Ellen gives her guests white-handled all-purpose clippers, claiming they are the best clippers for everything from chicken splitting to flower cutting.

We know nothing of tomorrow; our business is to be good and happy today.

—SYDNEY SMITH

Life is given us as a passion.

—JACQUES BARZUN

There are so many ways to extend yourself to let friends know how much they mean to you. With all of us so busy so much of the time, particularly when we're working and raising a family, it's precious to take a moment to make tangible your connection to friends.

GREAT ANTICIPATIONS

Spending extended time with others is a special event, and
we should try in any way we can to make a tradition of
this with those we love. One of my good friends, Baba,
lives on a farm in Maryland. Baba is like an adopted sister.
She loves our daughters Alexandra and Brooke, and she
extends her hospitality to us whenever we're
free to visit her at Mineral Spring Farm.
From the screened front door of her rambling Victorian house you can see straight
down the front hall, through the living
room and the sun porch, over the lawn, and
out onto the dock to the bay.

*Life is everywhere
life, life in ourselves,
not in what is
outside us. Live
positively.*

—FEDOR
DOSTOEVSKY

Baba always enjoys awaiting our arrival,
giving it a great sense of event as though we
were coming in by stagecoach, the journey
hard and unpredictable. With her slight yet theatrical
southern accent she tells us of her great anticipation, or
aynticipayshun, of our arrival. Baba insists that all summer
guests take off their watches upon arrival so they can begin
to live by the natural rhythms of sunrise and sunset. After
tossing our SportSacs into our respective cottage bedrooms, we enjoy a cool drink on the shady porch before
voting to go on a bird watch by boat. We take off for the
dock full of "great anticipation" of the sunset on the
Chesapeake Bay. The motorboat reminds me of the artful

boat Claude Monet used along the Normandy river where he painted over a hundred years ago; his was an ingenious floating studio. The sleepy motor glides us ever so slowly along the bay's glassy surface, where swans skim the water by a feather, reminding me of my backhand grazing the net on the tennis court.

The cups that cheer but do not inebriate.

—WILLIAM COWPER

Our bird watch by boat that day lasted hours. I sat at the bow hugging my knees, feeling the sun on my back and the wind all around me. I was aware that I had never felt so relaxed or happy. We were all in touch with our feelings that day, observing, soaking up the wonder and sacredness of the moment. Being with our family, with friends, "anticipating" a pleasurable evening made me inhale deeply, absorbing into my lungs this lovely atmosphere that filled me with a spirit of renewal. All this natural beauty, the unusual intensity of the day was mood-altering, transforming me to a state of pure happiness, pure peace.

There is a communion of more than our bodies when bread is broken and wine is drunk.

—M.F.K. FISHER

None of us had the slightest inclination to go anywhere or do anything else; where we were and what we were doing was perfect. Afternoon slipped gracefully into evening. The birds were flying into the sunset as if to remind us to soar in this moment. No one on that boat will ever forget the beauty of that day. We were happy, ripe because of our time together. The air was made sweeter by the affection we all felt for one another.

As always, it was wonderful being at Baba's. Baba is rather exceptional, often changing her colorful costumes several times a day. Often, so do I. I'd deliberately brought a fun selection of clothes with me, knowing that I would enjoy changing in response to the changes in the day. Peter and Baba's husband, Dan, however, were in a different, more traditional mood, rocking in antique wicker chairs on the front porch, sipping Chardonnay, and discussing world events. "Oh, a symposium," I teased. "Join us, darling Alexandra," Dan proposed as he popped up to bring another chair to form a circle, handing me a huge gubby-stemmed glass into which he poured some Kendall-Jackson. We toasted. Clink, clink. "Cheers." Judging by the position of the sun I suspect it was early evening. Baba arrived with a giant white terry cloth robe with a sash and hood. "Alexandra," she said, "take your wine to the shower. The light is perfect. There's shampoo, creams, and a stack of towels on the beach. Go. You'll be amazed."

The end of living in just living itself.
—LIN YUTANG

I rocked for a few minutes, listening distantly to "the boys." My heart was already on to the next wonderful ritual: the outdoor shower. I was drawn away, walking barefoot in the grass behind an open trellis to a wooden platform. I stripped away my dirty clothes and enjoyed being naked in the open air. I showered in the late sunlight, just before dusk. The shampoo container was sunwarm, as were the water and the towels. The cool breeze caressed me as I enjoyed this poignant moment. From where I stood I could see the dock with the boat. I could also watch the children playing croquet on the lawn several hundred feet away. Lush English ivy and honeysuckle climbed the trellis, providing privacy for a pale New Yorker who was raised to be modest at all times.

The coconut soap, the almond- and lemon-scented shampoo, the giant white towels, the beauty of the place, the setting sun on my naked body, all of these transported me to a higher plane of experience. The honeysuckle all around tempted me. I turned off the water, pulled a blossom from the bush, and sucked some of the nectar from the blossoms. I wrapped my hair in one towel, my body in another, put the robe on and, feeling like a Roman goddess, I floated to the porch to see how the boys were doing.

"Anticipation." The longer you wait for something, the more you can enjoy the anticipation of it. I was starved. Dinner. What would be served at our banquet? What would I wear? Dan insisted I dine in my robe. When I reached for my wineglass I realized my fingers were all wrinkled. How long had I been having my otherworldly shower experience? Ah, this was living. I suddenly felt inspired to run down to the cottage and slip on my white slacks, a silk tunic, and some ballet slippers. I was

Live in each season as it passes; breathe the air, drink the drink, taste the fruit, and resign yourself to the influences of each.

—Henry David
Thoreau

One crowded hour of glorious life is worth an age without a name.

—Sir Walter
Scott

squeaky clean, cooled off, hungry, happy, and ready for an evening of fun. We need so little to be happy.

The sun was setting. We all had a drink on the back terrace in the cool of the evening before dinner. No one had any idea what time it was. All of us were totally at ease, relaxed and made ecstatic by our fine connection to each other. Is this not the height of grace?

While we live, let us live.

— MEDIEVAL PROVERB

No one felt rushed. Pâté and cheese appetizers kept our tummies from growling for food. There was plenty of time for everything, including a heated discussion about politics and time for the roast to cook into caramel succulence. Eventually we sat down to dinner. Baba had set the table that morning. Because she enjoys preparing for an event, she set the stage for our private drama around the dining room table. There's something satisfying about a round table. We have one in our kitchen and in our Zen garden in Stonington. That evening, at Mineral Springs Farm, I felt we were all hugging each other as we toasted, tasted, teased, and told amusing stories to each other, about each other, endlessly, throughout Saturday night.

I sing of books, of blossoms,
birds, and bowers:
Of April, May, of
June, and July
flowers.

— ROBERT HERRICK

We had a wonderful evening: stimulating conversation, great food, lovely wine, and the pleasure of being with friends. I could hardly go to sleep even though when we finished it was two o'clock in the morning. I felt as though I'd been doing aerobics; I glowed with energy. I melted into the cool white bed linen. The paddle fan on the ceiling soothed me. I hugged my pillow and slept like an angel. The next time I was conscious, hot cinnamon buns and coffee had curled their aromas around my face; the sound of laughter rose up from the porch below our window. Saturday wasn't a dream that would disappear at dawn. It was indeed a glorious day. On Sunday, while swinging in the hammock on the porch by myself, I thought, This is what life is all about. Isn't it?

Celebrating the Passing of a Good Life

One made a climate within a climate; One made the days—the complexion, the special flavor, the special happiness of every day as it passed; one made life.

—Willa Cather

The summer before last, a little over five months after my brother Powell's death, Peter and I went to Powell's weekend house on Lake Michigan, which was his waterside retreat from the pressures of Chicago. His widow and children had decided to honor his wishes by spreading his ashes on Lake Michigan, near the public tennis courts where he loved to play at nine o'clock every Sunday morning with his wife, Fran, and two friends. We prepared for the celebration of Powell's life, doing errands which included going to the general store to buy supplies. At the store I wandered from aisle to aisle, certain that Powell had stood exactly where I was now standing, enjoying his time in this store that sold everything, just as I was enjoying it now. Recently, with tears in his eyes, one of Powell's best friends told me that my brother and I were two of a kind, only of the opposite sex. I smiled as I cast about in the store enjoying these moments of wandering, carrying Powell in my heart.

My attention was caught by some intensely bright balloons. I ended up buying a whole bag of balloons of different shapes and sizes and hot colors. When Fran saw me put the balloons on the checkout counter she smiled. "Oh, Alexandra, how wonderful. Balloons. Powell would love that." I remembered how there were always hundreds of balloons at parties and celebrations when we were children. It seemed appropriate to have them now. I also bought lots of ribbon in bright primary colors which I used to tie these colorful balloons everywhere our eyes could see. They danced around the sky weightlessly, bobbing gently in the wind. The sight of this playful abundance of colorful, luminous balls drawing our eyes up through the trees into the sky and out to the lake beyond was awesome. The balloons looked mysterious and mystical, vivid and

I have felt
'A presence that
disturbs me with
the joy
Of elevated
thoughts;
a sense sublime
Of something far
more deeply
interfused,
Whose dwelling is
the light of setting
suns,
And the round
ocean and the
living air
And the blue sky,
and in the mind
of men.

—William
Wordsworth

264 ✳ GRACIOUS LIVING IN A NEW WORLD

dynamic. It's a bit eccentric to fly balloons in trees to pay tribute to the life of someone you love who has died, but somehow the balloons lifted us up as they lifted our eyes to the sky.

Celebrating the
equality
of things,
Your every moment
will
be in truth.

—LAO-TZU

The day we spread Powell's ashes on the lake began with his children going out alone on a canoe. Afterward, we all met for breakfast at the inn where Peter and I were staying, and then together we drove to the tennis courts. Friends had planted a commemorative garden there for Powell with an eighty-foot oak tree with a circumference that seemed to have grown the width of eternity. The color of the daylilies seemed especially radiant that morning. There was a powerful feeling in the air. We sensed Powell's strong presence. Fran scattered the remainder of his ashes on the flower garden. Powell's essence, his soul, was at this sacred place that Sunday morning. Glancing over to the courts one

A divine Presence
engulfs us
unexpectedly and we
abound in joy.

—JOHN BOWEN
COBURN

could almost hear him calling, "Frannie, I've got it." He helped so many of us to keep the ball in play. Powell's maxim was "Just get the ball over the net and keep it in play." That day, I was so very conscious of his voice, his instruction.

We told jokes and held each other up in visible and invisible ways, each of us reexperiencing the many private celebrations we'd had with Powell. We celebrated Powell in a way that none of us will ever forget. We lifted him up, high in the sky, and loved him more that afternoon than anyone could ever express.

I know deep in my heart how valuable it is to celebrate our connection to each other. We don't need any particular reason to celebrate—being alive and together is enough. As the man in the news office often asks me, "Mrs. Stoddard, is today a balloon day?" Yes! Double thumbs up. I agree with William James who taught that effort is an opportunity to show affection from the center of our personal energy.

By celebrating our connection to others, we are appreciating the jubilee of life. For our personal fortune of love, and our human power to say yes in positive, optimistic affirmation of the world, we are tipping our hat to the Creator whose presence is everywhere, transcendent and eternal. As Joseph Campbell bluntly said just before his death, "*This is it*. If you don't get it here, you won't get it anywhere."

> *And all the windows*
> *of my heart*
> I open *to the day.*
> —JOHN GREENLEAF WHITTER

Eight

❊

New Horizons

PASSPORT TO A NEW PERSPECTIVE

I always know where my passport is. I reach for it whenever my wanderlust beckons. Time spent in new surroundings, whether near or far, gives us a fresh perspective on life. Just as we step back a few feet in order to see a painting or the patterns in an elaborate cloth more clearly, when we take a few steps onto distant soil our lives can become a little clearer, too. When we "get away" new vistas open up to us, just when we think we've seen it all.

If you live in the city, go to the country. If you live in the country, go to the city. The more different the place, the better. Widen your path, deepen your understanding, expand your interests, and expose yourself to new passions. By traveling, Peter learned to calm down and give himself over to the Zen of the journey. Traveling teaches you to accept that some things are out of your hands: You miss the plane and have to wait for another, or you're unfamiliar with native customs, so you just have to wing it. When you're in a foreign country and don't speak the language, there are inevitable misunderstandings where you get lost or end up on the wrong road because you don't understand all the signs. The whole adventure widens your path, expands your interests, and imparts important lessons about life and yourself.

The use of traveling is to regulate imagination by reality, and, instead of thinking how things may be, to see them as they are.

—SAMUEL JOHNSON

Travel teaches us that people perform similar rituals in different, diverse ways. They worship differently, their cuisine, architecture, way of dressing, and socializing are unique, giving the particular space a rich history, tradition, and spirit. By jumping into this complete change, you are cleansed of the feeling that you are in control. Some of the most disappointed travelers in the world want to stay in charge of events, resenting their position as uninvited guests in another land. I enjoy my trips from the minute I begin to plan them, by reading about my destination and deciding where to stay. I find it all thrilling, including the wait at the airport.

I've been on the go ever since I was a teenager playing the tennis circuit. I also had the great fortune, when I was sixteen, to travel around the world with my aunt Betty Johns—with stops in India, Japan, Burma, Hawaii, Greece, France, Italy, and Thailand. Aunt Betty was open, determined, and fascinated by life. She was then and has remained an inspiration to me; she gave me the world. When I took baby Alexandra to Basel, Switzerland, I was amazed at what I saw. There were cows in the streets wearing bells around their necks. The world is so varied. What a joy and a blessing for all to see.

This is a good world . . . which has a soul, a spirit, a fundamental relation to each of us deeper than all other relations—is a friendly world.

—JAN C. SMUTS

When I travel I like to absorb the spirit of a community and a country and live its specific, unique existence. Unfortunately, I don't pick up languages easily. But I often memorize phrases and learn to speak these few words in a flawless accent, sometimes fooling the natives themselves. I've found that I don't need to speak the native language fluently to explore a country. Language is only one way to communicate. There are so many unspoken avenues by which we discover each other.

We learn so much about a people when we eat their food, drink their wine, learn from their architecture, their art, their history, and their religion. Participating in the life of a people and learning their history brings us closer to them and gives us a deeper understanding of the meaning of life. The everyday things that we take for granted in our daily lives become a source of fascination when we travel. We see how people put their mark on the world by the specific ways they respond to the challenges and mysteries of life. I've seen how people sleep in Bombay, how they transport themselves in Tokyo, what people wear in Milan, how they talk to each other in Madrid, how they worship in Bangkok, how they dance in Rio, how they rush in Hong Kong. Necessity's genius as the mother of so many varied inventions never ceases to fill me with curiosity and wonder. How do cultural distinctions evolve? Why do we eat what we eat? How is it that some people eat with their fingers while others have a very precise and specific way of holding a knife and fork, or use wooden sticks to feed themselves? Gathering rice kernels at the end of pointed chopsticks isn't the easiest way to accomplish your mission. In some cultures, people remove their shoes before entering a house, but when a perfectionist "neatnik" in New York City insisted I remove my shoes before entering her home because she didn't want me to track in dirt, I was offended. When we have the grand-

Learning is a name superior to beauty; learning is better than hidden treasure. Learning is a companion on a journey to a strange county; learning is strength inexhaustible.

—THE HITOPADESA

children for supper in New York, we eat at six o'clock. In Acapulco we dine at nine, first sipping a glass of wine before we begin eating. In some countries it is customary to arrive at another's home with a gift, whereas hospitality in other cultures dictates giving a gift to everyone who enters your house. These cultural rituals, such as the ways people in different cultures greet each other, bowing, shaking hands, kissing on both cheeks or patting each other on the shoulder, bring order, identity, continuity, and a sense of serenity.

The woods are lovely, dark and deep,

But I have promises to keep,

And miles to go before I sleep,

And miles to go before I sleep.

—ROBERT FROST

I believe that "When in Rome, do as the Romans do" applies to all countries where we travel. We'll never learn anything unless we steep ourselves in their world, seeking out secret places tourists don't frequent in order to become fully absorbed in the adventure of the unknown.

When we travel, over and over again we are amazed by the inventive powers of the human imagination. Paradoxically, we learn more about ourselves when we are in unfamiliar surroundings. Though we note so many of our distinctions from others, often those distinctions express our common longings. Sometimes I wonder whether other ways of life might improve my own. At the same time, seeing different ways renews my appreciation for the way I am able to live. Learning from each other this way is a wonderful spiritual commerce. Each trip has helped to train me to be more discerning, more gracious, and more aware of the intriguing nuances of everyday life. This is how we widen our path.

THE LIGHT IN TUSCANY,
THE SCENT OF PARIS

Traveling is a feast for the senses. When we're in a new place, whether near or far, everywhere we turn we can see, smell, touch, hear, and taste a new world. The light in Tuscany, the colors of the Sinai desert, the noise of the Moroccan *souks,* the taste of spicy curry in India, and the smoky smell of the streets of Paris, all open us to new heights of appreciation for the sensory-rich world around us. I've participated in grand, colorful street fairs and parades bursting with life and celebration. I love the crowded streets of Hong Kong where the energy is intense. I also enjoy going to the Cairo bazaar where I barter for exotic fabrics. I've been in the bustle of life in the open markets of Paris and the street festival in Bali, where the dancing is mysterious and the costumes are chromatically intense.

When Peter and I were working in Singapore, we were fortunate to enjoy a visit to Bali, courtesy of Ambassador Koh, who arranged a pleasurable weekend for us there on the white beach of Bali's southeast coast where the water looks milky green. My memory of everything about this exotic place is still so vivid: the energy of the streets, the green mountains in the background, the silver dazzling sunlight that turns to

A refined simplicity is the characteristic of all high bred deportment, in every country.

—JAMES FENIMORE
COOPER

hues of glory at sunset. Everyone wore vivid, bright colors; my memory flashes up images of red, white, gold, and orange. The colors of the brilliant Balinese flags billowing in the breeze looked like ribbons of undulating color. Shaped like ice cream cones, but more strung out, they were as playful as kites. Everything and everyone was exotic, from the man outside our room who played cymbals of varied tones, to the handmade batik glimmering on the walls, ceiling, curtains, bed hangings and bedspreads of our seaside love nest, where the rooms were diminutive, and at the same time larger than life. The food was piquant, sensual, a combination of spicy, sweet, and sour, its aroma perfuming the air. Between the costumes, craft, dance, and rhythms, Bali's whole look and style is theatrical, otherworldly, and sublime.

Our difference of wit appears to be only a difference of impressionability, or power to appreciate faint, fainter, and infinitely faintest voice and visions.

—EMERSON

We walked around barefoot for the entire weekend. When I "dressed up" for dinner I put on a cotton Javanese batik sarong, which bore the suitable label, Batik Art. This intricate piece of cloth, two square yards in size, is one of the most beautiful textiles I own. When I bought the cloth I watched its maker, a veritable textile genius, design another piece of cloth with pure pigments of color. Watching the batik dying process was fascinating: Dye is applied to a piece of fabric which has been treated with melted wax. The waxed portions resist color and the rest of the fabric takes on beautiful fluid patterns of color.

Wrapping myself in this piece of fabric is always more thrilling than wearing any fancy designer evening dress. I have a pink tank bathing suit the same shade as the background of the cloth, which has eleven pure, clear colors: red, hot pink, purple, bright blue, yellow, white, and several different shades of green. The fabric has wide borders in diagonal stripes, which have a delicate swirly pine leaf

I feel no need for any other faith than my faith in human beings.

—Pearl S. Buck

design with giant butterflies. Large tulips and stylized roses dance all over this cloth filled with intricate details, including dainty veins on the leaves. Even the selvage, the horizontal edges of the material that are usually plain because they are hidden in the seam, has a rickrack design on the edge with a border of flowers, buds, and leaves in a small pattern, so it appears as a trim. Something that is a necessity, woven to prevent unraveling, can also be embellished to be beautiful. Batik sarongs also double as lovely table cloths for the garden and for the kitchen. I have inexpensively accumulated dozens of these lovely fabrics over many years. I have some pre-Columbian designs as well.

The first night we spent in Bali I wore my lovely cloth the way people in Malaysia, Indonesia, and the Pacific islands do. There are dozens of ways of tying this sarong around the waist. Holding the material with your arms stretched out to your right and left, wrap the sarong around your body once, tying it in a knot in the front. If I want to use it as a dress rather than a skirt, I tie it above my chest. Sometimes I fold the top over a foot or so, in order to shorten the length. If the cloth is too small to do this, tie a ribbon to each end, so you can make a bow. Once, when my suitcase never arrived for a ten-day vacation in the tropics, I learned lots of different configurations for graceful, elegant ways to make two-foot-square cloth look stylish. If you haven't inherited this tradition, you have to unabashedly experiment and let the beauty of the textile speak for you. I can remember how I felt, strolling through the streets with this lovely fabric wrapped around me. We dined outdoors under the twinkling stars, a three-quarter moon, and flickering candles. We enjoyed succulent grilled shrimp and I loved the feel of my toes in the sand. Peter added a polo shirt to his batik bathing trunks for our alfresco banquet.

Art flourishes where there is a sense of adventure, a sense of nothing having been done before, of complete freedom to experiment.

—ALFRED NORTH
WHITEHEAD

Our Bali beach shack was primitive and romantic. Every inch of the inside was shirred in batik. Imagine walking upstairs to a room entirely enveloped in shades of blue and pink batik. The ceiling's sunburst paddle fan cooled us on the bed below. We were so near the beach that we could see the dazzling reflections of the moon and the stars on the water below.

One day we moseyed down narrow streets to a temple

entrance to observe a festival. When the music began, dancers emerged adorned in elaborate headdresses and costumes. Their every movement captured the great spiritual powers honored at the festival. We then wandered around looking for more local color, guiding ourselves toward an authentic sense of the people and their history.

Going to Beijing to see the Forbidden City, the palace of imperial China, made us visualize the past glory of the emperors who lived there. Experiencing Brazil, where we participated in a very open and fascinating culture, and traveling to Egypt to explore the ruins of the cradle of civilization, were awesome adventures. Greece, with its subtle grace, poise, and beauty is a model for living today. When we go to Japan we learn how to care for our space, shape it, and make it an art form. Westerners could learn a great deal about the grace of understatement from the Japanese. Their word for subtle beauty is *shabui,* which addresses the inner energy of organic beauty.

> *In all things of nature there is something of the marvelous.*
>
> —ARISTOTLE

THE COLORS OF SPIRIT

The color of a place is vitally important to me. I have an insatiable appetite for childlike, clear colors. Every country I've been to teaches me more about the power and pleasure of color. The more colorful the location, the happier I feel. I love going to Greece, Bermuda, Acapulco, St. Barthélemy in the French Antilles, Provence, the New England coast, southern Spain, and the Amalfi coast of Italy, all chromatically intense and invigorating.

The spirit of a people and a place is most intensely and immediately reflected for me in their use of color. As an interior designer I consider myself a colorist. Textiles also have always been a passion for me. One of the fabric lines I designed, called Giverny, was inspired by the colors—pinks, yellows, purples, peaches, whites, reds, and greens—of Claude Monet's garden of that name. I also designed a ribbon fabric which is printed to look as though the colors are woven, and this was inspired by seeing so many colorful ribbons in Florence and Rome. When I was asked to produce color schemes for some eighteenth-century printed chintz documents, having seen so many stately houses in England, Italy, and France helped my eye to create the right combinations and tones.

Life was meant to be lived and curiosity must be kept alive.

—ELEANOR ROOSEVELT

Another designer, Inger McCabe Elliot, our neighbor in Stonington who lives across the street in the cornflower-blue house, has also brought the colors of foreign lands into her life and work. Her tangerine-colored door and matching shutters with bright white trim are evocative of Indochina. Inger, an enormously talented designer, is the founder of the design and textile firm, China Seas, which originally sold nothing but charming batik cloths. In her book, *Exteriors,* she quotes Le Corbusier: "A fundamental truth: man needs color. Color is the immediate, spontaneous expression of life. . . ." Inger developed French blue as the theme color of her business. I recall going to China Seas one sultry August day with a client. We instantly felt refreshed by the blue. It cooled us down from the heat outside. Indeed, color has a profound impact on our lives.

When we're in a new place we enjoy the color of people's clothing, the design of their houses, the exotic fruits, the native flowering plants and trees, the decoration of their vivid pottery, the elaborate way they decorate their tools, enameling, painting, and how they insert semiprecious stones. My heart pounds when I happen across colors that delight me; they take my breath away. Color fuels my energy and is my way of entering a new place. The islands of Bermuda and Mykonos, Greece, epitomize luminosity, where the energy and pleasure of self-generated light is clear. The tropical fish and hibiscus in the Caribbean make an indelible impression on the memory. The colors that remind us of Provence are the orange roofs, the violet hills, the silver-black olive trees, the blue water against an everchanging sky, and the towering evergreen cypress trees. The cool jade of China, the hot sunsets of Mexico, and Holland when the tulips burst forth—all these colors speak to me, wherever I am, and inform me.

Instead of being on automatic pilot, we can explore what's possible if we start to kindle the flame of being fully alive.

—JON KABAT-ZINN

I owe my color sense to every garden through which I've strolled; every landscape, seascape, and forest I've ever seen. The spirit of a people is expressed in their use of color. You can find color patterns in a people's customs, their mythology, their rituals, celebrations, and ceremonies. Color is spirit made visible.

THE QUALITY OF LIFE

Whenever I travel I'm always struck by the many special ways a city or a country looks and feels different, foreign. There is not only a different pace to life in other cities but each city has its own unique look. As we struggle to live graciously in the land of flux and haste that is modern America, we can learn a lot from other shores. One of the marvelous things we observe when we travel is how much people care about the quality of their lives. By their architecture, their art, their public spaces with beautiful parks and gardens, the organization of their transit systems, their schools, and by the rhythms of the day, we discover what a people care about, what they value in life. In Paris a fresh baguette is a serious quality-of-life issue. When we are in Paris we search for its crispiest baguettes and its flakiest croissants. In Mykonos the narrow alleys are whitewashed and so are the steps to the

Zen is consciousness, unstructured by particular form or particular system, a trans-cultural, trans-religious, trans-formed consciousness.

—THOMAS MERTON

houses. Everything is gleaming fresh white, brightening daily life. In Singapore the streets are immaculate; everywhere the eye looks is clean, improving the quality of life for everyone. From Rio to Rangoon, Burma, we witness the local devotion to holy days, where rich and poor participate with equal seriousness and enthusiasm. In Rome, the fountains are exuberant and well-maintained, making a stroll through the streets a sensuous, joyful event. Japan's raked-sand gardens and tea houses are calming and open to all, a cherished tradition. Most places where we travel, childhood is the most esteemed stage in life, which shows effervescently in children's carefree play; in Norway and Sweden children are the center of the home, participating in all family events.

All major cities in the world have museums that celebrate ancient and modern art and decorative objects of a culture, a great source of pride for the people. In Cairo we went to see Tutankhamen's tomb, discovered in 1921, a testament to the rich historical inheritance of the area. A year later it was at our front door at the Metropolitan Museum of Art, displayed in bright lights and fanfare.

Living in such a relatively young country as America, we lose sight of the fact that the cultural history of the

Beauty is, even in the beautiful, occasional,—or, as one has said, culminating and perfect only a single moment, before which it is unripe, and after which it is on the wane. But beauty is never quite absent from our eyes.

—Emerson

rest of the world is much older than our own, and many countries still retain some of the more gracious qualities of earlier times, particularly their slower rhythms. When we travel we have the opportunity to slow down and move in step with others.

Call it the siesta. Call it the midday break. Call it by any name, it's lunch at a leisurely pace, and around the world people structure their days around it. The midday meal is a perfect example of the respect people give to the rhythms of their day. Do other cultures place more value on enjoying life, day to day, than we do? In France or

He that travels much knows much.

—THOMAS FULLER

Italy, for example, you'll see hardly a soul on the street during the lunch hour. All the stores close; everyone pulls in their shutters because it's time to eat. As you walk down the street you hear the sounds of glasses clinking, the scratch of forks on plates, and the muffled voices of the people inside echoing out into the street. At midday you feel you know exactly where everyone is; there's almost a sense of communion. This midday break feels so respectful of human needs; there's a time to work and a time to rest. Whenever I slip into this rhythm while I'm traveling, I am filled with grace. In America we tend to race through our lunches, rushing to get back to work. We're always working. Portable phones are pulled out at restaurants, on buses, or when we're walking down the street. There's almost never a time when stores aren't open and business isn't being conducted.

Traveling in cities also makes you aware of the different

look of a town or city. Some cities invite you in, while others overwhelm and intimidate you. The scale of a city is determined by its architecture, and there are schools of architecture that are more mindful that buildings should serve our needs and not tower over us, blocking out the sunlight. A city's architecture and its public spaces express so much about its quality of life. If the streets are welcoming to walk in, it makes sense that you'd feel better living in that environment. In Italy, there are *piazzas;* in France, there are *places.* They're those lovely public squares we discover and fall in love with all over the world. In these grand plazas you can sit at a table and watch life go by. I adore these public spaces which seem to have been built exclusively with our need for elegance and a sense of community in mind. When I sit in a piazza I feel that I'm participating in the life of the city. Here people can stop, take a break, slide off the treadmill, and return to themselves for a moment, without too much effort. They can sit in a beautiful space and feel enriched by its formal beauty, its grace. Entering the Vatican City, through its majestic keyhole colonnade, makes us aware that we are being drawn into a sacred place of history, mystery, and power. Walking up the Spanish Steps in Rome, to tea at the famous Hassler hotel, and back down to the Via Condotti and the excitement of all the shops is a ritual of

As we acquire more knowledge, things do not become more comprehensible, but more mysterious.

—Albert Schweitzer

The world is its own magic.

—Shunryu Suzuki

great impact. In Venice, the experience of going to St. Mark's Square, people-watching at a café listening to the church bells and violins stays with us. Look in Paris for a café next to a church. Brooke and I have several such favorite places to hang out, and often go into the church to light a candle and feel spiritual illumination. The Seine provides public waterfront areas and the dozens of majestic bridges with gilded statues make daily strolls romantic.

You are free to question everything you were taught to believe and to acquire new perspectives. As your mind opens to change, you'll feel a new lightness and more joy.

—CHARLOTTE DAVIS KASL

Since air travel has become more available to Americans, and the prices are very competitive, we can travel to foreign countries more and more. With this exposure to other cultures we've developed an appreciation for slower, more graceful rhythms of daily life. Gradually, we're bringing these pleasures home. Coffee bars and tea houses are popping up everywhere. People care more about eating fine fresh foods, and more and better produce has become available. Farmers' markets and open-air bazaars are burgeoning throughout the country, in cities and in small towns alike. People are opening up to Eastern traditions, reducing stress by taking yoga classes and meditating. The Holland tulip festival and the celebrated London flower show remind us of the magnificent lift to the human spirit natural beauty brings. Little by little, these old, graceful, and respectful ways are changing our lives for the better.

Traveling like a Native

I like to travel like a native. I like to enter into a place and pretend I am living there—if only briefly. Once I've settled into our hotel or inn, I explore the immediate neighborhood. I might purchase some fruit from a tiny fresh produce market to add color to the room and as a way of participating in the daily life. I like to think of my hotel as a home away from home and here I am, doing the grocery shopping. If there's a stationery store nearby, I'll often buy some notepaper. It's amazing what you can learn when you're simply doing the things you'd normally do at home. There are vast differences in paper in each country. I notice the way it feels, its thinness or thickness. What does it feel like to write on this paper as the people who live here do? I even like to go into supermarkets just to look at foreign packaging. How do they sell their goods? What are they trying to promote? Everywhere I go I find that doing simple things like this is great fun and very stimulating, because it's rooted in real, everyday life.

No pessimist ever discovered the secret of the stars, or sailed to an unchartered land, or opened a new heaven to the human spirit.
—Helen Keller

I travel the way I live: very informally. I don't like taking tour buses or spending my days rushing from one sight to another. I follow my nose. I don't like feeling pressured by a group. When we were in the Soviet Union in 1984, the only way tourists were allowed to travel was in groups on buses. The government was concerned that, left on our own, we might see things we shouldn't see. Being so restricted, I really felt that I had missed out on a true experience in the country. I personally prefer to be my own tour guide. I like to make my own discoveries. There are exceptions, though. I like to travel with knowledgeable people. When my art history teacher Phyl Gardner took her class to a museum, I always appreciated seeing the art through her perceptive eyes.

During a trip to Italy some years ago with Peter and Brooke, we were guests of Arriego Cipriani, owner of Harry Cipriani and the famous Harry's Bar in Venice. He knew I loved the architecture of the sixteenth-century Italian architect, Andrea Palladio. Arriego arranged with a friend, who was a scholar of Italian architecture, to escort us through a glorious day during which we would be admitted into thirteen private houses not ordinarily open to the public. Seeing the Palladian villas in Venice with a scholar was an unrivaled stimulation. He located the villas and drove up past glorious sunflower fields to get there. That day, I felt a great sense of adventure and romance. We were whisked around like royalty. Our visits to these sixteenth-century

> *The world thus exists to the soul to satisfy the desire of beauty. This element I call an ultimate end. No reason can be asked or given why the soul seeks beauty. Beauty, in its largest and profoundest sense, is our expression for the universe.*
>
> —Emerson

homes transported us to another era. Seeing that little had changed in the way people lived in these homes from the time of their construction left me speechless and lost in another world. I felt very blessed and fortunate.

When we returned to our hotel room, we were greeted by magnificent flowers and a dozen books on Palladian architecture. There, at the elegant Gritti Palace on the Grand Canal, I sat on the balcony studying the architecture with Peter and Brooke. This unforgettable trip to Venice helped to trigger Brooke's decision to go to Florence to study Renaissance art in the fall of her junior year in college.

True contentment is a real, even an active virtue—not only affirmative but creative. It is the power of getting out of any situation all there is in it.

—G. K. CHESTERTON

When we travel, Peter and I never plan very much ahead of time. We prefer to let serendipity take charge, and, in the end, we make great discoveries by accident. Wherever I am I always like to get up early to walk to the marketplace to take photographs. Some of my best photographs of Paris were taken in the early morning when storekeepers are preparing the streets and shops for the new day. Paris is also my favorite place to watch the parade of people coming and going. Life is a theater in many respects, and we can learn so much just by being interested enough to watch and observe. Sitting quietly, seeing the daily dance, is one of the best ways I know to get a feeling for the spirit of a place and its people.

Participating in customs, such as tea ceremonies in Kyoto, Japan, or attending local religious services helps us to become more empathetic about a culture. Once when I was on a photographing mission on an island in Greece, I heard people wailing from a church, and I went over to have a look. I was somehow drawn inside, and listening to the beauty of the music intermingled with the crying, I realized I was at a funeral.

As you walk and eat and travel, be where you are. Otherwise you will miss most of your life.

—BUDDHA

When I went around the world with my aunt, we wore saris in India. Wherever Peter and I go, we dine at ethnic restaurants off the beaten path. In Venice, we went beyond the Lido to a tiny island of fishermen's homes, harboring one of the best fish restaurants in the world—naturally. We ate our fish on white waxed paper, seated at long picnic tables with benches. By asking the locals where to go, we inevitably run into a lot of colorful surprises. Peter and I always go native when we're near water. On the island of Cozumel, off the coast of the Yucatán in Mexico, we drove our jeep down the coast of mint ocean waves to a thatched hut, where we lunched on grilled sardines, conch, and lobster with our bare feet dug into the cool sand, light dappling down on our table amidst the roar of the ocean.

There are times when we enjoy going to parks, gardens, and museums on our own, and other times when we enjoy going around with friends, seeing what they think we'd enjoy seeing. There's nothing wrong, either, with hanging out in our hotel room for a few hours or more on some days. If a hotel room is conducive to taking Zen time, I look forward to spending lots of time there. Sometimes Peter and I don't leave our room until two o'clock in the afternoon!

A Passion for People

The human connection is so important to gracious living. When we travel, we are always guests, and meet people on their terms. We learn their ways and respect them as teachers. The best way to become knowledgeable about a place is to let those we meet along the way become our primary informers. Every experience is valuable, and when we show a genuine interest in their customs, food, and decorations, we are no longer strangers in a foreign land, but cousins from another homeland.

From the various people we meet at the hotel, to the person who gives us directions on the street corner, to the waitress in a restaurant who helps us with the menu, to the ticket salesman on the train, the people we encounter when we travel all add texture and flavor to our adventure. When I was in Florence in a tiny shop where they sold marbleized paper, the store owner sensed my passion and invited us to go watch the marbleizing process across the street, upstairs, hidden from tourists.

This world's not blot for us,
Nor blank; it means intensely, and means good.

— Robert Browning

In Venice I saw glass blown in a shop along the Grand Canal. The owner of the store recommended we go to the island of Murano to see glass-blowing on a grander scale. Not only did we go, but my affection for these cones of spun color has been important in my design work. In Positano on the Amalfi coast of Italy I loved the look of the olive dish in our hotel lobby so much that I inquired where it came from. When I learned that it was crafted in the Vietri factory nearby, we made a day trip out of it, and decided to have some pottery custom-made for a bank I was designing in Texas. Not everywhere can you find whimsical cows on earthy, colorful plates.

The soul of a journey is liberty, perfect liberty, to think, feel, do just as one pleases.

—William Hazlitt

Wherever we go we feel graced by the many extraordinary and generous people we meet. When people invite us into their homes or to visit the sights with them, their warmth and affection never fail to confirm my belief that people want to reach out to each other in kind and generous ways. You might meet a child or a student at a café and strike up an impromptu conversation about their lives. During our adventures we've met doctors and great chefs who have become friends. What a wonderful feeling to continuously make friends wherever your journeys take you! An architect in Singapore, knowing I was a designer, showed Peter and me more than a dozen of his houses, and, whenever we'd visit one, the owners would invite us to tea in their garden. Being able to sit and visit with local families is always a treat and privilege. Graciousness abounds abroad.

The "Hereness" of Special Places

When we arrive in places we've some previous knowledge of, we enter those places with a sense that there is a special spirit to this place, a sense of history. We're alert and alive, and we find meaning in everything we see. We can find this significance in the architecture, the literature, the history, the important men and women who have lived here, in whatever greatness has touched this special place. Nothing takes us out of our lives more dramatically than experiencing something important first hand.

Curiosity is free-wheeling intelligence . . . It endows the people who have it with a generosity in argument and a serenity in their own mode of life.

—Alistair Cooke

One of the places where I feel this "hereness" most strongly is when visiting the homes of my heroes. As if on a pilgrimage, we walk expectantly through the homes of people we've admired, hoping to make a special, more sensory connection with them. Standing in the rooms, looking out the windows of their homes makes them more real, more identifiable as people, like you and me. We feel we're looking through their eyes deepening our experience of them. When I imagine Roger and Line Mühl, our artist friend and his wife, walking through their gardens looking at the beauty all around them, I feel transported in time. We've visited Lord Mountbatten's house in the Bahamas, and in Bangkok we saw the home of Jim Thompson, the textile genius who mysteriously disappeared. In the Cotswolds, west of London, we've stopped off at the home of the Marquess and Marchioness of Aberdeen, both artists. On the Greek island of Corfu, off the coast of Italy, we made a trek to Lawrence Durrell's strawberry-pink house. Once we had the exciting opportunity to visit George and Barbara Bush when they were in the White House.

The tea-room was an oasis . . . where weary travelers could meet to drink from the common spring of art appreciation.

—OKAKURA KAKUZO

Claude Monet's gardens are a sacred place for me, a place where I feel "hereness." Monet created Giverny to be a place of intense natural beauty where he could paint. Having been to The Mount, Edith Wharton's home in Lenox, Massachusetts, I felt closer to her, knowing her interest in interior design, understanding how she was the spark that lead the way to the profession, and seeing her designing and decorating for myself. Observing where she sat, dined, and walked in the gardens, seeing her views from where she rested on the terrace, you can imagine being in her skin, and it's a powerful experience. I visualized her writing and reading in her library, and, when I went upstairs to her bedroom, I could envision her seated in bed writing her novels. I loved seeing the small freight elevator where

Traveling is almost like talking with men of other centuries.

—RENÉ DESCARTES

Henry James's trunks were transported upstairs. She had the elevator built especially for him because he never traveled lightly.

When I visited Emerson's house in Concord, the Old Manse, named by Hawthorne who had also lived there with his bride, I was moved. Seeing his desk, a simple, small, wall-hung slanted desk, where he wrote with a quill pen and faced a powder-blue wall near the door to the upstairs hall, allowed me to envision this writer as a real person who sat at this desk and recorded his insights and impressions. Noble intellects have the power to stretch our minds, exercise our potential, and put a fire in our belly. Knowing the look of Emerson's daily surroundings, where he wrote, where he ate dinner, and the china he used, made his work even more vividly alive to me. I've felt an affinity for Emerson ever since reading him in high school. It was while reading Emerson that I first felt an author speak directly to me on a wealth of different issues. Emerson was a minister and reminded me of my grandfather, also a preacher. His grace is always present in his writing, and he seems to be speaking to us in reference to today's world. He philosophy never seems dated, and I never tire of reading and rereading his compelling essays. I don't mind that he was elusive, mysterious, and complex. Of the many biographies written about him, *Emerson: Mind on Fire,* by Robert D. Richardson, Jr., is the one that brings

Real joy comes not from ease or riches or from praise of men,
But from doing something worth while.

—SIR WILFRED GRENFELL

us closest to him psychologically, providing amazing details about his behavior. I believe that the most a writer can do for himself and for us is to try to shed a little light on our path. Emerson is one of my great illuminators.

Seldom and slowly the mask falls, and the pupil is permitted to see that all is one stuff . . . the circumstances vary, the amount of happiness does not . . . different means, but the same quantity of pleasant excitement.

—EMERSON

I also revere Thomas Jefferson as one of my main teachers. My admiration intensified when I was exposed to his inventive, designing mind on my visit to Monticello, his home in Charlottesville, Virginia. This architectural masterpiece reinforces the importance of good residential design and architecture and how it can illuminate our consciousness.

I felt such awe when we visited the splendors of Pompeii's great murals with their spectacular designs and colors. The art was preserved for centuries under thick layers of lava from the cataclysmic volcanic eruption of Mount Vesuvius on a summer day in A.D. 79, excavated beginning in 1709. With their trompe l'oeil architectural details, these murals have influenced decorative taste ever since.

The first time I saw the Parthenon in Athens I almost fell to my knees, not because I had sprained an ankle on the crumbling rocks, but in astonishment at the grace of proportions. I feel this same sense of magnificence in a Japanese garden and other sacred places. I still go outside of Paris to visit Chartres, the thirteenth-century cathedral whose purity of stained-glass colors is so brilliant. The blues are incomparable. I light a few candles, sit, look up, and feel inspired. When I journeyed to Knossos, in Crete, I was struck by the imagination and ingenuity displayed in the ruins. Not only did the inhabitants have running water, but they had an air-conditioning system as well.

When we encounter the energy of these places, we are imbued by the spirit and intelligence of those who inhabited it, and this experience enlarges our understanding.

If we are to achieve a richer culture, rich in contrasting values, we must recognize the whole gamut of human potentialities, and so leave a less arbitrary social fabric, one in which each diverse human gift will find a fitting place.

—MARGARET MEAD

RED-LACQUERED CHOPSTICKS
FROM BANGKOK

I have carried back souvenirs, both material and spiritual, that mean a great deal to me from my travels. Perhaps my most important souvenir is the one I brought back from a lovely picnic where I sat, pregnant, beside a babbling brook in Canaan, New York. The beauty of this place was so moving, so inspiring that it led us to name our second daughter, Brooke. As to more tangible souvenirs, on the window ledge of our Stonington cottage are Greek pottery dolls I purchased thirty-four years ago while traveling. To me, they have a human heart and soul. They spoke to me about the Greek spirit then, and they continue to speak to me still. They were even sketched in my first book, *Style for Living*.

While we don't necessarily go to these faraway places to shop, often I find wonderful local art and other souvenirs that I treasure. Bringing things home is a fun way to extend the vacation, to recreate the favorite places of our journeys. There isn't a corner of a room in our home that doesn't reflect our love of travel. My treasured Indonesian sarong keeps our romantic Balinese weekend forever alive. Our cottage is loaded with these objects that remind us of happy places, sundrenched days and starry nights. We also discover, in the objects people make, a sense of their passions and their idea of beauty.

I love to sail forbidden seas, and land on barbarous coasts.

—Herman Melville

Bringing something home from a place where you've been happy, where you've received positive energy and good feelings, is an excellent way to transfer that energy into your daily life. Whether we buy a silk scarf in Rome, Moravian ginger cookies in Winston-Salem, North Carolina, indigo-blue elastic bands in a department store in Paris, or a Shaker chair in Massachusetts, these objects tell us a story. When I shop to find an object that especially represents the spirit of a place, I try to avoid gift items from stores that cater to tourists. I want the most authentic objects to bring home, whether they are items to wear, to grace our cottage or apartment, or to give to family or friends as gifts. Which objects speak for the people? Which represent the land and the spirit of the country?

In China I found blue and white porcelain rice bowls

to give as token souvenirs to friends. In Bangkok I found red-lacquered chopsticks from a street vendor for under twenty-five cents for a dozen pairs. I've dragged home everything but a live elephant from all corners of the world. I remember where I found each item, and, often, how pleased I was to have found a bargain. In Mexico I bought several silver rings decorated with round balls. I recently wore the rings at a talk I gave and a woman complimented me on their chic style. I was glad to be able to tell her they cost only a dollar each. Peter and I have made some mistakes. We brought some brightly colored miniature houses in Brazil, only to discover the wood was full of worms.

If you approach each new person you meet in a spirit of adventure you will find yourself endlessly fascinated by the new channels of thought and experience and personality that you encounter.

—ELEANOR ROOSEVELT

I remember the teeming rain in Siena in 1963 when I was caught in the square without an umbrella. Some local entrepreneur sold me a gigantic green farm umbrella for a few dollars. I dragged this crude, raw, wooden-handled monster around Italy in the sunshine and brought it home to New York City as a reminder of that downpour, and that lost afternoon we spent eating grilled truffles instead of sightseeing.

Ever since I wore screamingly intense colored silk saris when I was in India for a month in 1959, I've picked up fabrics from all over the world. I wear silk from Thailand as cummerbunds and as bandannas in my hats. I have flaming chromatically intense tunic blouses I wear over white cotton slacks as a summer uniform or on island escapes. In Thailand in 1959, I purchased an exquisite, brightly colored, horizontally striped blouse in brilliant shades of blue and white, with silver metallic threads woven into the design, falling permanently in love with the exotically beautiful silk fabric and design. When the Singapore government hired me to decorate their permanent residence in New York City, I told Ambassador Tommy T. B. Koh that I felt I needed to travel to Singapore before beginning my design work. He arranged for Peter and me to go on an extensive buying trip throughout Southeast Asia. All the textiles we selected came from Bangkok: pure Thai silk, a favorite of mine since first seeing this fabric in my teens.

The world is its own magic.

—SHUNRYU SUZUKI

When I catch a glimpse of the exotic textiles I've collected from around the world, when I handle the pottery I brought home from Italy, when I study the crystals I discovered in Brazil, when I use my red-lacquered chopsticks from Bangkok, I can sense the original energy I felt when I was *there*, bringing my experiences into the present day.

While the world is full of suffering it is also the overcoming of it.

—HELEN KELLER

DEEPENING OUR UNDERSTANDING OF LIFE

I reexperience the extraordinary, awe-inspiring awareness of beauty whenever I recall special places: seeing the Taj

Mahal with its precious stones gleaming through white alabaster in the brilliant sunlight, and visiting Claude Monet's garden at Giverny for the first time were both powerful experiences for me. Sitting on the beach on the Greek island of Corfu with Peter and the children at five A.M., watching the sunrise on the Ionian Sea had a magical quality. Crunching through the woods and climbing a mountain in Massachusetts in

Encounter is always a potentially creative experience.
—ROLLO MAY

October when the foliage was at its peak was unforgettable. Several years ago I found myself in Norfolk, Virginia, in May. Feeling nostalgic for my Zen garden in Stonington, I made a pilgrimage to their botanical gardens. To my great fortune, my spontaneous visit was timed perfectly for the peak of the rose season. Walking in the sunlight through the arched trellises crowded with colorful, sweet-smelling, huge, blooming roses was an experience of such delight that I will carry it with me forever. Each travel experience has a way of opening us up to absorb even more of the life that surrounds us. We are drawn to places where we forget ourselves and be-

You must be willing to let life itself become your teacher.
—JON KABAT-ZINN

come awestruck, spellbound, lost in a boundless, ever-regenerating astonishment at how truly marvelous the universe is. All we have to do is show up and *be there* in a state of appreciation, and grace will follow.

But I have also seen terrible poverty. I have witnessed people living in inhuman conditions. I remember as a teenager watching the rickshaw puller in India and wondering if I could bear to have him to pull the cart for me, my aunt, and all our luggage. I've also seen the saddest places covered with garbage and graffiti, where people aren't living in joy at all, but are trapped in hopelessness. What can we say about this, except to remind each other that life is precious and we must try to look out for each other. Travel deepens our humanity. It reminds us that human beings are capable of acts of great kindness as well as acts of mean neglect. There is no place that is so beautiful that we never find deprivation in its midst. Nor should we try to avoid it or hide it away. Rather we must face it and learn to understand it better than we do in order to make a difference, and to teach our children about injustice. Even in the exotic Caribbean islands there is extensive poverty mixed in with the native cultures. In many parts of Mexico and India the children are taught to beg at an early age. This is a reality. But poverty in material wealth does not mean spiritual and cultural poverty. I've been in orphanages in India where the children's happiness was infectious. Seeing people transcend their surroundings teaches us respect for the dignity of all human life. We breathe deeply, recognizing the ever present grace, reminded of how fortunate we are, how blessed our lives are, and how truly appreciative we should be.

The world is all outside; it has no inside.

—EMERSON

I have here only made a nosegay of culled flowers, and have brought nothing of my own but the thread that ties them together.

—MICHEL DE MONTAIGNE

BON VOYAGE!

I'll continue to hit the road, absorb the local color. Though travel can be costly, going to foreign places is more possible today than ever before. It is possible to take more and more different kinds of trips, from safaris in Africa to treks across the Sahara Desert, if you're so inclined. You can bicycle through river towns in northern Portugal or hike from village to village on public paths throughout the English countryside. What a wonderful way to get into the landscape and really get to know a country.

One of the pleasantest things in the world is the journey.

—WILLIAM HAZLITT

Travel opens our hearts and our minds. A little bit of each town or city, each country or each island, stays with you and fills your mind and your soul. Travel is my designer's capital. Travel is also my writer's capital. I draw on it for uplift and inspiration. Every experience we expose ourselves to improves our lives in every way. We are broadened by our understanding of what a rich, diverse world we inhabit. We can live more graciously when we've looked through the wide-angle lens of life. I'm always ready for a good view, just tell me where and when.

Nine

❊

Let Us Live as Poets

THE ESSENCE OF GRACE

To live with grace today, despite the strain of modern life often causing us to act against our own nature, requires a steady vision. To hold fast to the basic things, the enduring simple pleasures, is the surest way I know to sustain that vision. Following the rhythms of our heart, believing in and using our own power, rediscovering the wonder of nature and the sensory world around us, finding satisfaction in our labor, sustaining closeness and connection to family and friends while also taking time for solitude to feed our inner well, and remembering always to celebrate, all these comprise a gracious vision of life. This is my ideal, my goal. Though we may never perfectly realize these ideals, by keeping our gaze fixed in this direction we will never lose our way for long.

One day we may look out the window and, slowly but surely, as if watching a negative developing into a picture, we can see how beautifully a bird flies across the pale blue sky. We know this happens hundreds of times a day, yet now this sight reveals a transcendent presence to us. On another day we may speak with a friend and, suddenly, overcome by feelings of love and gratitude, we say, "I'm so glad you're my friend; it's good to have you in my life," and our relationship gains strength and deepens. This feeling gives meaning to our journey.

Know the true value of time; snatch, seize, and enjoy every moment of it.

—LORD
CHESTERFIELD

"The individual human is still the creature who can wonder, who can be enchanted by a sonata, who can place symbols together to make poetry to gladden our hearts, who can view a sunrise with a sense of majesty and awe," wrote Rollo May. Life yields up to us its meaning if we are open and appreciative.

I spoke of the village as the place where, because of its smaller scale, I learned to take a calmer, gentler, slower path, not rushing past essential joys of life. As spiritual sages have taught us through the ages, we must establish our link to what makes life meaningful to be spiritually fulfilled. Too many of us tend to race off our path when confronted with the challenges of today's often tumultuous world, and now we are looking to set our feet upon a gentler road.

POETRY AS WONDER

The poet sees everything, from the common to the rare, through a lens of wonder; there is an inner dynamic, a meaning in all things. The poet looks at the world with a perceptive eye. She looks for the hidden connections between things. Similar to an X ray, the vision of the poet penetrates the predictable surface of life to the awesome inner truths hidden beneath it. This is the poet's insight.

I am simply what I am, or I begin to be that. I live in the present. I only remember the past and anticipate the future. I love to live.

—HENRY DAVID
THOREAU

My fascination with poets has something to do with this urge to seek the essence of things, to live in this expanded awareness. We cannot always secure that meaning directly so the poet finds metaphors that coax it out indirectly. This language, paradoxically, has the capacity to reach us more profoundly. When we experience the poetic moment, when we taste one of these "ah-hah" moments as we tap into something true, we say, "Here, here. Yes."

There is poetry in everything: from the crack in the sidewalk where a flower grows to the rising of the sun;

from the way the light falls on a staircase to a beautiful musical score. Poetry is "the synthesis of hyacinths and biscuits," said Carl Sandburg. John Kennedy expressed the great potential in poetry, explaining, "When power narrows the areas of man's concern, poetry reminds him of the richness and diversity of his existence." Poetry speaks to us all.

Let us be poets. Let us be fixed and focused on finding and sustaining meaning in every aspect of our lives. To live graciously in the modern world, or any time, for that matter, we must remain alert as poets do, mindful of the wonder that brings grace.

Time flows for ever; the past cannot be recaptured and the future is uncertain; only the day, the present hour, is a solid good.

—Lin Yutang

"Crossing bare common, in snow puddles, at twilight, under a clouded sky, without having in my thoughts any occurrence of special good fortune, I have enjoyed a perfect exhilaration," explained Emerson. "When the poet can hold fast to this connection," writes Robert Richardson in his new biography, *Emerson: Mind on Fire*, "he has access—through his own poor power—to the world's power and beauty. Not only did [this insight] never leave him, it never lost its sweet urgency, its sensuous hold on him, its ability to lift the common moments of everyday life on the updrafts of awareness. . . ."

I confess I'm in awe of poets. I read them the way I sip tea or a good wine, slowly, savoring the subtleties, the richness, the bouquet. My imagination is fired by the powerful personal vision that poetry expresses. I'm astounded by the clarity, the pleasure, the inexpressible truths that poetry can manifest. "A poem begins in delight," Robert Frost confided, "and ends in wisdom."

The butterfly counts not months but moments, and has time enough.

—Rabindranath
Tagore

Living as a Poet

How can we become poets, taking disparate elements from our lives to form a whole bringing fresh meaning to each part? How do we connect to the wavelength of the poet? Is it possible for us to live as poets do, with this heightened awareness? I think we can. Once we discover the joys that lie in wait every day beneath the most mundane things—from shopping at the farmers' market, baking a cake, or hammering a nail, to lingering over a candlelit dinner—we can move toward a vision where we see grace, as the poets do, in life around us.

All poetry is putting the infinite within the finite.

—Robert
Browning

One of my favorite poets, Rainer Maria Rilke, said, "As bees gather honey, so we collect what is sweetest out of all things and build. . . ." Robert Frost says, "A poem begins with a lump in the throat; a homesickness or a lovesickness." Poetry is a reaching-out toward expression; an effort to find fulfillment in communicating.

You don't have to *be* a poet to enjoy the poet's sensibility. There are many poets in my life. They may not be published poets, they may not even write poetry, but all, in their way, in their hunger for understanding and appreciation of the gifts in everyday life, are poets. My spiritual guide and friend John Coburn is such a poet. His prayers are always rich with meaning. More than twenty years ago when he left New York City to become a bishop, I asked him why he chose to become a spiritual leader. He'd been an English professor for years before going into theology. "Alexandra, English just wasn't enough," he replied. "It didn't deal with the mystery." One day Peter and I had lunch with John Coburn and Mrs. Brown's son, Louis, in Boston. Crunching through snowdrifts, walking to his office on Joy Street, I realized the poet's need to dwell in the mysterious. Poets are

The art of art, the glory of expression and the sunshine of the light of letters, is simplicity.

—Walt Whitman

distinguished by special imaginative and creative powers, insights, and sensibilities. Dr. Coburn believes, "The journey inward is always—at its best—a road toward action." Poets are makers and creators.

Dr. Coburn teaches us, "Life is an ongoing process. You can never tell. Every moment has the potential for meaning. Every moment has, therefore, an eternal meaning. . . . Perhaps all any of us can learn—really learn so that our lives are changed—is what we learn from our own personal experience. As we accept more of life, become more open to ourselves and learn to trust our deepest selves more, we come to trust life more." I've seen people become tearful during particularly stirring moments in Bishop Coburn's sermons. His prose is poetic, ethereal, and moving.

Our friend Anthony Petro, a surgeon, is also a poet. He lives in Jackson, Mississippi, with his wife, Mary Ann, and two daughters, Melanie and Michelle. We first met when I came to town to lecture for a fund-raiser for the local symphony in the late 1980s. I was touched that he came to the event and stayed through lunch. As we sat together, I could sense his compassion, understanding, and tenderness. The following year, Anthony met Peter, who also felt his presence as a poet. His unobtrusive manner is one of caring. He and Mary Ann have stayed in close touch with us over the years, occasionally visiting us in New York and hosting us in Mississippi. In between these visits we catch up on the phone and exchange letters. Anthony's letters are always tender and heartfelt. They are poems of appreciation, wonder, and grace.

When you're a poet, you're a poet first. When it comes, it's like an angel.

—MAY SARTON

Anthony is a peaceful man. He and Mary Ann live in a house overlooking a lake, and I've often seen him rocking in a chair for hours on his front porch, gazing into nature, full of appreciation, content. As the sun sets he takes in the sounds of crickets, watches the swans, and admires the relaxed, lush English garden he created. We speak often and I've come to know and appreciate the pleasure he takes in simple things. One

My days are swifter than a weaver's shuttle.

—JOB 7:6

afternoon Peter and I were sitting in the living room of their beautiful Georgian house when we heard the most amazing music blasting at full volume. I felt I was in a cathedral with great acoustics. "Who is this singing 'Amazing Grace'?" I inquired. "Jessye Norman, the opera singer," he answered, with a gentle, understanding smile of appreciation. He knew we wanted to melt into the chintz upholstered

You will not find poetry anywhere unless you bring some of it with you.
—JOSEPH JOUBERT

chairs, lean our heads back, look around, and absorb the beauty of the moment. After "Amazing Grace," we listened to Vivaldi's *Spring*. Anthony opened all the French doors that lead to the porch from the living room to let the wind blow though the house as though inviting the birds and swans to listen, too. He seems to forget there are walls between him and the beauty beyond.

Early in the morning you can see him watching with his binoculars as the swans build their nest. He loves to feed the ducks and swans. When he returns home from the hospital, the loud noise of his 1965 Corvette alerts the birds to come feed. By the time he reaches the garage, he has dozens of two-legged friends on the lawn to greet him and follow him around.

Imagination in the morning, memory is the evening of the mind.
—EMERSON

Anthony plants periwinkles and pansies in the huge terra-cotta pots on his porch, and after dark, under the stars, he listens to music. He loves Ray Charles and the blues, as well as Vivaldi's *Four Seasons* and Frank Sinatra. I can picture him putting on

"The Mashed Potato," reaching for Mary Ann's hand, and bopping around the porch under the stars in the glow of the moon. After dinner he sits in a comfortable swivel chair in his music room and listens to Beethoven quartets, Mozart operas, and Chopin preludes as he reads.

"How's the poet?" I always ask his wife, Mary Ann, whenever we talk. Anthony works hard as a doctor, but he is serene and calm at his core. I feel his peacefulness whenever we're together.

I have a friend who lives in Athens whom I met at a dance in Connecticut in 1956 and we've stayed in touch all these years. Tony Lykiardopoulos lives his daily life with a poetic awareness. He has a refined sense of taste and style, and willingly opens up all his senses to the stim-uli that surround him. One of the attributes of this spirit is an unabashed love of beauty and a sensitive eloquence. His love of life is vigorous, and I feel his sense of wonder and joy in every moment. Poets come in all shapes and sizes, and the quality they have in common is an uncommon reverence for life. Tony also loves photography, and his pictures are taken through the lens of a person who sees life as a beautiful gift, a dance to dance, a song to sing, a moment to savor.

He who makes time precious lives forever.

—Peter Megargee Brown

It's not how long you live, but how much you can enjoy each day. Poets are creators of grace-filled moments, and whether their journey on earth is long or short, their poetic mark lives on through us and future generations.

Who are these people who opened up to the wonder and wisdom of each day?

Consider the enormous impact these giants continue to have on the world. They "walked the walk," taught us about love, and opened us up to understanding eternal issues of morality, transcendence, and the pursuit of truth and grace for the soul. Who are the men and women who left tracks on your path that shimmer, sparkle, and expand your vision of what's possible in one human life span? When I think of my heroes, the people who left us with their immortality through their children, their writings, their

The dream was always running ahead of me. To catch up, to live for a moment in unison with it, that was the miracle.

—ANAÏS NIN

artwork, their causes, or their discoveries, I realize that none of these stars knew ahead of time when their time was up. Aristotle lived to be thirty-eight, considered a long life at the time. Saint Augustine lived to be seventy-six. Marcus Aurelius, fifty-nine, Confucius, seventy-two. Socrates lived to be sixty-nine, as did Seneca, but Sophocles lived to be eighty-five, and Plato eighty. Lao-Tzu, a favorite of mine, was born in 604 B.C. and lived until 531 B.C. That's a long life indeed. He's the one who taught us we're dying prematurely, centuries before the buzz word "stress" came into our vocabulary. My favorite essayist, Michel de Montaigne, who lived in the sixteenth century, died at fifty-nine, and in the same century the Spanish author Miguel de Cervantes died at sixty-nine.

I was fascinated to learn that Blaise Pascal died at

thirty-nine, Jane Austen at forty-two, and John Keats at only twenty-six. Percy Bysshe Shelley was thirty, Søren Kierkegaard, forty-two. Henry David Thoreau lived to be forty-five, and Emerson died at seventy-nine. Emily Dickinson lived eleven years longer than Thoreau, dying at fifty-six, but Louisa May Alcott died at fifty-five. Anton Pavlovich Chekov lived to be forty-four.

To burn always with this hard, gemlike flame, to maintain this ecstasy, is success in life.

—Walter Pater

Edith Wharton died at seventy-five, Beatrix Potter at seventy-seven, Marcel Proust at fifty-one, and both Sir Winston Spencer Churchill and Somerset William Maugham died at ninety-one, Albert Schweitzer at ninety.

Think about Eleanor Brown becoming a centenarian, spreading beauty far and abundantly, believing she would die when her usefulness was over. Reviewing a few dozen people who lived, became useful, and died illustrates to me the importance of finding your passion, your innate gifts and talents, and focusing on using them as your energy and power, using all the moments you have, grateful for the gift of each single day.

Real generosity toward the future consists in giving all to what is present.

—Albert Camus

John Ruskin believed work should be in praise of what you love. By avoiding many irrelevancies, by increasing time to *be*—that space we provide for personal transcendence, by simplifying—we will dignify our accumulated time. When we comprehend our ingenious ability to have a poetry of thoughts, formulating beliefs that bear fruits of goodness, that ring true and are right for us, we are not wasting our time, we are magnifying it. Our character and worth can expand higher, deeper, and broader and be universally valid, even supreme, when we tap into the wider affairs of life. We are improving our ability to make the most of our lives. How we use time defines us.

Poetry is simply the most beautiful, impressive, and widely effective mode of saying things.

— MATTHEW ARNOLD

John Coburn calls people who cherish every moment of life as a gift, "grace-bearers." These grace-filled spirits have made the effort and have taken the time available to them each day to find meaning. "We measure ourselves by many standards," wrote William James. "Our strength and our intelligence, our wealth and even our good luck, are things which warm our heart and make us feel ourselves a match for life. But deeper than all such things and able to suffice unto itself without them, is the sense of the amount of effort we put forth. . . . He who can make much is a hero." We can all make a commitment to be grace-bearers and poets. Living with the awareness of the poet is our way of surrendering our hesitations and joining forces with the universe to discover life as a sacred gift.

Every day is a little life, and our whole life is but a day repeated. Therefore live every day as if it would be the last.

—JOSEPH HALL

EMILY DICKINSON: A LIFE AS POET

*A good poem is a
contribution to
reality. The world is
never the same once
a good poem has
been added to it. A
good poem helps to
change the shape
and significance of
the universe, helps
to extend everyone's
knowledge of himself
and the world
around him.*

—DYLAN THOMAS

The poems of Emily Dickinson are among my favorites. She speaks in darts and flickers of sublime perception in ways I cannot. Her spare words help connect me to a universal spirit and remind me of our common humanity and our need for one another. I read William Blake, John Donne, William Wordsworth, Henry Wadsworth Longfellow, Edgar Allan Poe, Walt Whitman, W. B. Yeats, and William Shakespeare. But of all these masters, Emily Dickinson perhaps moves me the most because I can identify with her domesticity and her struggle for inner strength. She was intrepid to the core.

"The story of modern literature," writes Cynthia Griffin Wolff in her definitive biography, "bears recurring witness to the conversion of loss into gain, to radical deprivation leading to great creative accomplishment. But nowhere in our literary annals is that conversion more striking than with Emily Dickinson."

Emily Dickinson found her poetry in the focus of domesticity. She lived in intimate contact with the details of ordinary life, and there she found powerful feelings. "For each ecstatic instant/We must an anguish pay / In keen and quivering ratio / To the ecstasy." Dickinson's breathless, mysterious aliveness, her questioning mind, her strangeness, her whimsy, her powerful idiosyncratic imagination could transform the intimate details of the personal in such a way that they became universal, and an inspiration to us all.

John Coburn shares my passion for Dickinson. After he became Episcopal bishop of Massachusetts, he preached a sermon about her at St. Paul's Cathedral on Easter Sunday, invoking "her divine intoxication, her tender majesty," and her ability to be exalted. Bishop Coburn then urged us all to "exalt, rejoice, give thanks . . ."

OUR TIME OUT OF TIME

Emerson had it right: "Time does not pass, we pass." His philosophy was Zenlike. "The present moment is in your power," he wrote. "But the past is inalterable, the future is inscrutable. . . . All that can be done for you is nothing to what you can do for yourself." Gracious living is about understanding our own power and the importance of living in the moment.

"The present moment is not limited from one point

There is symbolic as well as actual beauty in the migration of the birds, the ebb and flow of the tides, the folded bud ready for the spring. There is something infinitely healing in the repeated refrains of nature—the assurance that dawn comes after night, and spring after the winter.

—RACHEL CARSON

of the clock to another," wrote Rollo May. "The moment is always ready to give birth, to open up. The moment always has its finite side (which the mature person never forgets). But the moment also always has its infinite side, it always beckons with new zest. Time for the human being is not a corridor; it is a continual opening out." I can always find my core of peace when I let go of my preoccupation with the passage of time. When we're inside this soft, luminous glow, we see the universe through the soul of our imagination, and it is as though this was the first time we ever understood the mystery of life. When we mediate, or however we allow ourselves to become one with the moment, time is infinite. This is grace.

The language that serves as the poet's tool kit is the stuff of our own minds.

—GLENN DIXON

One September morning I found myself wide-awake at five-thirty. Out my window I could see a sparkling light dazzling on the harbor. Boats were coming and going under full sail, canvas flapping in the crisp breeze. I was ready to hit the day. I tiptoed down the stairs so I wouldn't wake Peter. Barefoot, in my long white nightgown, I walked through the Zen garden to the inner gate. As I looked around I saw that fall was almost here; summer was coming to a close.

All men are poets at heart.

—EMERSON

I returned to the kitchen, ground some French-roast coffee beans, squeezed some oranges, poured the juice into some hand-blown glasses, washed some dishes by hand, and rearranged the glasses in the cabinet. Once the coffee was ready I went out to greet the three "New Dawn" roses. I read a bit and wrote some letters.

I anticipated Peter's appearance, which heightened my pleasure. By six o'clock I'd settled nicely into the Zen garden. Before going to the round table with my coffee I sat down on the cold moist stone of the meditation bench. A seven-year-old young lady once asked me what meditation was all about and I answered, "Sit still, be quiet, be open, be present."

Being in the garden at dawn brought me back to early memories of my own garden when I was seven years old. Today, I noticed the dew on the rose petals, the sense of peace. The calm I experienced was, for those moments, complete. The whole day lay before me as a precious treasure. There were no obligations, no commitments, no schedules, no agenda, no deadlines. It was six o'clock in the morning on a September day and I felt totally free. This serenity flowed through my body. I felt it as a physical sense of well-being.

A poet dares be just so clear and no clearer . . . He unzips the veil from beauty, but does not remove it.

—E. B. WHITE

I then watered, raked, and swept the stone terrace. Emerson and I agree about gardens. They're pretty to look at but the real exhilaration comes with being the gardener. Getting soil under your fingernails, getting down there with the worms, the bees, the fragrances, and the colors, lifts you up. I was in my own world, yet I had never felt less alone. I was in the moment, surrounded by its richness.

By being open to the here and now, a wealth of enjoyment is revealed to us naturally. In these intensely focused, yet simple moments, we notice the
color of a flower, its fragrance, beauty, and
delicacy, and we lose our fear of life and
loss.

"[E]very morning began with infinite
promise," wrote Richardson in his biography of Emerson. "Any book may be read,
any idea thought, any action taken. . . . On
a day no different from one now breaking,
Shakespeare sat down to begin *Hamlet* and
Fuller began her history of the Roman revolution in 1848. Each of us has all the time there is; each
accepts those invitations he can discern."

Peter finally arrived in the garden, kissed me good
morning, took a deep breath of the fresh sea air, and
admired the beauty of the roses and the view out to sea.
He sipped the freshly squeezed juice and spoke of happiness. "A new day is dawning indeed. How good it
all is."

*Every wakeful step,
every mindful act is
the direct path to
awakening. Wherever
you go, there
you are.*

—BUDDHA

✤

Ten Principles of a Gracious Life

KINDNESS

When we show sympathy and understanding toward each other, when we have a warmhearted nature, and when we show tenderness, we are kind. No matter what accomplishments we achieve over our lifetime, gentleness and goodness are the most helpful influences of good will. When we are naturally kind, we will be thought of favorably by others, and our kindness will induce an aura of happiness.

ELEGANCE

When we are sensitive to beauty in simplicity and mildness in manners, and choose to conduct ourselves in this consciousness, elegance results. Being refined in appearance, form, and style indicates that we not only respect and care for ourselves, but that we take others seriously as well. Showing interest and concern for and being receptive and responsive to those we come into contact with makes us examples of grace.

OPENNESS

Whenever we open up, we are extended and expanded, ready to communicate to our heart and mind through our five senses. Without reserve and false pretense, we're accepting, sincere, and free. Whether we embrace someone with open arms, open our hand to another, or keep our eyes and ears open to a flower or to the symphony of birds singing, we reveal our true feelings. When we keep the day open for any purpose, go out in the open air, open a door, a window, a box, or a letter, we are spreading open our heart and thoughts to bounteous discoveries and new beginnings.

A UTHENTICITY

When we are true to ourselves and to others, when our character is one of integrity, we have the quality of being authentic. Our personality is genuine, absolute, and reliable, and
therefore worthy of trust and credibility. When we believe in
ourselves, we are free to grow in our own soil, in the direction of our pure nature, which is grace-filled.

G ENEROSITY

When we are magnanimous, liberal in our giving as well
as in sharing of our self, we show noble character and an
abundance of spirit and strength. A generous person is
stimulating, exalting, and beneficent, understanding that
when we are free to give courageously, our lives will be
overflowing with grace. Whether we provide a generous
table for breaking bread together or sing someone's
praises, when we are generous, we live "over the top" and
our own cup is mysteriously replenished.

E ASE

Whenever we experience freedom from constraint, pain,
agitation, or worry, we sense the pleasant satisfactions of

naturalness. When we're not making an effort, when we have relief from labor and are able to be carefree, we can feel rested, be quiet and tranquil, secure in the ease and comfort of our mind and heart. We need relaxation and a moment's peace in order to live graciously, and when we do find this sense of calm, we experience greater dexterity in our performance. By backing away we move forward with grace.

Contentment

If we can attain satisfaction with what we have in our lives, it will bring us happiness and grace. In our present condition, if we're able to solve our inner problems and affirm life, we will be in harmony with our expectations. In any situation, we can be appeased and self-contained, and gratify ourselves with realistic desires. Whenever we make the best of whatever situation we find ourselves in, we are essentially living a gracious life.

Fairness

To be a straightforward, honest person who is reasonable, impartial, and nonjudgmental, culminates in a fine, rare quality of character and intellect which is the foundation of fairness. Fairness requires being consistently unprejudiced, just, and tolerant, and with this honorable attitude a gracious life naturally unfolds.

Geniality

Whenever we have a warm, cheerful, positive disposition, we're not only contributing to, but sympathizing with the enjoyment of life. People who inspire joy or happiness, who affirm and confirm others, are marked with genius, belonging to a higher nature. When we have a pleasant, friendly personality, we glow with a gracious, giving spirit, spreading the energy of light all around us.

Appreciation

When we have a quick recognition of excellence, when we're able to value someone or something, fully aware of the magnitude of their qualities, our illumination leads to being thankful, increasing the value of esteem. Being aware of the worth of appreciation is key to a gracious life. Whenever we esteem highly, we are validating life, its merit and worth. When we are thankful, we ourselves increase in value, transcending time and place, becoming one with eternity. Of all the qualities of a gracious life, appreciation is the most essential. When we're conscious of all the good and beautiful things and people in our lives, not judging, but living in continuous gratitude, we're free to connect with the great, timeless truths. When we show appreciation, we're recognizing the divinity within us, our true identity.

Acknowledgments with Love and Appreciation to:

Carl, Toni, Ellen, Marysarah, Julie, Elisabeth,
and Peter